THE TROJAN WOMEN
AND OTHER PLAYS

EURIPIDES was born in Attica (the country whose main city was Athens) about 485 BCE. By the time of his death in 406 BCE he had written at least eighty plays, which were performed at the Great Dionysia, the Athenians' major drama festival. Seventeen of these survive complete. He was one of the three outstanding figures—with Aeschylus and Sophocles—who made fifth-century Athens pre-eminent in the history of world drama. While he lived his apparently reclusive life Euripides was less successful than the other two tragedians, winning the festival's prize only five times. But his vigorous, immediate, controversial, and flamboyantly theatrical plays soon became by far the most popular and frequently revived works in the ancient repertoire. The universality of the conflicts he explores, and the startling realism of his characterization, ensure that he has also been by far the most often adapted, staged, and filmed of the ancient dramatists from the Renaissance to the present day. In the three great war plays contained in this volume Euripides subjects the sufferings of Troy's survivors to a harrowing examination. We weep for the aged Hecuba in her name play and in *The Trojan Women*, yet we respond with an at times appalled admiration to her resilience amid unrelieved suffering. Andromache, the slave-concubine of her husband's killer, endures her existence in the victor's country with a Stoic nobility. Of their time yet timeless, these plays insist on the victory of the female spirit amid the horrors visited on them by the gods and men during war.

JAMES MORWOOD is retired Grocyn Lecturer in Classics and Fellow of Wadham College at Oxford University. He has translated four volumes of Euripides' plays for Oxford World's Classics, and his other books include *A Dictionary of Latin Words and Phrases* and works on Sheridan.

EDITH HALL is Professor of Classics and Drama, Royal Holloway, University of London and co-director of the Archive of Performances of Greek and Roman Drama at the University of Oxford. She has published widely on ancient Greek drama and society and has written introductions for the Oxford World's Classics editions of Euripides' *Medea and Other Plays*, *Bacchae and Other Plays*, *Heracles and Other Plays*, and *Orestes and Other Plays*.

OXFORD WORLD'S CLASSICS

For over 100 years Oxford World's Classics have brought readers closer to the world's great literature. Now with over 700 titles—from the 4,000-year-old myths of Mesopotamia to the twentieth century's greatest novels—the series makes available lesser-known as well as celebrated writing.

The pocket-sized hardbacks of the early years contained introductions by Virginia Woolf, T. S. Eliot, Graham Greene, and other literary figures which enriched the experience of reading. Today the series is recognized for its fine scholarship and reliability in texts that span world literature, drama and poetry, religion, philosophy and politics. Each edition includes perceptive commentary and essential background information to meet the changing needs of readers.

OXFORD WORLD'S CLASSICS

EURIPIDES

Hecuba
The Trojan Women
Andromache

Translated and Edited by
JAMES MORWOOD

Introduction by
EDITH HALL

OXFORD
UNIVERSITY PRESS

OXFORD

UNIVERSITY PRESS

Great Clarendon Street, Oxford OX2 6DP

Oxford University Press is a department of the University of Oxford.
It furthers the University's objective of excellence in research, scholarship,
and education by publishing worldwide in

Oxford New York

Athens Auckland Bangkok Bogotá Buenos Aires Cape Town
Chennai Dar es Salaam Delhi Florence Hong Kong Istanbul Karachi
Kolkata Kuala Lumpur Madrid Melbourne Mexico City Mumbai Nairobi
Paris São Paulo Shanghai Singapore Taipei Tokyo Toronto Warsaw

with associated companies in Berlin Ibadan

Oxford is a registered trade mark of Oxford University Press
in the UK and in certain other countries

Published in the United States
by Oxford University Press Inc., New York

Introduction and Bibliography © Edith Hall 2000
Translation and Notes © James Morwood 2000

The moral rights of the author have been asserted

Database right Oxford University Press (maker)

First published as an Oxford World's Classics paperback 2001
Reissued 2008

British Library Cataloguing in Publication Data

Data available

Library of Congress Cataloging in Publication Data

Euripides
[Hecuba. English]
Hecuba; The Trojan women; Andromache / Euripides / translated with explanatory notes by
James Morwood; with an introduction by Edith Hall.
p. cm.
Includes bibliographical references (p.).
1. Euripides—Translations into English. 2. Hecuba (Legendary character)—Drama.
3. Andromache (Legendary character)—Drama. 4. Troy (Extinct city)—Drama.
5. Trojan War—Drama. I. Title: Hecuba; The Trojan Women; Andromache.
II. Morwood, James. III. Euripides. Trojan women. English.
IV. Euripides. Andromache. English. V. Title: Trojan women.
VI. Title: Andromache. VII. Title.
PA3975.A2 2000b 882'.01—dc21 00–059816

ISBN 978-0-19-953881-2

1

Typeset by Hope Services (Abingdon) Ltd.
Printed in Great Britain by
Clays Ltd, St Ives plc

ACKNOWLEDGEMENTS

The translator would like to acknowledge his considerable debt to Professor Christopher Collard and Professor James Diggle. Any errors or misjudgements are due to his own obstinacy or negligence.

CONTENTS

ABBREVIATIONS

AJP	*American Journal of Philology*
BICS	*Bulletin of the Institute of Classical Studies*
CA	*Classical Antiquity*
CJ	*Classical Journal*
CP	*Classical Philology*
CQ	*Classical Quarterly*
CR	*Classical Review*
G&R	*Greece & Rome*
GRBS	*Greek, Roman, and Byzantine Studies*
HSCP	*Harvard Studies in Classical Philology*
JHS	*Journal of Hellenistic Studies*
PCPS	*Proceedings of the Cambridge Philological Society*
RSC	*Revista di Studi Classici*
SO	*Symbolae Osloenses*
TAPA	*Transactions and Proceedings of the American Philological Association*
YCS	*Yale Classical Studies*
s.d.	*stage direction*

INTRODUCTION

EURIPIDES AND HIS TRADITION

In the fourth century BCE the people of Pherae in northern Greece were oppressed by an inhumane tyrant named Alexander. He had murdered his own uncle, but his reputation for unusual cruelty rested especially on the way he treated his enemies. He buried them alive, or encased them in animal hides before setting his hunting dogs upon them. Moreover, when putting down rebellious cities he had twice surrounded all the men in full assembly and butchered every single one, including the youths. A man incapable of pity, or so it would seem. Yet the pathos of Euripidean tragedy proved too much even for him. At a production of *The Trojan Women* he felt compelled to leave the theatre abruptly, 'because he was ashamed to have the citizens see him, who had never taken pity on any man that he had murdered, weeping over the sorrows of Hecuba and Andromache' (Plutarch, *Life of Pelopidas* 29.4–6).

This story shows that the ancient Greeks already recognized the extraordinary emotive power of Euripides' *Trojan Women*, one of three tragedies in this volume dealing with the consequences of the fall of Troy for its female population. All the tragic playwrights of the fifth century BCE repeatedly found materials for their plots in the story of the Trojan War. While Thebes provided the mythical exemplar of a city riven by internal strife, explored theatrically to great effect by Euripides in his *Phoenician Women*, Troy served in the Athenian imagination as the site of the archetypal war against an external adversary. The siege of Troy was felt to prefigure both the wars Greece had fought with Persia in the early part of the century, and subsequently the Peloponnesian War of the last three decades, which tore the Greek world apart. Troy thus functioned as a mythical prism through which the fifth century refracted its own preoccupation with military conflict. In the earlier half of the century the tragedian Aeschylus composed a famous trilogy which put Achilles centre-stage in dramatizing the plot of the *Iliad*, and Sophocles' surviving plays include the pathbreaking Trojan War tragedy *Philoctetes* (409 BCE), with its all-male cast of super-heroes. Euripides composed many plays set against the same backdrop, but one of his most distinctive contributions to this type of tragedy seems to have been consistently to turn the focus away from the dilemmas facing the illustrious male warriors, and onto the women—especially the mothers Hecuba and Andromache—whose lives were wrecked by male violence. As the chorus of *The Trojan Women* sing, 'Sing, O Muse, a new song about Ilium' (511–14).

Many of Euripides' most important dramas, including others dealing with aspects of the Trojan War, have not even survived. One of the ancient audience's favourite plays, much parodied in comedy and painted on numerous vases, was his exciting *Telephus*. Although this drama survives only in fragments, it is instructive to think about the reasons for its extraordinary popularity and to compare it with the tragedies dealing with the women of Troy. Telephus, the hero destined to guide the Greeks to Ilium, was disabled by a war wound, masqueraded as a beggar, worked as a lowly porter in Agamemnon's palace, and displayed phenomenal rhetorical skill in a debate where he challenged the motives of the 'heroic' campaign against Troy. Moreover, in a melodramatic climax, he grabbed the baby Orestes from his cradle, and threatened to kill him if the Greeks did not help heal his wound.[1]

Although dealing with an episode in the heroic legend of the Trojan War, *Telephus* seems to have been such a favourite piece in the ancient repertoire precisely because it displayed several of Euripidean drama's typically 'unheroic' qualities. This poet was clearly fascinated by the theatrical potential of disability, poverty, lower-class occupations, disguise, iconoclastic rhetoric, and vulnerable infants. Euripides' understanding of the emotive effect of putting children in life-threatening situations—most famously in *Medea*—is also evident in every play in this volume. In *Hecuba* the queen's attendant women slaughter the two young sons of her one-time ally Polymestor; in *The Trojan Women* the baby Astyanax is brutally cast from the city walls; in *Andromache* the heroine's small son is nearly murdered. The tragedies are further connected by the interest they share with the lost, much-loved *Telephus* in portraying aristocrats suffering the ignominy of servitude. The major difference, however, between *Telephus* and these plays is the gender of the protagonists. *Telephus* was produced in 438 BCE, whereas *Hecuba*,

---

[1] For a translation and discussion of the fragments of *Telephus*, see C. Collard, M. J. Cropp, and K. H. Lee (eds.), *Euripides: Selected Fragmentary Plays*, vol. i (Warminster, 1995).

The Trojan Women, and *Andromache* all date from the period of the Peloponnesian War, which broke out in 431 BCE, and during which the treatment of war captives became increasingly brutal. The practice of rounding up and slaughtering the entire male population of city-states (as Alexander of Pherae was somewhat later to do) became almost unexceptional: at Plataea in 427 BCE the Spartans executed two hundred and twenty-five men in succession, enslaved the women, and razed the city to its very foundations; they then methodically melted down even the metal fixtures in the city wall to make couches for the goddess Hera (Thuc. 3.67). It is scarcely surprising that this type of brutality made an impact on contemporary drama.

The Greeks and Romans were passionate about the innovative and emotive Euripides. A character in a comedy announced that he would be prepared to hang himself for the sake of seeing this (by then dead) tragedian (Philemon fr. 118).[2] Aristotle's formalist discussion of tragedy complains about Euripides' use of the *deus ex machina*, his unintegrated choruses, and the 'unnecessary' villainy of some of his characters. Yet even Aristotle conceded that Euripides was 'the most tragic of the poets', meaning that he was the best at eliciting both fear and the pity which traumatized Alexander, tyrant of Pherae (*Poetics* 56ᵃ25–7, 54ᵇ1, 61ᵇ21, 53ᵃ20).

In his *Rhetoric*, Aristotle also revealingly states that Euripides was the first tragic poet to make his characters speak naturally in everyday vocabulary; it so happens that Theodorus, the very same actor whose emotional delivery so affected the tyrant Alexander was also held, according to Aristotle, to excel in the 'naturalistic' enunciation of this revolutionary type of dramatic diction (Aristotle, *Rhet.* 3.1404ᵇ18–25).[3] For the single most significant reason underlying Euripides' astonishing ancient popularity was probably the accessible, fluent, and memorable poetry in which his characters expressed themselves: even Alexander the Great, no professional actor, is supposed to have been able to perform a whole episode of a Euripidean tragedy off by heart as a party trick (Athenaeus, *Deipnosophists* 12.537d–e). The audiences adored the accessibility and psychological immediacy not only of the diction but of the *sentiments* Euripides

---

[2] Fragments of comedy are cited throughout from R. Kassel and C. Austin (eds.), *Poetae Comici Graeci* (Berlin, 1983–95).

[3] Aelian, *Varia Historia* 14.40, although the tragic heroine Theodorus was playing in Aelian's version of the story was the protagonist of Euripides' *Aerope*.

attributed to his Bronze Age heroes: a good example is the bathos of Menelaus' response to Hecuba in *The Trojan Women*, when she pleads with him not to allow Helen to travel on board his ship. Hecuba fears that he will be seduced into commuting the death sentence he has passed on his errant wife. But he deliberately misunderstands and responds by asking, with withering black humour, whether his wife has put on weight (1050). Thus Trojan queens and Spartan heroes, paupers and demi-gods, practitioners of human sacrifice, incest, bestiality, and child-murder: Euripides made them all 'speak like human beings' (see Aristophanes, *Frogs* 1058).

Euripidean tragedy became 'classic' almost immediately after his death, and was consistently revived not only in the theatre attended by the tyrant Alexander in the fourth century BCE, but across the entire Greek-speaking world and the Roman empire into the Christian era. Euripides was imitated by Roman tragedians—versions of *The Trojan Women* are attributed to both Ennius and Seneca—and made a huge impact on the non-tragic literature of succeeding generations, especially Menander, Virgil, Ovid, and both Greek and Roman orators. All three of the plays in this volume survived because they were regarded as sufficiently important in the first or second century CE to be chosen among the ten Euripidean tragedies selected for study in the schools of the ancient world; the reason was probably that they contain some of his most spectacularly rhetorical speeches, which made good models for an education centred on oratory. Moreover, his plays are everywhere apparent in the *visual* culture of the Mediterranean. Homer apart, no author stimulated the arts more. The Romans painted Euripides' scenes on their walls and carved them on their sarcophagi; the Byzantines commissioned elaborate mosaics, keeping his pagan myths alive in the visual imagination of Christendom.

The nineteenth-century scholar Benjamin Jowett said this tragedian was 'no Greek in the better sense of the term',[4] for after his revivification in the Renaissance Euripides often suffered by comparison with the structural perfection, 'purity', and 'Hellenic' spirit perceived in his rival Sophocles. This is, however, to simplify the complex and largely unwritten story of Euripidean reception and performance. Once Erasmus had translated *Hecuba* into Latin (1524), its status as archetypal 'revenge tragedy' made it one of the

---

[4] See A. N. Michelini, *Euripides and the Tragic Tradition* (Madison, 1987), 11 n. 40.

more popular ancient plays of the Renaissance; it was subsequently performed several times, in adapted form, on the neoclassical stages of Europe. In unadapted form, moreover, it has lately been revived in some important professional productions;[5] one reason is certainly that the recent dissolution of the former Eastern bloc has created profound contemporary resonances for the play's depiction of what we would call 'war crimes', and of reciprocal violence between three different ethnic groups.

The Trojan Women was long overshadowed by the tragic portrayal of the fall of Troy in the second book of Virgil's *Aeneid*, adapted, for example, by Hector Berlioz in the first two acts of *Les Troyens* (composed 1856-8). But during the twentieth century it has become one of the most frequently performed of all Euripides' plays. The women of Troy have often been made to protest against modern wars or to commemorate their victims. In 1919 and 1920 *The Trojan Women* was performed to mark the formation of the League of Nations; 1945 saw important productions in both Germany and England; Jean-Paul Sartre's adaption *Les Troyennes* (1965) expressed his abhorrence of French conduct in Algeria; his director, Michael Cacoyannis, subsequently made a powerful cinematic version (1971), starring Katharine Hepburn and Vanessa Redgrave, which was regarded as a comment on the war in Vietnam; the set of Tadashi Suzuki's stunning Tokyo production of 1974 was almost transparently Hiroshima. *Andromache*, in contrast, has remained in the shadow of Virgil's account of the heroine's life after the Trojan war as described in the third book of the *Aeneid*, and subsequently of Jean Racine's hugely influential *Andromaque* (1667). Euripides' own tragedy has been only occasionally performed, although it was one of the cycle of plays adapted in 1979 as *The Greeks* in a Royal Shakespeare Company production.[6]

Yet in general the century has smiled on Euripides more than any era since antiquity. One reason is his approach to myth, which has been characterized as subversive, experimental, playful, and eccentric in an identifiably modern way. Although he has occasionally been seen as a formalist or mannerist, the term 'irony'

---

[5] For example, Lawrence Boswell's acclaimed production at the Gate Theatre, London, in 1992. See the review in *Times Literary Supplement* no. 4668, p. 20.

[6] On the production history of *Trojan Women* see Oliver Taplin, *Greek Fire* (London, 1989), 261-3; for the RSC *Andromache* see John Barton and Kenneth Cavander, *The Greeks: Ten Plays Given as a Trilogy* (London, 1981).

dominates criticism. 'Irony' is taken to describe Euripides' poly-
tonality—his ability to write in two simultaneous keys. This 'irony',
however, is conceived in more than one way: sometimes it describes
the hypocritical gap between the rhetorical postures which
Euripidean characters adopt and their true motives: an outstanding
example is the smugly platitudinous Agamemnon of *Hecuba*.
Alternatively, 'irony' defines the confrontation of archaic myths
with the values of democratic Athens, a process which deglamor-
izes violence, casting heroic stories of bloodshed and conflict—for
example, the Greeks' reprisals against the Trojans, or Orestes' murder of Neoptolemus in *Andromache*—as sordid 'gangland killings'.[7]

Another reason for Euripides' modern popularity is that his sup-
ple and multi-faceted works easily adapt to the agendas of different
interpreters. Euripides has been an existentialist, a psychoanalyst, a
proto-Christian with a passionate hunger for 'righteousness', an
idealist and humanist, a mystic, a rationalist, an irrationalist, and
an absurdist nihilist. But perhaps the most tenacious Euripides has
been the pacifist feminist.

'Radical' Euripides was born in the first decade of this century
with Gilbert Murray as midwife. This famous liberal scholar, later
Chairman of the League of Nations, initiated in Edwardian London
a series of performances of Euripides in his own English translations.
The Trojan Women (1905) was interpreted by many as a retrospec-
tive indictment of the concentration camps in which the British had
interred and starved Boer women and children during the Boer
War, especially since Murray had been an ardent campaigner
against the British government's hardline policy in South Africa;[8]
as a result of *Medea* (1907) the heroine's monologue on the plight
of women (see below, 'Athenian Society') was recited at suffragette
meetings.[9] Murray's political interpretations of Euripides, developed
in performance, found academic expression in *Euripides and his Age*
(1913). This book has fundamentally conditioned all subsequent
interpretation, whether by imitation or reaction. A decade later
Euripides' radicalism had become apocalyptic: 'not Ibsen, not
Voltaire, not Tolstoi ever forged a keener weapon in defence of

[7] This phrase is borrowed from W. G. Arnott's excellent article, 'Double the
Vision: A Reading of Euripides' *Electra*', *G&R* 28 (1981), 179–92.

[8] W. H. Salter, *Essays on Two Moderns* (London, 1911), 9.

[9] See further Edith Hall, 'Medea and British legislation before the First World
War', *G&R* 46 (1999), 42–77.

womanhood, in defiance of superstition, in denunciation of war, than the *Medea*, the *Ion*, the *Trojan Women*'.[10]

EURIPIDES THE ATHENIAN

What would Euripides have made of his modern incarnations? The reliable external biographical information amounts to practically nothing. No dependable account of Euripides' own views on politics, women, or war survives, unless we are arbitrarily to select speeches by characters in his plays as the cryptic 'voice of Euripides'. Aristophanes and the other contemporary Athenian comic poets, who wrote what is now known as 'Old Comedy', caricatured Euripides as a cuckold and a greengrocer's son, but their portrait offers little more truth value than a scurrilous cartoon.

The problem is not any dearth of evidence but a dearth of factual veracity. For the student of Euripides has access to a late antique 'Life' (*Vita*) and a fragmentary third-century biography by Satyrus. There are also the so-called 'Letters of Euripides', a collection of five dull epistles purporting to be addressed to individuals such as Archelaus (King of Macedon) and Sophocles, but actually written in the first or second century CE. Collectively these documents provide the first example in the European tradition of the portrait of an alienated artist seeking solace in solitude. This Euripides is a misogynist loner with facial blemishes who worked in a seaside cave on the island of Salamis, and retired to voluntary exile in Macedon as a result of his unpopularity. Unfortunately, however, this poignant portrait is demonstrably a fiction created out of simplistic inferences from Euripides' own works or from the jokes in Athenian comedy. Beyond what is briefly detailed below, the only aspect of the 'Euripides myth' almost certain to be true is that he possessed a large personal library (see Ar. *Frogs* 943, 1049).

Euripides' lifespan was almost exactly commensurate with that of democratic Athens' greatness. He was born in about 485 BCE, and was therefore a small boy when the city was evacuated and his compatriots thwarted the second Persian invasion in 480 BCE. He spent his youth and physical prime in the thriving atmosphere of the 460s and 450s, a period which saw the consolidation of Athens' empire and position as cultural centre of the Greek-speaking world.

[10] F. L. Lucas, *Euripides and his Influence* (London, 1923), 15.

He was witness in 431 BCE to the outbreak of the Peloponnesian War, fought between Athens and her rival Sparta over hegemony in the Aegean. He lived through the turbulent 420s, having opportunity to observe at first hand the ambition and brilliant oratory of Athenian leaders such as Pericles and Cleon; he witnessed the Athenians' brutal treatment of opponents of their imperialist policy, such as the islanders of Melos (416 BC); he lived through the Athenians' worst catastrophe ever, when in 413 the fleet and many thousands of men were lost at Syracuse in Sicily after an attempt to extend Athenian imperial influence westward. Thucydides, near-contemporary of Euripides and author of the *History of the Peloponnesian War*, saw the significance of the calamity (7.87): it was 'the greatest action of this war, and, in my view, the greatest action that we know of in Greek history. To its victors it was the most brilliant of successes, to the vanquished the most catastrophic of defeats.' Athens never fully recovered from this blow to her resources and her morale.

Euripides died in 406 BCE, thus narrowly avoiding the humiliating events of 404, when his city lost the war, her empire, and (briefly) her democracy and her pride. He wrote at least eighty plays, and possibly ninety-two. Nineteen have been transmitted from antiquity under his name. Of these *Rhesus* is probably not by Euripides himself, and *Cyclops* is a satyr play (a comic version of a heroic myth sporting a chorus of sex-starved satyrs). The poet first competed in the drama competition in 455 BCE, was victorious in 441, and won again in 428 with the group including *Hippolytus*, and posthumously (in ?405) with *Bacchae* and *Iphigenia at Aulis*. All the plays in this volume probably date from approximately the penultimate decade of Euripides' life, from 425 to 415 BCE, when conflict with Sparta or her allies was a semi-continuous fact of Athenian life. *Hecuba* was first performed before 423 BCE, probably a few years after the outbreak of the Peloponnesian War. *The Trojan Women* was certainly performed in 415 BCE, when the group to which it belonged won second prize. *Andromache* is printed last in this volume because its action takes place later in mythical time than that of *Hecuba* or *The Trojan Women*. But although the play itself is undated, there are metrical and other reasons (including the vehemence of the rhetoric against Sparta) for assigning it, like *Hecuba*, to the mid-420s.

It is tempting to speculate on Euripides' own reaction to the unfolding story of the Peloponnesian War, and to ask whether it affected the evolution of his dramatic technique. As we have seen, the masculine focus of *Telephus*, which dates from 438 BCE, seems to have been rather different from Euripides' heartbreaking portrayals, composed after the Peloponnesian War began, of the misery which warfare inflicts on women. Warlords committing or justifying unspeakable atrocities feature not only in *Hecuba* and *The Trojan Women*, but also in *Phoenician Women* (409) and *Iphigenia* at *Aulis* (?405). Yet these unforgettable plays, however shocking their portrayal of 'war crimes', lend no substantial support to the widely held view that Euripides, after initially supporting Athenian expansionism, despaired and retreated from the contemporary scene as the promoters of war became more powerful. It may be that truth lies behind the biographical tradition that he spent his last two years at the Macedonian court of Pella, supposedly writing plays including *Bacchae* and *Iphigenia at Aulis*; it may be that the very existence of the 'Macedonian exile' tradition reveals Euripides' anti-democratic (and therefore anti-imperialist) sympathies. On the other hand, the lack of evidence for a political career, in contrast with Sophocles' attested appointments to high office, may suggest a neutral emotional detachment from public affairs.

Yet Euripides was profoundly engaged with the intellectual and ethical questions which the war had asked and which underlay the policy debates in the Athenian assembly. For these appear in thin disguise in his tragedies, which repeatedly confront notions of patriotism, pragmatism, expediency, and *force majeure* with the ideals of loyalty, equity, justice, and clemency. Such ethical disputes echo closely the agonizing debates in Thucydides which decided the fates—usually death or slavery—of the citizens of rebel states on both sides in the Peloponnesian War, including Mytilene, Plataea, and Melos. Indeed, many scholars have believed that in *The Trojan Women* Euripides was using myth to comment on, or even protest against, the punitive action taken by his compatriots against the islanders of Melos in 416, the year before the play's first production. The Athenians, in the eloquently plain diction of the historian Thucydides, 'put to death all the men of military age whom they took, and sold the women and children as slaves' (5.116).

While such a straightforward theatrical substitution of mythical Greeks for contemporary Athenians is unlikely to have been Euripides' method (especially since the Greek persecutors in the play are emphatically Spartan), it is certain that, intellectually, he was a child of his time. Every significant field studied by the professional intellectuals ('sophists') in contemporary Athens surfaces in his tragedies: ontology, epistemology, philosophy of language, rhetoric, moral and political theory, medicine, psychology, and cosmology. There is thus a kind of truth in Aulus Gellius' statement that Euripides studied physics with Anaxagoras, rhetoric with Prodicus, and moral philosophy with Socrates (*Noctes Atticae* 15.20.4); in the first version of Aristophanes' *Clouds* (fr. 401) it was even alleged that Socrates provided Euripides with the ideas for his clever tragedies! And Euripidean characters certainly adopt the new philosophical *methods*: they subtly argue from probability and relativism, and formulate their points as antilogy, proof, and refutation. All Euripidean tragedies are influenced by the developing sophistic 'science' of rhetoric, or 'persuasion', especially those composed after the arrival in Athens in 427 BCE of the great Sicilian sophist and rhetorician Gorgias, famous for his verbal pyrotechnics and ability to make a tenuous argument appear overwhelmingly convincing, 'to make the weaker argument appear the stronger'. The plays in this volume contain some of Euripides' most ostentatious rhetorical displays, for example Cassandra's demonstration in *The Trojan Women* that the defeated Trojans were actually more fortunate than their Greek conquerors (365–405), and Helen's speech in self-defence in the same play (914–65). This almost certainly echoes Gorgias' exhibition piece, *Encomium of Helen*, which proved it was possible 'to defend the indefensible' by exonerating Helen of Troy of all blame for the Trojan War.[11]

EURIPIDES IN PERFORMANCE

Most Euripidean tragedies were first performed at an annual festival in honour of Dionysus, the Greek god of wine, dancing, and theatrical illusion, who is the protagonist of Euripides' most obviously 'Dionysiac' tragedy, *Bacchae*. The Great Dionysia was held in the spring when sailing became feasible. It was opened by a religious procession in which a statue of Dionysus was installed in the theatre, along with sacrifices and libations. Yet the Dionysia was also a political event. It affirmed the Athenian citizenry's collective iden-

---

[11] See the translation in D. M. MacDowell (ed.), *Gorgias' Encomium of Helen* (Bristol, 1982).

tity as a democratic body with imperial supremacy: front seats were reserved for distinguished citizens, and only Athenians could perform the prestigious benefaction of sponsorship (*chorēgia*). The spectators included representatives from Athens' allied states. The allies displayed their tribute in the theatre, where they also witnessed a 'patriotic' display by the city's war orphans—an aspect of the performance context which must be borne in mind when considering how the original audience might have reacted to a 'war play' such as *Trojan Women*. The plays were expected to befit this audience: insulting Athens at the Dionysia may have been a prosecutable offence (Aristophanes, *Acharnians* 501–6). It is not certain whether women attended the drama competitions, although most scholars assume that if women were present at all it was in small numbers, perhaps consisting only of important priestesses.

The tragedies were performed over three successive days in groups by three poets: each poet offered three tragedies plus one satyr play. In 431 BCE, for example, Euripides took third place with three tragedies (*Medea*, *Philoctetes*, and *Dictys*), followed by a satyr play called *Theristai*, 'Reapers': the other two competitors were Euphorion (Aeschylus' son), who won first prize, and Sophocles, the runner-up. The plays were judged by a panel of democratically selected citizens, and care was taken to avoid juror corruption, but the audience's noisy applause and heckling influenced the outcome (Plato, *Republic* 6.492b5–1).

The plays were performed in the Theatre of Dionysus on the south slope of the Athenian acropolis. Individual actors probably performed their speeches and songs most of the time on the stage (*skēnē*), while the chorus of twelve sang and danced to forgotten steps and gestures in the dancing arena (*orchēstra*). All the performers were male, and all were masked; little is known about the degree to which actors in female roles attempted to disguise their true gender. For performance conventions we have to rely on the characters' words, since the Greeks did not use stage directions. The last two decades have produced important work on the visual dimension and its contribution to the meaning of tragedy: scholarship has focused on physical contact, and on entrances and exits. The evidence for the material resources of the theatre as early as the fifth century is slight, although the poets had access to a machine which permitted the airborne epiphanies *ex machina*, such as Thetis at the end of *Andromache*. There was also the *ekkyklēma*, a

contraption allowing bodies to be wheeled out of the doors of the
palace or tent forming the 'backdrop' to most surviving tragedies:
it may have been used to bring Polymestor's dead children from the
Trojan women's tent in *Hecuba*. Vase-paintings offer a stylized
reflection of the costumes, masks, and scenery, and some are
directly inspired by individual tragedies, including a powerful illus-
tration of *Hecuba* on a vase painted perhaps a hundred years after
the play's original production: it portrays the blinded Polymestor
staggering towards the viewer between the figures of Agamemnon
and a white-haired Hecuba, her faced deeply etched with pain.[12]

HECUBA

One of the bleakest of all Euripides' dramas, *Hecuba* is a study in the
repercussions of international war on individual families. In the
immediate aftermath of the fall of Troy, it brings the Greek king
Agamemnon, the Thracian warlord Polymestor, and the Trojan
queen Hecuba into a perverted form of intimacy born of reciprocal
brutality. While Hecuba's former friend Polymestor becomes her bitterest enemy, and her deadly opponent Agamemnon becomes a
temporary ally, the tragedy emphasizes the volatility of loyalties and
coalitions in such times of crisis. As the chorus comments, it is
strange how 'the laws of necessity determine men's relationships,
making friends of bitter enemies and enemies of those who once
were friends' (846–9). This vicious triangular plot is played out on
the harsh, snowy, marginal region of the Thracian Chersonese,
where Asia turns into Europe across the straits from the Trojan
mainland; by a type of pathetic fallacy this atmospheric setting
seems reflected in the tragedy's major psychological interests: in the
processes by which humans harden themselves to commit crimes of
chilling barbarity, in the darker edges of the self, in the disintegra-
tion of social boundaries, and in strange mental and physical trans-
formations.

Hecuba places the psyche of the Trojan queen under a theatrical
microscope: already multiply bereaved, she is confronted with two

[12] The picture is reproduced in A. D. Trendall and T. B. L. Webster, *Illustrations
of Greek Drama* (London, 1971), no. III.3.19. The continuing popularity of *Hecuba* in
the century after its original production is also suggested by the probability that the
great orator Aeschines, ex-actor and rival of Demosthenes, had once played the role
of Polymestor (Dem. 18.267, 19.337).

further excruciating losses which precipitate her own mutation into a vindictive aggressor. The first part of the play dramatizes her reactions to the news that her daughter Polyxena must be sacrificed to appease the ghost of the Greek Achilles; the second part presents her with the corpse of her son Polydorus (who has been murdered by Polymestor, king of the wild Thracian land where the play is set), and enacts the dreadful reprisal she exacts. The ancient Greeks were more capable than we are today of emotional honesty in articulating the human drive for revenge: Thucydides' account of the Peloponnesian War draws repeated attention to the importance of this impulse in the shaping of history. In a famous speech to the Syracusans before battle with the invading Athenian imperial army, for example, Thucydides' Gylippus urged them that 'in dealing with an adversary it is most just and lawful to claim the right to slake the fury of the soul on the aggressor', and adds that vengeance provides the 'greatest of all pleasures' (7.68). No Greek tragedy concentrates to such a degree as *Hecuba* on the psychology of revenge, or rather on the psychological *process* by which a victim turns into an avenger, a process some psychoanalysts would call 'the internalization of the oppressor'.

The Greeks in the play, with the single exception of the herald Talthybius, display a casual brutality as shocking to the audience as to their victims on stage. Although Hecuba once saved Odysseus' life, he is responsible for persuading the Greeks to carry out the sacrifice of Polyxena, and makes his most shameful appearance in ancient literature when he arrives to justify arresting her. Agamemnon, to whom Hecuba turns for assistance against Polymestor, is a self-serving moral invertebrate, quick with a platitude on the nature of virtue but incapable of virtuous action. He agrees to turn a blind eye to Hecuba's actions against Polymestor, while refusing, lest he incur the disfavour of his army, to provide her with any active support. The Thracian Polymestor is one of the most unmitigatedly unpleasant characters on the ancient stage—a barefaced liar, a cynical opportunist, and the only tragic villain whose crime is motivated solely by avarice. And Hecuba herself, although she has far more excuse than the male characters for her atrocious behaviour, is transformed by her psychological trauma into as culpable a villain as any of them; she instigates not only the blinding of Polymestor, but also the killing of the two sons with whom he was unwise enough to enter the women's tents. The

penalty exacted for the life of Polydorus is not one but *two* lives: it
is as if Hecuba's need to avenge Polyxena is displaced into
Polymestor. This is a brilliant piece of psychology on Euripides'
part: it is the Greeks who are responsible for by far the greatest part
of Hecuba's suffering, but they are too powerful for her to oppose,
and the psychological violence she has endured simply has to find
expression somewhere.

The play includes several passages which show why Euripides
was regarded by Aristotle as the absolute master of the tragic emotion of pity: the last parting of Polyxena from her mother is one of
the most painful moments in western theatre. Indeed, it can be
argued that this play makes its audience consciously meditate upon
the tragic aesthetics of pity. Unlike the drama of the Renaissance,
Greek tragedy did not use 'metatheatrical' figures of speech, such as
'all the world's a stage', perhaps because its authors were attempt-
ing to avoid anachronism in their portrayal of a Bronze Age world
when theatre had not yet been invented.[13] But they did use analo-
gies with the visual arts, which force the audience into thinking
about the *visual* dimension of tragic theatre. Thus Talthybius'
shocking account of the beautiful princess's dignity and courage, as
she bared her breast for the sacrificial sword, memorably likens her
appearance to that of a beautiful statue (560–1); later, Hecuba asks
Agamemnon to pity her, standing back from her 'like a painter' to
scrutinize her suffering (807). Passages such as these remind the
spectators that they are colluding in the theatrical process precisely
by gazing upon anguish and atrocity. Such poetic figures were probably also responsible for producing the ancient tradition that
Euripides had himself been an artist, and that pictures of his were
on display in the city of Megara (*Life of Euripides* 17–18).

One of the most powerful theatrical moments in the play is the
blinded Polymestor's gory entrance on all fours, 'crawling like a
four-footed beast of the mountain', and expressing in nearly inar-
ticulate song a bloodthirsty desire to glut himself on the flesh and
bones of the 'savage beasts' he deems the women of Troy to be
(1056–1106). Polymestor has become as like an animal as a
human can, thus not only reinforcing one of the most important
images in the play's poetic repertoire, but bodily demonstrating that

[13] See Patricia Easterling, 'Anachronism in Greek Tragedy', *JHS* 105 (1985),
1–10.

all the social boundaries dividing human from beast can disintegrate when the human psyche is placed under sufficient pressure. Hecuba, whose children have been slaughtered by Greek and Thracian alike, and who is treated with no more respect than an animal, comes to behave like a beast herself when her emotions get out of control. The process of psychological 'bestialization' culminates in Polymestor's prediction that she will actually be transformed into a dog, and her tomb, 'Poor Dog's Tomb', will serve as a landmark to help sailors navigate (1265-73).

It is not only on an individual level that this play shows the boundaries between human and beast disintegrating. It dramatizes the total failure of those social practices, such as deliberative and judicial procedures, which are supposed to regulate the expression of human passions. The Greek assembly is revealed to be no dignified arena of debate, but an unthinking mob, manipulated into sanctioning the outrage of human sacrifice by Odysseus, 'that cunning-hearted, logic-chopping, sweet-tongued courtier of the people' (131-3). Polymestor's show trial in Agamemnon's 'kangaroo court', so hastily convened at the end of the play, is shown to have nothing whatsoever to do with the administration of justice. Despite Agamemnon's nauseating insistence on the inherent superiority of Greek legal procedures (1129-31, 1248), the trial takes place only *after* Hecuba has taken the law into her own hands and exacted her terrible penalty.

As if to underline the emotional isolation inflicted upon Hecuba by serial atrocities, Polymestor is condemned to end his days alone on a deserted island. But the play never lets its audience forget the future awaiting Agamemnon, either. The sacrifice of Polyxena is designed to remind the audience of the sacrifice of Iphigenia, especially since it is caused by the becalming of the Greek fleet near Troy, just as they were becalmed ten years before at Aulis. Hecuba discusses Agamemnon's relationship with Cassandra, implicitly reminding the audience of the reception that awaited this couple at Argos (826-32); moreover, the blinded Polymestor infuriates Agamemnon by accurately foreseeing that his real wife, Clytemnestra, will murder him with an axe in his bath (1279-81). Few ancient tragedies culminate in such unmitigated hopelessness for all the principal characters concerned; even fewer imply that the terrible fates awaiting them are quite so richly deserved.

THE TROJAN WOMEN

In spite of its high ancient reputation, this play was held in low critical estimation from the Renaissance until the twentieth century. Its
lack of an identifiably Aristotelian 'plot' involving error and reversal prompted the judgement of A. W. Schlegel, which was profoundly to influence reactions until well into the twentieth century,
that 'the accumulation of helpless suffering, without even an opposition of sentiment, at last wearies us, and exhausts our compassion'. He was offended both by the famous debate between Helen
and Hecuba, which he saw as 'an idle altercation, which ends in
nothing', and by the protagonist Hecuba, represented throughout
'in sackcloth and ashes, pouring out her lamentations'.[14] It is interesting that Schlegel saw as weaknesses what are now believed to be
this remarkable play's great strengths—its uncompromising
despair, concerted lyrical lamentation, elaborate rhetoric, and the
commanding, central figure of Hecuba.

For the corrective to this modern view of *The Trojan Women* was
not to come until the twentieth century, when the play began to be
performed. One scholar wrote in 1930 of his 'conversion' to a work
he had previously seen as 'a most unpleasant play to read' after
watching a performance which proved to him that 'the incidents
which seemed like disconnected scenes when read appeared to be
much more closely knot together, so that there actually seemed to
be a plot which advanced steadily to a climax'.[15] For it is only a
performance that makes it possible to appreciate the *cumulative*
effect of the sequence of scenes revealing the appalling effect of the
war on the female inhabitants of Troy: Hecuba's pain at her multiple bereavements and humiliation at her enslavement, Cassandra's
psychotic 'celebration' of impending sexual union with her con-
queror, Andromache's anguish at the loss of her baby son
Astyanax, Helen's desperate—but successful—bid to save her own
life, and the climax in which the Greeks set fire to Troy itself and
Hecuba attempts to charge headlong into the flames. For it is the

[14] Augustus W. Schlegel, *A Course of Lectures on Dramatic Art and Literature*, 1st
German edn. 1825, cited from the 2nd edn. trans. John Black (London, 1840),
i. 179–80.
[15] William N. Bates, *Euripides: A Student of Human Nature* (1930), 199–200. The
performance was almost certainly a staging of Gilbert Murray's translation, produced
by Harley Granville Barker's company when it toured the United States with the
play, sponsored by the US Women's Peace Party, in 1915.

reactive presence of the widowed old queen which draws into a coherent vision all the other characters' perspectives: she dominates the stage from the beginning to the end, and her role must have challenged even the greatest of ancient actors. Her part requires not only a powerful signing voice and the ability to deliver elaborate, pointed rhetoric, but considerable physical stamina. Her body seems to symbolize Troy itself: first seen by Poseidon prostrate with grief, she alternately struggles to her feet and collapses to the ground throughout the entire action. At the close she is trying to raise herself from the earth, which she has been pounding in a formal dirge, in order to stumble off to her fate in slavery.

The Trojan Women is unusual in that we know just a little about the other Euripidean plays produced at the same time. The sequence consisted of the lost *Alexandros* and *Palamedes*, the surviving *The Trojan Women*, and a lost satyr play, *Sisyphus*. It is clear that the three tragedies were to a certain extent interconnected. They were all set at or near Troy and treated episodes from the war in chronological order; some characters (for example Hecuba, Cassandra, and Odysseus) appeared in more than one of them. In *Alexandros* the poet dramatized the Trojans' mistake in exposing Paris as a child (obliquely alluded to in *The Trojan Women* 597) and his eventual reunion with his family; *Palamedes* enacted the Greeks' wrongful prosecution of the innocent Palamedes at Troy after Odysseus (apparently at least as unpleasant a character as in *The Trojan Women*) laid false evidence against him. The tragedies as a group thus contained some kind of unity, and some of the original resonances of *The Trojan Women* must be lost on us, who have access only to the third. But it is possible to overstate this problem, since most of antiquity read or watched *The Trojan Women* as an independent artwork, just as we do today.

In three of the plays dating from the last decade of Euripides' life Helen appears as a character (*The Trojan Women*, *Helen*, *Orestes*). In his *Helen* of 412 BCE he was to use the version of her myth which claimed that it was not the heroine herself who went to Troy, but a cloud-carved simulacrum; through this device he was able to use the mythical heroine to explore questions raised by contemporary philosophers in the fields of ontology (what is being?) and epistemology (how do we know things?). But the Greeks had another, even more pressing philosophical question—'how should we live?'—and before Plato, from the *Iliad* onwards, the ethical debates fought in mythical narratives over culpability for the carnage at Troy—debates in which the name of Helen insistently recurred—were the most important forerunners of Greek *moral* philosophy. In *The Trojan Women* Euripides makes his characters strain their intellectual and theological muscles as they attempt to find a reason for the catastrophe, an impulse which the pressure of bereavement quickly transforms into a quest for a single scapegoat—the Spartan Helen—to shoulder all the blame.

On the superhuman level Hecuba, in her more reflective moments, can see abstract forces such as 'necessity' and 'chance' at work (616, 1204), in addition to the particular hatred the gods felt against Troy (612–13, 696, 1241). The chorus is suspicious that Zeus himself, the supreme Olympian, has betrayed the city he once loved well (1060–70); Poseidon himself blames the goddesses Hera and Athena for the destruction of Troy (8–12, 24); others sometimes allege that the war-god, Ares, is individually responsible for the carnage (376, 560). But blaming metaphysical and divine forces does not satisfy the traumatized women of Troy. Nor does acknowledging the culpability of the male players in the drama of the war, whether Odysseus who had the idea of killing the infant Astyanax (1225), Paris who first offended the sons of Atreus (598), or even the collective Greek invaders, denounced by Andromache in a famous paradoxical apostrophe: 'O you Greeks, you who have devised atrocities worthy of barbarians' (764). In a moment of profound psychological insight Hecuba can see that it has been the Greeks' *fear*, fear above all of what Astyanax might one day become, which has made them behave so abominably (1159–65). But not even these male hate figures prove adequate to the Trojan women's need for a focus for their rage. It is Helen above all whom Hecuba blames for the death of Priam and all her personal misery (130–7, 498, 969–1032, etc.), the chorus agrees with her (1111–17), and the overwrought Andromache goes even further, denouncing her lovely sister-in-law as the offspring of a series of malign forces—'the Avenging Spirit . . . Envy and Murder and Death and all the evils that the earth breeds' (768–9).

The issue of blame is most heavily underscored by Helen's astonishing defence speech (see also above, 'Euripides the Athenian'), in which she exploits to the full the ancient rhetoricians' defence technique of *antikatēgoria*—or defence through counter-attack—by blaming others for the very crime of which she stands accused.

Helen finds nearly everyone other than herself guilty of causing the
Trojan War: Hecuba for giving birth to Paris, Priam for failing effi-
ciently to implement the exposure of his infant son (917–22),
Aphrodite for exerting an overwhelming power, and Paris for 'forc-
ing' her into the marriage anyway (959–65). The play thus shows
with devastating clarity not only how men in wartime treat women
and children, but how women barbarized by men blame other
women, and how humans in desperate straits exhaust their emotional energies on attributing blame and exacting punishment
rather than on thinking constructively about the future. But for
Troy, of course, there is to be no future: as the chorus sings in the
closing dirge, 'Like smoke on the wings of the breezes, our land, laid
low in war, now vanishes into nothingness' (1297–9).

ANDROMACHE

Hecuba and *The Trojan Women* both dramatize the effects of the fall
of Troy on its female population; *Andromache* takes one of those
women, Hector's widow, and reveals what happens to her in her
life as a slave in Greece. It thus shows how war informs the lives of
its victims even in times of peace. The conflict in *Andromache* is not
international combat, but a domestic dispute—the bitter war waged
by a man's wife against his mistress. The husband is Neoptolemus,
killer of Priam and son of Achilles; the wife is Hermione, daughter
of Helen; the mistress is the widow of Hector. It is little wonder,
then, that the ghosts of the Trojan War haunt the triangular psychological landscape of the drama. Andromache, for example,
warns Hermione against trying to outdo her mother Helen 'in the
love of men' (229–31).

Fundamentally the plot is similar to that of the *Odyssey* and
many Greek tragedies: it is a 'homecoming' play, in which the male
householder is away but awaited, and a crisis develops in his
absence. In *Andromache* Euripides stretches to extremes this familiar
plot-type by making his audience wait for the hero (who could
return from the Delphic oracle at any moment to discover Spartans
throwing his mistress and son into deadly jeopardy) until three-
quarters of the play have passed. Moreover, when Neoptolemus
finally makes his long-awaited entrance, it is on a funeral bier
(1166). Yet his name and absence have dominated much of the
foregoing action, thus lending emotional coherence to the play's

two earlier movements: the persecution of Andromache and her
rescue by Peleus, followed by Hermione's fear of persecution and
her rescue by Orestes. The 'Hermione' sequence is itself a 'mirror'
scene, offering a distorted reworking (complete with her own nurse
and exaggerated laments) of the foregoing 'Andromache' sequence.
This complex structure, which used to dismay unitarian critics, has
recently been better understood as one of Euripides' subtler experiments with plot-type—or rather, with his audience's *expectations* of
plot-type: *Andromache* mutates from suppliant drama to escape play
to a tragedy of divine vengeance for human misdemeanour. Within
this fluid structure, the action pushes emotional crises and rhetoric
to their limits: the poet strains for 'effects produced by extreme and
wilful distortion of both situation and character'.[16]

The play is set in a relatively remote district in Thessaly, known
as 'Thetideion' because the goddess Thetis lived there with her mortal husband Peleus before she abandoned him (19–20). Marriage—
or rather, marital breakdown—is a crucial theme: Neoptolemus'
marriage to Hermione is disastrous; he finds her sexually unattrac-
tive (157), and she has failed to become pregnant by him. In terms
of the immanent 'rules' of Greek tragedy, Neoptolemus has courted
disaster by expecting his wife and concubine to share one roof: all
the men in the genre who do so (the other two are Agamemnon in
Aeschylus' *Agamemnon* and Heracles in Sophocles' *Trachiniae*) are
dead by the end of the play. As Orestes says here, it is a very bad
thing for one man to live with two women he sleeps with (909, see
also 464–6). This seems to reflect Greek popular ethics: although
male adultery was not condemned, an Athenian legal speech attributed to Demosthenes praises a man for keeping his mistress away
from his marital home out of respect for his wife and old mother
(59.2).

Neoptolemus actually dies at the hand of his rival for Hermione's
hand—the young Argive murderer Orestes. Other ill-omened mar-
riages featuring prominently include Menelaus' union with the
adulterous Helen (680–6) and Agamemnon's even more catastrophic marriage to Clytemnestra (1028–30). It comes as a relief,
therefore, when the play concludes on a note slightly less pes-
simistic about matrimony: Thetis bestows immortality on the hus-

[16] See Anne Pippin Burnett, *Catastrophe Survived: Euripides' Plays of Mixed
Reversal* (Oxford, 1971), 131.

band she once forsook, thus effecting a type of reconciliation, and moreover implies that Andromache's forthcoming marriage to the Trojan exile Helenus will at least be uneventful (1231-49).

Euripidean tragedy was performed by men before a male audience, and it is therefore striking to find him writing a scene where a wife and a mistress quarrel in front of a female 'internal' audience (the chorus). Such theatrical 'eavesdropping' on the secluded and excluded sex is a typical Euripidean technique: in *Hippolytus* Phaedra and her nurse discuss matters of the heart; the heroine of *Electra* has a terrible argument with her mother. But no other Greek tragedy features what today might be termed a 'cat-fight', an altercation between two women, unrelated by blood, over a sexual partner. Indeed, this quarrel is almost without parallel in ancient literature until the Augustan Roman elegist Propertius. He describes, in comic vein, how his mistress Cynthia gatecrashed a party where he was finding solace with two foreign women, attacked them, chased them away, and returned to upbraid her two-timing boyfriend (4.8.59-80).

For humour was one option open to ancient authors, including the versatile Euripides, when dealing with strong 'feminine' emotions. Hermione, a spoilt teenager with pathologically extreme reactions, verges on the laughable. Sexual jealousy makes her lambast Andromache with preposterous rhetoric, until she senses danger to herself and lurches into terror and self-recrimination. Threatening suicide by several means, teetering on the edge of insanity, she is rescued from emotional breakdown only by the appearance of Orestes, a murderous young man to whom she seems to be ideally suited. Yet Hermione's emotional incontinence, comical and dangerous by turns, nevertheless conforms with the beliefs held by Euripides' contemporaries about the effect of puberty on the female psyche. The gynaecological texts attributed to Hippocrates show that young women between the menarche and their first pregnancy were regarded as vulnerable to all manner of physical and psychological disorders; a doctor of Euripides' day would have suspected that Hermione's womb was wandering through her body, causing her to become literally 'hysterical' (the word in Greek signifies a disorder of the uterus). The treatment prescribed would undoubtedly have included sexual intercourse and serial pregnancies.[17]

[17] See A. E. Hanson, 'The Medical Writers' Woman', in D. M. Halperin, J. Winkler, and F. I. Zeitlin (eds.), *Before Sexuality: The Construction of Erotic*

This dark fantasia on the theme of a marriage entails a series of head-on rhetorical collisions between Greek characters from Thessaly, Sparta, and Argos, in addition to Andromache and her nurse, who are not Greek at all. An interest in ethnic provenance is signalled in the entrance song of the local Greek chorus, who tell Andromache that they want to help her 'even though' she is Asiatic (119); the play subsequently demonstrates how personal hatred is often conflated with and expressed by what would today be called 'racial prejudice' and 'racial abuse'. Hermione alleges that Andromache's sexual relationship with Neoptolemus is a sordid quasi-incestuous sexual deviation typical of barbarians (170–6); to Menelaus Andromache expresses a trenchant denunciation of the Spartan character (445–53), a theme which Peleus vituperatively elaborates, with a focus on the promiscuity of Spartan females (595–601). The prominence of the ethnicity theme may in turn be connected with the circumstances of the play's composition. According to an ancient piece of testimony, *Andromache* was not originally performed in Athens. Scholars have suggested various venues, including Argos and Thessaly, but the most probable answer is that the play was written for the royal house of the northern kingdom of Molossia, and thus may represent a unique example of an important sub-genre of ancient tragedies commissioned by patrons outside Athens.

At the end of the play the goddess Thetis announces that Andromache's child (called Molossos in the ancient cast list) will go to Molossia and there found a dynasty of kings (1247–8). In the 420s the ruling member of that dynasty was the young king Tharyps, who was keen to 'Hellenize' his semi-barbarian country and came to Athens for an education, where he was granted citizenship.[18] It is not unlikely that *Andromache* was intended to pay Tharyps a theatrical compliment. For it enacts a myth which bestows upon him a genealogy going back not only to one of the greatest Greek heroic lineages—Peleus, his son Achilles, and his grandson Neoptolemus—but also, through Neoptolemus' 'interracial' union with Andromache, to the royal house of Troy.

Experience in the Ancient Greek World (Princeton, 1990), 309–37, 320; Helen King, *Hippocrates' Woman* (London, 1998).

[18] See further Edith Hall, *Inventing the Barbarian: Greek Self-Definition through Tragedy* (Oxford, 1989), 181.

ATHENIAN SOCIETY

Euripides' plays were first performed in Athens at a festival celebrating Athenian group identity, and consequently often reveal an 'Athenocentrism' manifested, for example, in the famous praise in *Medea* of the beauty of Athens' environment, the grace of its citizens, and its cultural distinction (824–45). In this volume the chorus of *The Trojan Women* fervently wish that if they must be enslaved in Greece, their home will be the famous land of Theseus, who was an Athenian hero (207–9); they later describe in honorific language the Attic island of Salamis and its hero Telamon (799–801).

Yet the social fabric of the city which Euripides inhabited was heterogeneous. In 431 BCE an estimated three hundred thousand human beings lived in the city-state of Attica. But at least twenty-five thousand were resident non-Athenians ('metics'), including businessmen and professionals; a third were slaves, the majority of whom came from beyond Hellenic lands—from the Balkans, the Black Sea, Asia, or Africa. This ethnic pluralism perhaps finds expression in the 'multi-ethnic' casts of tragedy. The characters in these plays, with their Trojan focus, are less ethnically varied than the Phoenicians, Egyptians, Colchians, and Crimeans who appear in some other works by Euripides, but even so *Hecuba* introduces the audience to the Thracian Polymestor and his sons in addition to the Trojans of 'Phrygia' in Asia Minor.

Slavery was fundamental to Athenian economy and society, and tragedy reminds us of this unfortunate portion of the population. In *Acharnians* Aristophanes commented on the intelligence Euripides imputed to his slaves (400–1), and his plays include slaves with important roles as well as mute attendants: the first dialogue of *Andromache* reveals the mutual respect and affection marking the relationship between Andromache and her old slave woman, who is touchingly sensitive to her mistress's humiliating change in status. The institution of slavery is itself much discussed: a character in a lost play affirmed that a noble slave is not dishonoured by the title, because 'many slaves are superior to the free' (fr. 511).[19] In this volume there are several heartbreaking accounts of what life could be like from the perspective of a slave who had known better

---

[19] This and all subsequent references to the fragments of Euripides are cited from A. Nauck, *Tragicorum Graecorum Fragmenta*, 2nd edn., with supplement by B. Snell (Hildesheim, 1964).

circumstances: Hecuba meditates on the degrading tasks that await her, on the discomfort of sleeping on the floor with a bad back, on the mortification of having nothing with which to cover her ageing flesh but tattered rags (*The Trojan Women* 494–7).

The ethical dilemmas and emotional traumas in Euripides are never wholly inseparable from the decidedly unheroic pressures of finance and economics. It is not just that the metaphorical fields draw colour from monetary transactions (Talthybius speaks of a hypothetical punishment of Cassandra in terms of her earning a wage, *The Trojan Women* 409). Money or lack of it colours the characters' experiences; it is an important issue in *Andromache*, where Hermione, the daughter of the fabulously wealthy Spartan royal house, is disgruntled by the simpler lifestyle of the family into which she has married. Some Euripidean characters express lucid insights into the economic basis of society: the most striking example by far is Medea's first monologue in *Medea*, which clarifies the socio-economic imperatives underlying her own and other women's predicament:

Of everything that is alive and has a mind, we women are the most wretched creatures. First of all, we have to buy a husband with a vast outlay of money—we have to take a master for our body . . . divorce brings shame on a woman's reputation and we cannot refuse a husband his rights . . . I would rather stand three times in the battle line than bear one child (*Medea* 230–51).

She trenchantly exposes the jeopardy in which marriage placed women: besides the insulting dowry system, they were subject to legalized rape in marriage, a hypocritical double standard in divorce, and agonizing mortal danger in childbirth.

This kind of speech outraged the Christian writer Origen, who criticized Euripides for inappropriately making women express argumentative opinions (*Contra Celsum* 7.36.34–6); in *Frogs* Euripides claimed to have made tragedy 'more democratic' by keeping his women—young ones and old ones—talking alongside their masters (948–50). It is indeed a remarkable feature of Euripidean tragedy that many of his best thinkers and talkers are women: as the Byzantine scholar Michael Psellus observed with some consternation, in the first debate scene of *Hecuba* Euripides brings the captive Trojan queen on stage 'as antagonist to Odysseus, a man of noble birth and oratorical skill'. Although Euripides 'has Odysseus declaim not without charm', it is the woman to whom the poet 'gives the prize of honour' (*Euripides and George of Pisidia* 95-9).

Women are of course prominent in tragedy generally: patriarchal cultures often use symbolic females to help them imagine abstractions and think about their social order. It is also relevant that women performed the laments at funerals (a reality reflected in the serial dirges of both *Hecuba* and *The Trojan Women*), that Dionysus' cult in reality (as well as in *Bacchae*) involved maenadism and transvestism, and that women were perceived as more emotionally expressive, psychologically erratic (like Hermione in *Andromache*), and susceptible to divine possession (like Cassandra in *The Trojan Women*). They were also regarded as lacking moral autonomy: Athenian men were obsessed with what happened in their households behind their backs, and all the badly behaved women in tragedy—for example Medea, or Hermione in *Andromache*—are permanently or temporarily husbandless. The plays are products of an age where huge sexual, financial, and affective tensions surrounded the transfer of women between the households that made up the city-state. Clytemnestra's appeal to Agamemnon in *Iphigenia at Aulis* describes the vulnerability of women in such a society with pungent accuracy (1146-65). But there was certainly a feeling in antiquity that Euripides' focus on women was sharper than that of either Aeschylus or Sophocles; until recently critics were debating whether Euripides was a misogynist or a feminist. But the only certainties are that he repeatedly chose to create strong and memorable female characters, and that as a dramatist he had a relativist rhetorical capacity for putting both sides of the argument in the sex war.

The position of women in the real world of Athens has itself long been a contentious issue, especially the degree of confinement to which citizen women were subject. But it is clear that most men would have preferred their wives and daughters to stay indoors, to be little discussed in public, to practise thrift, to possess unimpeachable sexual fidelity, and serially to produce healthy sons. Many in the audience would have agreed with Andromache's self-referential description in *The Trojan Women* of the ideal wife, who stays at home, abjures gossip, keeps quiet in the presence of her husband, and knows exactly what are male and female spheres of influence respectively (645-56): they might, however, have felt that Euripides was caricaturing the idealized image of the perfect wife in *Andromache*, when he makes the same heroine boast that she had even aided and abetted Hector in his extra-marital affairs, and breastfed his illegitimate children (222-5)!

Women could not vote or participate in the assembly; nor could they speak for themselves in the courts of law or normally conduct financial transactions except through the agency of their male 'guardian' (*kyrios*)—father, husband, or nearest male relative. A woman known to articulate views in front of men might be regarded as a liability: even the female chorus of *Andromache* rebukes the heroine, during her altercation with Menelaus, for speaking too much as 'a woman talking to a man' (364). But women did of course negotiate with the existing power structures (we hear hints in the orators of the need for men to seek their womenfolk's approval), and were prominent in the central arena of public life constituted by religion. This is reflected in an important ode in *The Trojan Women* describing how the women of Troy had celebrated the dedication of the wooden horse to Pallas Athena by singing and dancing in her honour (545-55). Other Euripidean tragedies feature important priestesses, such as Iphigenia, a priestess of Artemis in his *Iphigenia among the Taurians*, the Egyptian priestess Theonoe in his *Helen*, and the 'Pythia' of Apollo at the Delphic oracle in his *Ion*. In a lost play the wise woman Melanippe defended women against practitioners of misogynist rhetoric like Hippolytus (*Hippolytus* 616-68); one of her strategies was to list the Panhellenic cults which women administered (fr. 499):[20]

Men's criticism of women is worthless twanging of a bowstring and evil talk. Women are better than men, as I will show . . . Consider their role in religion, for that, in my opinion, comes first. We women play the most important part, because women prophesy the will of Zeus in the oracles of Phoebus. And at the holy site of Dodona near the sacred oak, females convey the will of Zeus to inquirers from Greece. As for the sacred rituals for the Fates and the Nameless Ones, all these would not be holy if performed by men, but prosper in women's hands. In this way women have a rightful share in the service of the gods. Why is it, then, that women must have a bad reputation?

[20] Translation taken from M. R. Lefkowitz and M. B. Fant, *Women's Life in Greece and Rome: A Source Book in Translation* (London, 1992), 14.

EURIPIDES AND RELIGION

Melanippe's words are a fitting introduction to the category of *dramatis personae* constituted by the gods. What is to be deduced about Euripides' religious beliefs from his on-stage divinities in these plays (Poseidon, Athena, Thetis), and the Apollo, Death, Aphrodite, Artemis, Madness, Hermes, Dioscuri, and Dionysus who physically appear in others? One function of Euripides' gods from the machine, such as Thetis in *Andromache*, is certainly to provide a metatheatrical 'alienation' device drawing attention to the author's power over his dramatic narrative. But does that mean that he was an atheist?

Allegations that Euripides was a religious radical began in his lifetime. Aristophanes' caricature includes the charge that Euripides' tragedies had persuaded people 'that the gods do not exist' (*Women at the Thesmophoria* 450-1), and portrays him praying to the Air ('Ether') and 'Intelligence' (*Frogs* 890-2). By later antiquity it was believed that it was at Euripides' house that Protagoras, the great relativist and agnostic thinker, read out his famous treatise on the gods, beginning 'Man is the measure of all things' (fr. 80 B 1 Diels-Kranz; Diog. Laert. 9.8.5).

Some characters in Euripides undoubtedly articulate views which must have sounded modern and 'scientific' to his audience. They depart from traditional theology by attributing the workings of the universe either to physical causes or to the power of the human mind. In *The Trojan Women*, for example, Hecuba wonders whether Zeus should be addressed as 'the necessity imposed by nature, or human intelligence' (884-6). In one lost play a character asserted that 'the mind that is in each of us is god'; in another the first principle of the cosmos was said to be Air, which 'sends forth the summer's light, and makes the winter marked with cloud, makes life and death'; in a third Air was explicitly equated with Zeus (frr. 1018, 330.3-5, 941).

There has always been a critical tendency to see Euripides as seeking to overturn or challenge traditional religion, especially belief in the arbitrary, partisan, and often malevolent anthropomorphic gods of the Homeric epics. It has been argued that in figures such as Aphrodite and Artemis in *Hippolytus*, or Poseidon and Athena in *The Trojan Women*, Euripides put on stage the most 'Homeric' of all Greek tragic gods precisely to undermine them. Thus his theatrical divinities, the argument goes, are a literary throwback to the old anthropomorphism, constituting a consciously reductive enactment of the commonly accepted personalities of the Olympians. Alternatively, Euripides is interpreted as a humanist who denies any but human motivation to human action and whose works operate on a similar principle to Thucydides' rationalist and atheological determination that it is human nature, *to anthrōpinon*, which drives and conditions history. Critics have even seen Hecuba in *The Trojan Women* as a kind of proselyte advocating a new Euripidean doctrine, emphasizing her assertion that whatever the name 'Zeus' may really mean—necessity or intelligence—it is that principle which disposes 'all human affairs according to justice' (886, see also Theonoe's words in *Helen* 1002–3). This view, allegedly, suggests a belief in a new religion of peace and justice, which Euripides is urging should replace the old Olympian cults.

Yet it is mistaken to confuse Euripidean characters' more innovative theological opinions with his (unknown) personal views. Moreover, many of the expressions of scepticism are more complicated than they seem. One rhetorical function of scepticism is to *affirm* the belief being doubted simply by raising it to consciousness.[21] Hecuba may doubt the existence of an anthropomorphic god called Zeus, but her scepticism brings the difficulty in understanding the reasons for human misery to the forefront of the audience's minds. Moreover, her words must be heard against the background of the play's opening scene, in which two important Olympians brutally explain the past, present, and future sufferings of both Trojans and Greeks in terms of divine omnipotence, feuds, spite, and vindictiveness.

For the overall impact of Euripidean tragedy does nothing to disrupt the three fundamental tenets of Athenian religion as practised by its citizens: that gods exist, that they pay attention (welcome or unwelcome) to the affairs of mortals, and that some kind of reciprocal allegiance between gods and humans was in operation, most visibly instantiated in sacrifice. The tragic performances were framed by the rituals of the Dionysia, and ritual fundamentally informs tragedy's imagery, plots, and songs: a study of wedding and funeral motifs, for example, has shown how they become conflated into sinister variations of the figure of the 'bride of death', a strik-

---

[21] See T. C. W. Stinton, ' "Si credere dignum est": Some Expressions of Disbelief in Euripides and Others', *PCPS* 22 (1976), 60–89.

ingly important poetic figure, especially in relation to Polyxena in *Hecuba* and Cassandra in *The Trojan Women*.[22] Ritual, moreover, brings group consolidation and profound consolation, as a collective human response in the face of catastrophe. As the chorus of *The Trojan Women* sing, 'When misfortunes come, how sweet are tears and sorrowful songs and grief-laden music' (608-9).

The plays themselves stage ritual, and frame accounts of it. In *Hecuba* the terrible sacrifice of Polyxena is duly accompanied by a ritual libation and a prayer to the recipient, before mutating into a funeral rite, complete with the heaping of leaves and pinewood to make the funeral pyre (527-9, 573-5). In *The Trojan Women* the crazed Cassandra performs a ritual wedding song in anticipation of her union with Agamemnon (308-40), and Hecuba actually prepares the corpse of the baby Astyanax for burial in front of the audience (1218-50). In *Andromache* a messenger relates how Neoptolemus had prepared for an animal sacrifice at Delphi (1102-13). The *history* of religion certainly seems to have fascinated Euripides, who includes in his tragedies numerous descriptions of specific cults. In *Hecuba* Polymestor has consulted the local Thracian oracle of Dionysus (1267). In *The Trojan Women* the chorus refer to Athena's revelation of the olive tree on the Athenian acropolis (801-3), and describe in some detail the Trojan cult of Zeus and the rituals in his honour which they practised before the destruction of their city (1060-76). In *Andromache* the heroine explains that the locality is named after the goddess Thetis because she had married Peleus there (19-20), and the end of the play provides a mythical explanation for the cult of the hero Peleus on the nearby coastline (1263-9).

Euripidean plots are repeatedly driven by violations of the great taboos and imperatives constituting popular Greek ethics, the boundaries defining unacceptable behaviour which Sophocles' *Antigone* calls the 'unwritten and unshakeable laws of the gods' (*Ant.* 454-5), and which Euripidean characters are more likely to call 'the laws common to the Greeks' (e.g. *Heraclidae* 1010). These regulated human relationships at every level. In the family they proscribed incest, kin-killing, and failure to bury the dead: although neither incest nor kin-killing is prominent in the plays in this

[22] Rush Rehm, *Marriage to Death: The Conflation of Wedding and Funeral Rituals in Greek Tragedy* (Princeton, 1994).

volume, there are several references to the murders within the family of Agamemnon (e.g. *Hecuba* 1279–81), in *Hecuba* Polymestor's failure to bury Polydorus compounds the crime of murder, and the women of Troy are heartbroken because they are unable to give their husbands burial (*The Trojan Women* 1081–4). At the level of relationships between members of different households and cities these 'common laws' ascribed to Zeus the protection of vulnerable groups, such as suppliants and parties engaged in the compact of reciprocal trust required by the guest/host relationship.

Supplication is a formal entreaty, accompanied by ritualized touching of knees, hand, and chin, which is intended to put the recipient under a religious obligation to accede to the suppliant's requests. Supplication in Euripides characterizes numerous crucial scenes. Polyxena's pride is underscored by her conspicuous *refusal* to supplicate Odysseus or to beg him not to lead her away to her death in the early part of *Hecuba* (345), although Hecuba has no such scruples about supplicating Agamemnon when persuading him to help her wreak vengeance on Polymestor. Indeed, she rhetorically wishes that her entire body could be turned into a vehicle for supplication by possessing voices in her arms, her hands, her hair, and her feet, 'so that they could all weep together and clasp your knees, urging arguments of every kind' (836–40). At a crucial moment in *Trojan Women*, when Menelaus has just passed a sentence of immediate death upon his adulterous wife Helen, she predictably supplicates him. In this particular case, of course, it is the physical contact with the suppliant, rather than a religiously conceived obligation, that seems to be the decisive factor (1042–57). In *Andromache* both the heroine and Hermione use supplication in their appeals to male rescuers (573, 892). The regulation of hospitality is also apparent in these plays: in Hecuba Polymestor has utterly betrayed his relationship with the Trojan royal house by murdering his guest Polydorus, and in *Andromache* a major topic of discussion is the nature of the relationship, created by the marriage of Hermione to Neoptolemus, between the Spartan and Phthian royal houses.

MUSIC, CHORUS, SONG

We have lost the melodies to which the lyrics of tragedy were sung to the accompaniment of pipes (*auloi*). But it is possible partially to decipher what John Gould has called 'strategies of poetic sensibility'[23] within the formal, conventional media open to the tragedian: besides the choral passages, which were danced and sung, the tragedian had several modes of delivery to choose from for his individual actors. In addition to set-piece speeches and line-by-line spoken dialogue (*stichomythia*), they included solo song, duet, sung interchange with the chorus, and an intermediate mode of delivery, probably chanting to pipe accompaniment, signalled by the anapaestic rhythm ($\cup \cup -$). Euripides' songs were extremely popular: the ancients believed that some Athenians in Sicily saved themselves after the disaster at Syracuse in 413 BCE by singing some of his songs to their captors (Plutarch, *Life of Nicias* 29). In a lost comedy named *Euripides-Lover* (Axionicus fr. 3) a character discusses people who hate all but Euripidean lyrics.

In this edition the sung and chanted sections have been labelled and laid out in shorter lines so that the reader can appreciate the shifts between speech and musical passages. In *Hecuba*, when Polymestor crawls out of the tent, blinded and bereaved, he sings to express the agony he is suffering and the extremity of his emotional turmoil (*Hecuba* 1056–1106); in *Andromache* the heroine sings a sad lament for Hector, Troy, and her own present plight, rendered unusually poignant by her use of an elegiac metre unique to surviving tragedy (103–16). Awareness of the intermittent use of the singing voice matters because it mattered in antiquity. The musicologist Aristoxenus said that speech begins to sound like song *when we are emotional* (*El. Harm.* 1.9–10). It certainly affects our appreciation of Hecuba's desolation, for example, that Euripides chose to make her *sing* about her plight throughout both *Hecuba* and *The Trojan Women*; Helen, on the contrary, is the only female lead never to sing in *The Trojan Women*, a sign, perhaps, of the difference between her calculating and manipulative character and the emotional depth of the women of Troy. Or perhaps the difference articulated is connected with ethnicity: the Greek Helen's spoken rhetoric, like that of her Greek husband Menelaus, contrasts sharply with the songs of the Trojan chorus and the dirges performed antiphonally with them by Hecuba and Andromache.

The chorus can also speak, and even function as an 'umpire' between warring parties in a debate (*Andromache* 232–3, 691–2).

[23] John Gould, 'Dramatic Character and "Human Intelligibility" in Greek Tragedy', *PCPS* 24 (1978), 43–67, esp. 5–8.

Sometimes the chorus' songs 'fill in' time while actors change roles, or 'telescope' time while events happen off stage (e.g. *Hecuba* 444–83, *Andromache* 1009–46). Often the chorus sings forms of lyric song derived from the world of collective ritual. Passages of choral song may have their roots in hymns of praise to the gods; in *The Trojan Women* venerational songs are subtly turned into lyric critiques, when the women of Troy sing to Eros about the destruction sexual love has brought on the country (840–59), and to Zeus about the failure of their cult in his honour (1060–80).

Some choral odes present a mythical narrative functioning as a form of memory; in *Andromache* the chorus traces the sorrows of Andromache back beyond the Trojan War to the judgement of Paris on Mount Ida (274–308). Other choral songs may be more firmly rooted in the time of the action taking place, but likewise offer valuable contextualizing material. In an exquisite ode at the heart of *Hecuba*, the Chorus of Trojan widows sing of the night that Troy fell, how they first heard the shouting from the streets when their husbands had fallen asleep, and they were preparing for bed, arranging their hair, and 'gazing down the gleaming perspective of my golden mirror' (914–27). The ode thus reminds the audience that Hecuba's emotional pain is as multiple as the widows of Troy: as they say to Andromache in *Trojan Women*, 'Your tragedy is the same as ours. As you lament your own fate, you teach me where I stand in my woes' (684–5). Yet some choral odes are more philosophical or contemplative in orientation, and meditate in general terms on the issues which have been explored in the concrete situation of the play's previous episode. Thus the chorus of *Andromache*, witnesses to the domestic conflict between the householder's two women, reflect on the similar problems caused by rival claimants to the position of 'top dog' in politics, poetry, and seafaring (464–93).

SPEECH

In Aristophanes' *Frogs*, a prominent feature of Euripidean tragedy is the 'programmatic' prologue delivered by a leading character, which is characterized in the comedy as predictable in both metrical form and in 'scene-setting' function. But the Aristophanic caricature was unfair: the prologue characteristically establishes expectations, themes, and images which will subsequently become central to the drama. Euripides, moreover, varied the impact by his choice of speaker. Choosing to open *Hecuba* with the ghost of her son Polydorus not only establishes the play's important focus on the relationships between the living and the dead—he informs the audience that another ghost, that of Achilles, has demanded Polyxena's blood—but by a brilliant stroke of dramatic irony allows the omniscient spectators subsequently to concentrate on Hecuba's emotional *response* to the news of the death of her son, with which they are already cognizant. In *The Trojan Women* it is a god, Poseidon, who explains the background to the tragedy, and thus sets the whole action within a theological frame of reference which fundamentally alters the audience's perspective on the human immorality and amorality which they are about to witness. Only *Andromache* in this volume opens with the Aristophanic caricature of the protagonist's prologue, and it is crucial to the audience's reactions to the ensuing action that the wise and emotionally mature heroine is allowed to stake her claim to their sympathies at her play's outset.

The Roman rhetorician Quintilian judged Euripides of more use than Sophocles to the trainee orator (10.1.67), and the modern reader will undoubtedly be struck by the series of peculiarly formal debates in these plays: Hecuba versus Odysseus and versus Polymestor in *Hecuba*, Helen versus Hecuba in *The Trojan Women*, Andromache versus Hermione and Peleus versus Menelaus in *Andromache*. The debate (*agōn*) is one of the features which Athenian tragedy assimilated from the oral performances which characterized two other great institutions of the democracy: the lawcourts and the assembly. To meet the increasing need for polished public speaking and its assessment under the widened franchise, the study of the science of persuasion, or the art of rhetoric, developed rapidly around the middle of the fifth century (see also above, 'Euripides the Athenian'); this is reflected in tragedy's increased use of formal rhetorical figures, tropes, 'common topics' such as pragmatism and expediency, and hypothetical arguments from probability. One form of exercise available to a trainee orator was the 'double argument'—the construction or study of twin speeches for and against a particular proposition, or for the defence and prosecution in a hypothetical trial. As a character in Euripides' lost *Antiope* averred, 'If one were clever at speaking, one could have a competition between two arguments in every single case' (fr. 189). In assessing Euripidean rhetoric it must be remembered that his audience had become accustomed to startling displays by litigants in lawsuits (Aristophanes, *Wasps* 562–86); by the 420s political oratory sometimes descended into competitive exhibitionism in which the medium had superseded the message (Thuc. 3.38).

Euripides' gift for narrative is perhaps clearest in his 'messenger speeches', vivid mini-epics of exciting action, whether it is Talthybius' heart-rending account of the sacrifice of Polyxena in *Hecuba* (518–82), or the messenger's report of the death of Neoptolemus at Delphi in *Andromache* (1086–65). All Euripides' poetry is marked by exquisite simile and metaphor, often traced thematically through a play (in *Hecuba* maritime imagery, in *Trojan Women* vivid personifications of violence, in *Andromache* stitching, weaving, ropes, and textiles). Euripides' picturesque style was much admired in antiquity ('Longinus', *de Sublim.* 15.1–4).

Euripides showed infinite versatility of register, and was capable of selecting rare poetic words for special effect (Ar. *Poet.* 58^{b}19–24). Yet he still revolutionized the diction of tragedy by making his characters speak in his distinctively 'human way'. Aristotle affirms that it was not until Euripides wrote roles using language drawn from everyday conversation that tragedy discovered natural dialogue. This ordinary quality to the language spoken by Euripides' characters attracted emulation by able poets even within his lifetime, yet in Aristophanes' *Frogs* Dionysus dismisses them as insignificant 'chatterers' in comparison (89–95). For Euripides was really doing something extremely difficult in making his unforgettable characters express themselves plausibly and 'like human beings'. Thus the author of an encomium to Euripides in the *Palatine Anthology* justifiably discourages the aspiring imitator (7.50):

> Poet, do not attempt to go down Euripides' road;
> It is hard for men to tread.
> It seems easy, but the man who tries to walk it
> Finds it rougher than if it were set with cruel stakes.
> If you even try to scratch the surface of Medea, daughter of Aeetes,
> You shall die forgotten. Leave Euripides' crowns alone.[24]

[24] I am extremely grateful to James Morwood and Lindsay Hall for their insightful help with this Introduction.

NOTE ON THE TRANSLATION

This is a prose translation. However, lyrical and choric passages—intended for sung or chanted performance—have been laid out on shorter lines. These will inevitably have the appearance of free verse, but the translator's aim has been simply to denote the distinction between the spoken and sung or chanted areas of the play.

The translations are from James Diggle's Oxford Classical Text. I have put square brackets round passages of any serious significance which Professor Diggle believes are not by Euripides or are highly unlikely to be by him. Corrupt passages where the meaning is seriously in doubt are placed between † signs. I have kept discussion of both kinds of passage to an absolute minimum in the notes.

Asterisks (*) signify that there is a note on the words or passages so marked.

I have generally used the Latinized spellings of the Greek names but allowed the Greek spellings where the Latinized equivalent would have appeared strange.

Line numbers refer to the Greek text.

SELECT BIBLIOGRAPHY

GENERAL BOOKS ON GREEK TRAGEDY

P.E. Easterling (ed.), *The Cambridge Companion to Greek Tragedy* (Cambridge, 1987); Simon Goldhill, *Reading Greek Tragedy* (Cambridge, 1986); Rush Rehm, *Greek Tragic Theatre* (London, 1992); Charles Segal, *Interpreting Greek Tragedy: Myth, Poetry, Text* (Ithaca/London, 1986); Oliver Taplin, *Greek Tragedy in Action* (London, 1978); J. P. Vernant and P. Vidal-Naquet, *Tragedy and Myth in Ancient Greece* (English trans., Brighton, 1981); John J. Winker and F. I. Zeitlin (eds.), *Nothing to do with Dionysos? Athenian Drama in its Social Context* (Princeton, 1990).

GENERAL BOOKS ON EURIPIDES

P. Burian (ed.), *New Directions in Euripidean Criticism* (Durham, NC, 1985); Christopher Collard, *Euripides* (G&R New Surveys in the Classics 24; Oxford, 1981); D. J. Conacher, *Euripidean Drama* (Toronto, 1967); *Euripide* (Entretiens sur l'antiquité classique, 6; Fondation Hardt, Vandouvres-Geneva, 1960); Helene P. Foley, *Ritual Irony: Poetry and Sacrifice in Euripides* (Ithaca, 1985); G. M. Grube, *The Drama of Euripides*, 2nd edn. (London, 1962); M. Halleran, *Stagecraft in Euripides* (London, 1985); A. N. Michelini, *Euripides and the Tragic Tradition* (Madison, 1987); Judith Mossman (ed.), *Oxford Readings in Euripides* (Oxford, 2000); E. Segal (ed.), *Euripides: A Collection of Critical Essays* (Englewood Cliffs, 1968); P. Vellacott, *Ironic Drama: A Study of Euripides' Method and Meaning* (Cambridge, 1976); C. H. Whitman, *Euripides and the Full Circle of Myth* (Harvard, 1974).

EURIPIDES' LIFE AND BIOGRAPHIES

Hans-Ulrich Gösswein, *Die Briefe des Euripides* (Meisenheim am Glan, 1975); J. Gregory, *Euripides and the Instruction of the Athenians* (Ann Arbor, 1991); P.T. Stevens, 'Euripides and the Athenians', *JHS* 76 (1956), 87–94; M. R. Lefkowitz, *The Lives of the Greek Poets* (London, 1981), 88–104, 163–9; R.E. Wycherley, 'Aristophanes and Euripides', *G&R* 15 (1946), 98–107.

OPINIONS AND INTERPRETATIONS

R. B. Appleton, *Euripides the Idealist* (London/Toronto/New York, 1927); Robert Eisner, 'Euripides' Use of Myth', *Arethusa*, 12 (1979), 153–74; for 'historicist' approaches see E. Delebecque, *Euripide et la guerre du Péloponnèse* (Paris, 1951), and V. Di Benedetto, *Euripide: teatro e società* (Turin, 1971); E. R. Dodds, 'Euripides the Irrationalist', *CR* 43 (1929), 97–104; H. Reich, 'Euripides, der Mystiker', in *Festschrift zu C. F. Lehmann-Haupts sechzigsten Geburtstage* (Vienna, 1921), 89–93; K. Reinhardt, 'Die Sinneskrise bei Euripides', *Eranos*, 26 (1957), 279–317—Euripides as a nihilist; in his *Existentialism and Euripides* (Victoria, 1977) William Sale draws on both Heidegger and Freud; A. W. Verrall, *Euripides The Rationalist* (Cambridge, 1895).

RECEPTION OF EURIPIDEAN TRAGEDY

Peter Burian, 'Tragedy Adapted for Stages and Screens: The Renaissance to the Present', in Easterling (ed.), *The Cambridge Companion to Greek Tragedy* (see above), 228–83; Stuart Gillespie, *The Poets on the Classics* (London/New York, 1988), 90–4; Edith Hall, 'Medea and British Legislation before the First World War', *G&R* 46 (1999), 42–77; K. Mackinnon, *Greek Tragedy into Film* (London/Sydney, 1986); Fiona Macintosh, 'Tragedy in Performance: Nineteenth and Twentieth-Century Productions', in Easterling (ed.), *The Cambridge Companion to Greek Tragedy* (see above), 284–323; Martin Mueller, *Children of Oedipus and other Essays on the Imitation of Greek Tragedy 1550–1800* (Toronto, 1980), 46–63; F. L. Lucas, *Euripides and his Influence* (London, 1923).

VISUAL ARTS

Vase-paintings illustrating scenes from Euripides are collected in A. D. Trendall and T. B. L. Webster, *Illustrations of Greek Drama* (London, 1971), 72–105, and supplemented in the articles under the names of each important mythical character (e.g. 'Odysseus') in the multi-volume ongoing *Lexicon Iconographicum Mythologiae Classicae* (Zurich/Munich, 1984–?). See also Richard Green, *Theater in Ancient Greek Society* (London, 1994); Oliver Taplin, 'The

Pictorial Record', in Easterling (ed.), *The Cambridge Companion to Greek Tragedy* (section 1 above), 69-90; Kurt Weitzmann, 'Euripides Scenes in Byzantine Art', *Hesperia*, 18 (1949), 159-210.

PRODUCTION AND PERFORMANCE CONTEXT

Giovanni Comotti, *Music in Greek and Roman Culture* (English trans., Baltimore/London, 1989), 32-41; E. Csapo and W. J. Slater, *The Context of Ancient Drama* (Ann Arbor, 1995), 79-101; S. Goldhill, 'The Great Dionysia and Civic Ideology', in J. Winkler and F. I. Zeitlin (eds.), *Nothing to do with Dionysos? Athenian Drama in its Social Context* (Princeton, 1990), 97-129; John Gould, 'Tragedy in Performance', in B. Knox and P. E. Easterling (eds.), *The Cambridge History of Classical Literature*, vol. i (Cambridge, 1985), 258-81; Edith Hall, 'Actor's Song in Tragedy', in Simon Goldhill and Robin Osborne (eds.), *Performance Culture and Athenian Democracy* (Cambridge, 1999), 96-122; Nicolaos C. Hourmouziades, *Production and Imagination in Euripides: Form and Function of the Scenic Space* (Athens, 1965); Maarit Kaimio, *Physical Contact in Greek Tragedy* (Helsinki, 1988); Solon Michaelides, *The Music of Ancient Greece: An Encyclopaedia* (London, 1978), 117-19; A. Pickard-Cambridge, *The Dramatic Festivals of Athens*, 3rd edn., revised by J. Gould and D. M. Lewis (Oxford, 1988); Erika Simon, *The Ancient Theater* (London/New York, 1982); Oliver Taplin, *The Stagecraft of Aeschylus* (Oxford, 1977), and 'Did Greek Dramatists Write Stage Instructions?', *PCPS* 23 (1977), 121-32.

On satyr drama see P. E. Easterling, 'A Show for Dionysos', in Easterling (ed.), *The Cambridge Companion to Greek Tragedy* (see above), 36-53; Richard Seaford (ed.), *Euripides' Cyclops* (Oxford, 1984), 1-45; E. Hall 'Ithyphallic Males Behaving Badly: Satyr Drama as Gendered Tragic Ending', in M. Wyke (ed.), *Parchments of Gender: Deciphering the Bodies of Antiquity* (Oxford, 1998), 13-37.

SOCIAL AND HISTORICAL CONTEXT

See J. K. Davies, *Democracy and Classical Greece* (Glasgow, 1978), 63-128, and 'Athenian Citizenship: The Descent Group and the Alternatives', *CJ* 73 (1977-8), 105-21; Anton Powell, *Athens and Sparta: Constructing Greek Political and Social History from 478 BC*

(London, 1988); Paul Cartledge, *The Greeks* (Oxford, 1996) and (ed.), *The Cambridge Illustrated History of Ancient Greece* (Cambridge, 1997).

For an overview of the problems in reconstructing Athenian women's lives, see Josine Blok's review in J. Blok and H. Mason (eds.), *Sexual Asymmetry: Studies in Ancient Society* (Amsterdam, 1987), 1–57. For a recent range of views on gender issues see D. Cohen, *Law, Sexuality, and Society: The Enforcement of Morals in Classical Athens* (Cambridge, 1991); John Gould, 'Law, Custom, and Myth: Aspects of the Social Position of Women in Classical Athens', *JHS* 100 (1980), 38–59; Virginia Hunter, *Policing Athens* (Princeton, 1994), 9–42; R. Just, *Women in Athenian Law and Life* (London/New York, 1989); Elaine Fantham *et al.* (eds.), *Women in the Classical World* (New York/Oxford, 1994).

SPECIFIC ASPECTS OF EURIPIDEAN DRAMA

Rachel Aélion, *Euripide. Héritier d'Eschyle*, 2 vols. (Paris, 1983); W. G. Arnott, 'Euripides and the Unexpected', *G&R* 20 (1973), 49–63; Luigi Battezzatto, *Il Monologo nel teatro di Euripide* (Pisa, 1995); Francis M. Dunn, *Tragedy's End: Closure and Innovation in Euripidean Drama* (New York/Oxford, 1996); H. Erbse, *Studien zum Prolog der euripideischen Tragödie* (Berlin, 1984); M. Fusillo, 'Was ist eine romanhafte Tragödie? Überlegungen zu Euripides' Experimentalismus', *Poetica*, 24 (1992), 270–99; Richard Hamilton, 'Prologue, Prophecy and Plot in Four Plays of Euripides', *AJP* 99 (1978), 277–302, and 'Euripidean Priests', *HSCP* 89 (1985), 53–73; Rosemary Harriott, 'Aristophanes' Audience and the Plays of Euripides', *BICS* 9 (1962), 1–9; Martin Hose, *Studien zum Chor bei Euripides* (Berlin, 1990–1); E. O'Connor-Visser, *Aspects of Human Sacrifice in the Tragedies of Euripides* (Amsterdam, 1987); Bernd Seidensticker, 'Tragic Dialectic in Euripidean Tragedy', in M. S. Silk (ed.), *Tragedy and the Tragic: Greek Theatre and Beyond* (Oxford, 1996), 377–96; Sophie Trenkner, *The Greek Novella in the Classical Period* (Cambridge, 1958), 31–78; R. P. Winnington-Ingram, 'Euripides: *poiētēs sophos*', *Arethusa*, 2 (1969), 127–42.

For the lost plays of Euripides see C. Collard, M. J. Cropp, and K. H. Lee (eds.), *Euripides: Selected Fragmentary Plays*, vols. i–ii (Warminster, 1995, 1999); T. B. L. Webster, *The Tragedies of Euripides* (London, 1967).

On slaves in Euripides see H. Kuch, *Kriegsgefangenschaft und Sklaverei bei Euripides* (Berlin, 1974); K. Synodinou, *On the Concept of Slavery in Euripides* (Eng. trans., Ioannina, 1977); E. Hall, 'The Sociology of Athenian Tragedy', in Easterling (ed.), *The Cambridge Companion to Greek Tragedy* (see above), 93–126; D. P. Stanley-Porter, 'Mute Actors in the Tragedies of Euripides', *BICS* 20 (1973), 68–93. On children see G. Sifakis, 'Children in Greek Tragedy', *BICS* 26 (1979), 67–80. On women see H. Foley, 'The Conception of Women in Athenian Drama', in H. P. Foley (ed.), *Reflections of Women in Antiquity* (London/New York, 1981), 127–67; Ruth Herder, *Die Frauenrolle bei Euripides* (Stuttgart, 1993); Nicole Loraux, *Tragic Ways of Killing a Woman* (English trans.; Cambridge, Mass., 1987); Richard Seaford, 'The Structural Problems of Marriage in Euripides', in A. Powell (ed.), *Euripides, Women and Sexuality* (London/New York, 1990), 151–76; Nancy Sorkin Rabinowitz, *Anxiety Veiled: Euripides and the Traffic in Women* (Ithaca/London, 1993); Froma Zeitlin, *Playing the Other: Gender and Society in Classical Greek Literature* (Chicago/London, 1996).

For religion in Euripides see C. Sourvinou-Inwood, 'Tragedy and Religion: Constructs and Meanings', in Christopher Pelling (ed.), *Greek Tragedy and the Historian* (Oxford, 1997), 161–86. For sceptical discussions see M. R. Lefkowitz, 'Was Euripides an Atheist?', *Studi Italiani*, 5 (1987), 149–65, and ' "Atheism" and "impiety" in Euripides' dramas', *CQ* 39 (1989), 70–82; G. E. Dimock, '*God or Not God, or between the Two*': *Euripides' Helen* (Northampton, Mass., 1977)—Euripides' evangelism; Harvey Yunis, *A New Creed: Fundamental Religious Beliefs in the Athenian Polis and Euripidean Drama* (= *Hypomnemata*, 91; Göttingen, 1988). On supplication scenes, see J. Gould, 'Hiketeia', *JHS* 93 (1973), 74–103.

On the sophists, philosophy, and the intellectual background see D. J. Conacher, *Euripides and the Sophists: Some Dramatic Treatments of Philosophical Ideas* (London, 1998); J. H. Finley, 'Euripides and Thucydides', in *Three Essays on Thucydides* (Cambridge, Mass., 1967), 1–24; S. Goldhill, *Reading Greek Tragedy* (Cambridge, 1986), 222–43; G. B. Kerferd, *The Sophistic Movement* (Cambridge, 1981); W. Nestle, *Untersuchungen über die philosophischen Quellen des Euripides* (*Philologus* suppl. 8.4; 1901), 557–655, and *Euripides: der Dichter der griechischen Aufklärung* (Stuttgart, 1901); F. Solmsen, *Intellectual Experiments of the Greek Enlightenment* (Princeton, 1975), 24–31, 132–41.

On rhetoric see V. Bers, 'Tragedy and Rhetoric', in I. Worthington (ed.), *Greek Rhetoric in Action* (London/New York, 1994), 176-95; Richard Buxton, *Persuasion in Greek Tragedy* (Cambridge, 1982); C. Collard, 'Formal Debates in Euripidean Drama', *G&R* 22 (1975); D. J. Conacher, 'Rhetoric and Relevance in Euripidean Drama' *AJP* 102 (1981), 3-25; E. Hall, 'Lawcourt Dramas: The Power of Performance in Greek Forensic Oratory', *BICS* 40 (1995), 39-58; M. Lloyd, *The Agon in Euripides* (Oxford, 1992).

On characterization, see H. P. Stahl, 'On "Extra-Dramatic" Communication in Euripides', *Yale Classical Studies*, 25 (1977), 159-76; J. Griffin, 'Characterization in Euripides', in C. Pelling (ed.), *Characterization and Individuality in Greek Literature* (Oxford, 1990), 128-49.

On speech, language, style, and imagery, see Shirley Barlow, *The Imagery of Euripides* (London, 1971); I. J. F. de Jong, *Narrative in Drama: The Art of the Euripidean Messenger-Speech* (Leiden, 1991); P. T. Stevens, *Colloquial Expressions in Euripides* (Wiesbaden, 1976); Ernst Schwinge, *Die Verwendung der Stichomythie in den Dramen des Euripides* (Heidelberg, 1968).

INDIVIDUAL PLAYS

Hecuba

Commentaries: M. Tierney (ed.), *Euripides' Hecuba* (Dublin, 1946, repr. Bristol, 1979); Christopher Collard (ed.), *Euripides' Hecuba* (Warminster, 1991).

Studies: A. Adkins, 'Basic Values in Euripides' *Hecuba* and *Hercules Furens*', *CQ* 16 (1966), 193-219; Stephen Daitz, 'Concepts of Freedom and Slavery in Euripides' *Hecuba*', *Hermes*, 99 (1971), 217-26; George Gellie, '*Hecuba* and Tragedy', *Antichthon*, 14 (1980), 30-44; M. Heath, 'Iure principium locum tenet: Euripides' *Hecuba*', *BICS* 34 (1987), 40-68; J. Jouanna, 'Realité et théâtralité dans l'Hécube d'Euripide', *Ktema*, 7 (1982), 43-52; Katherine King, 'The Politics of Imitation: Euripides' *Hekabe* and the Homeric Achilles', *Arethusa*, 18 (1985), 47-66; D. Kovacs, *The Heroic Muse: Studies in the Hippolytus and Hecuba of Euripides* (Baltimore/London, 1987); C. A. E. Luschnig, 'Euripides' *Hecabe*: The Time is out of Joint', *CJ* 71 (1976), 227-341; R. Meridor, 'Plot and Myth in

Euripides' *Heracles* and *Troades*', *Phoenix*, 38 (1984), 205-15;
Judith Mossman, *Wild Justice: A Study of Euripides' Hecuba* (Oxford,
1995); Martha Nussbaum, 'The Betrayal of Convention: A Reading
of Euripides' *Hecuba*', in *The Fragility of Goodness* (Cambridge,
1986), 397-422; R. Meridor, 'The Function of Polymestor's Crime
in the *Hecuba* of Euripides', *Eranos*, 81 (1983), 13-20; C. Segal,
'Violence and the Other: Greek, Female and Barbarian in Euripides'
Hecuba', *TAPA* 120 (1990), 109-31; Theodore Tarkow, 'Tragedy
and Transformation: Parent and Child in Euripides' *Hecuba*', *Maia*,
36 (1984), 123-36; F. I. Zeitlin, 'Euripides' Hekabe and the
Somatics of Dionysiac Drama', *Ramus*, 20 (1991), 53-94.

The Trojan Women

Commentaries: K. H. Lee (ed.), *Euripides, Troades* (London, 1976);
S. A. Barlow (ed.), *Euripides: Trojan Women* (Warminster, 1986).

Studies: A. P. Burnett, ' "*Trojan Women*" and the Ganymede Ode',
YCS 25 (1977), 291-316; N. Croally, *Euripidean Polemic: The Trojan
Women and the Function of Tragedy* (Cambridge, 1994);
J. Fontenrose, 'Poseidon in the *Troades*', *Agon*, 1 (1967), 135-41;
K. Gilmartin, 'Talthybius in the *Trojan Women*', *AJP* 91 (1970),
213-22; J. Gregory, 'The Power of Language in Euripides' *Troades*',
Eranos, 84 (1986), 1-9; G. L. Koniaris, 'Alexander, Palamedes,
Troades, Sisyphus: A Connected Tetralogy?', *HSCP* 77 (1973),
83-124; Gilbert Murray, 'Euripides' Tragedies of 415: The
Deceitfulness of Life', in his *Greek Studies* (Oxford, 1948), 128-48;
Michael Lloyd, 'The Helen Scene in Euripides' *Troades*', *CQ* 34
(1984), 303-13; E. J. O'Neill, 'The Prologue of the *Troades* of
Euripides', *TAPA* 72 (1941), 288-320; A. Poole, 'Total Disaster:
Euripides' *Trojan Women*', *Arion*, 3 (1976), 257-87; P. Pucci,
'Euripides: The Monument and the Sacrifice', *Arethusa*, 10 (1977),
165-95; R. Scodel, *The Trojan Trilogy of Euripides* (*Hypomnemata*,
60; Göttingen, 1980); J. Sicalin, 'Die Krise der traditionellen
Weltanschauung in der trojanischen Tragödien des Euripides', in
H. Kuch (ed.), *Die griechische Tragödie in ihrer gesellschaftlichen
Funktion* (Berlin, 1974), 103-14; T. Sinkiewicz, 'Euripides' *Trojan
Women*: An Interpretation', *Helios*, 6 (1978), 81-95; T. C. W.
Stinton, *Euripides and the Judgement of Paris* (London, 1965); R. H.
Waterfield, 'Double Standards in Euripides' *Troades*', *Maia*, 34
(1982), 139-42.

Andromache

Commentaries: P. T. Stevens (ed.), *Euripides, Andromache* (Oxford, 1971); Michael Lloyd (ed.), *Euripides: Andromache* (Warminster, 1995).

Studies: U. Albini, 'Un dramma d'avanguardia: l'Andromaca di Euripide', *Maia*, 26 (1974), 83–95; Keith M. Aldrich, *The Andromache of Euripides* (Lincoln, Nebr., 1961); W. Allan, *The* Andromache *and Euripidean Tragedy* (Oxford, 2000); P. N. Boulter, '*Sophia* and *sophrosyne* in *Andromache*', *Phoenix*, 20 (1966), 51–8; A. P. Burnett, *Catastrophe Survived: Euripides' Plays of Mixed Reversal* (Oxford, 1971), ch. 6; H. Erbse, 'Euripides' *Andromache*', *Hermes*, 94 (1966), 276–97; K. H. Lee, 'Euripides' *Andromache*: Observations on Form and Meaning', *Antichthon*, 9 (1975), 4–16; Judith Mossman, 'Waiting for Neoptolemus: The Unity of Euripides' *Andromache*', *G&R* 43 (1996), 143–56; C. Pagani, 'La figura di Ermiona nell'Andromaca euripidea', *Dioniso*, 42 (1968), 200–10; D. L. Page, 'The Elegiacs in Euripides' *Andromache*', in *Greek Poetry and Life* (*Studies for Gilbert Murray*; Oxford, 1936), 206–30; D. S. Robertson, 'Euripides and Tharyps', *CR* 37 (1923), 58–60; I. C. Storey, 'Domestic Disharmony in Euripides' *Andromache*', in I. McAuslan and P. Walcot (eds.), *Greek Tragedy* (Oxford, 1993), 180–92.

A CHRONOLOGY OF EURIPIDES'
WORK AND TIMES

Dates of productions of extant plays (adapted from C. Collard, *Euripides* (Oxford, 1981), 2)		Dates in the history of Athens	
		462	Radical democracy established in Athens
455	First production		
		448	Building of Parthenon begun
441	First prize (play unknown)		
438	*Alcestis*—second prize		
431	*Medea*—third prize	431	Outbreak of Peloponnesian War between Athens and Sparta
430–428	*Heraclidae*	430	Outbreak of plague in Athens
428	*Hippolytus* (revised from earlier production)—first prize		
?425	*Andromache*		
before 423	*Hecuba*		
?423	*Supplices*		
?before 415	*Hercules Furens*		
before 415	*Electra*		
		416	Slaughter by the Athenians of the men of the island of Melos and the enslavement of its women and children
415	*Trojan Women*—second prize	415–413	Disastrous Athenian expedition to Sicily
before 412	*Iphigenia at Tauris*		
?before 412	*Ion*		
412	*Helen*		
?412	*Cyclops* (satyr play)		
411–408, ?409	*Phoenissae*—second prize	411	Oligarchic revolution in Athens
408	*Orestes*		
after 406	*Iphigenia at Aulis* and *Bacchae*—first prize		
		404	Defeat of Athens by Sparta in the Peloponnesian War

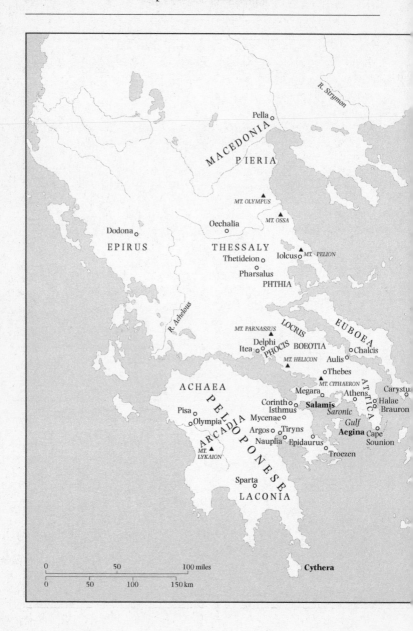

HECUBA

Characters

The ghost of POLYDORUS, son of Hecuba and Priam
HECUBA, widow of Priam, king of Troy
POLYXENA, daughter of Hecuba and Priam
ODYSSEUS, a Greek general
TALTHYBIUS, a Greek herald
SERVING WOMAN, an attendant of Hecuba's
AGAMEMNON, the Greek commander-in-chief
POLYMESTOR, king of Thrace
CHORUS of captive Trojan women

The play is set on the shore of the Thracian Chersonese (the Dardanelles). The stage building represents the tent set aside for AGAMEMNON's *captives.*

The ghost of POLYDORUS *appears above the stage building.*

POLYDORUS. I have left the gates of darkness where the dead are hidden and Hades* dwells apart from the gods, and come to this place. My name is Polydorus and I am the son of Hecuba, the daughter of Cisseus,* and of Priam. When it seemed dangerously likely that the Phrygians' city* would fall to the might of Greece, fear led my father to smuggle me out of the Trojan land to the house of Polymestor, his Thracian guest-friend,* who cultivates this fertile steppe of the Chersonese* and rules a horse-loving people by the spear.* My father covertly sent out a vast quantity of gold   10 with me so that, if ever the walls of Ilium* should fall, there would be no lack of money for his surviving children to live on.

I was the youngest of Priam's children*—and that was why he smuggled me from the land. For my boyish strength was not sufficient to carry armour or the spear. Now as long as the boundaries of our country remained secure, the towers of the Trojan land stood unshattered, and my brother Hector still triumphed with his spear, I was treated

splendidly at the house of my father's guest-friend. I flour- 20
ished like a sapling*—to my sorrow. But when Troy was lost
with Hector's life and my father's hearth was utterly
destroyed, and Priam himself had fallen at the god-built
altar,* slaughtered by the blood-polluted hand of Achilles'
son,* my father's guest-friend killed me, unhappy boy, for
the sake of the gold. He killed me and flung me into the surging salt sea so that he could keep the gold in his own house.
And I lie sometimes on the shore, sometimes in the rolling
waters, carried on the constant ebb and flow of the waves.*
There is no one to weep over me, no one to bury me.   30

Now I have left my body empty and I flit about above my
dear mother Hecuba. This is now the third day on which I
have hovered here—and all that time my miserable mother
has been near by on the land of the Chersonese after leaving Troy. All the Achaeans* are sitting idle on the shores of
this Thracian country, their ships at rest. For Achilles, son
of Peleus, appeared above his tomb* and held back the whole
Greek expedition as they steered their sea-dipped oars for
home. He is demanding to take my sister Polyxena as a pre- 40
cious blood-offering to bring honour to his tomb. And his
demand will be met. He will not be denied this gift by men
who love him. No, my sister's fate is leading her to her death
on this day.*

My mother will see the two corpses of two of her children,
myself and the unhappy girl. For in order that I, wretched
Polydorus, can win my burial,* I shall be seen in the rippling
waves at a slave-woman's feet. I asked and gained this
favour from those who hold power below,* that I should fall 50
into my mother's hands and be buried in a tomb. For myself
then, all that I wished to gain will be granted.

But I shall get out of the way of old Hecuba. Panic-
stricken by my ghost, she is coming here from the tent of
Agamemnon.* Alas! O my mother, a palace was once your
home and now you have seen the day of slavery. Your sorrows are as great now as was your prosperity then! One of
the gods is balancing your former happiness with your
destruction.

The ghost of POLYDORUS *goes out.*

HECUBA *is led on by Trojan captive women.**

HECUBA (*sings*). Lead out, my girls, lead out the old woman in
    front of the tent,
prop up your fellow slave—   60
you Trojan women—who was once your queen,
[take me, carry me, guide me, support me,]
clasping me by my aged hand.
And I, leaning on my bent arm as on a stick,
will set one foot before the other
as I stir my slow limbs to speed.

O day's bright radiance, O darkness of the night,
why, oh why am I roused like this
by terrifying night phantoms? O sovereign Earth,   70
mother of black-winged dreams,
I hurl from myself my vision of the night,*
[my dreams about my son who lives in safety here in Thrace,
and about Polyxena, my beloved daughter.
†Yes, how terrifying the vision that I saw, I heeded, I
    grasped!†]

O gods of the underworld, keep my boy safe!
Now he is the sole anchor of my house   80
and he lives in snowy Thrace,
guarded by his father's guest-friend.

Some new disaster lies in store.
A fresh song of woe will come to woeful women.
Never before now has my heart
shuddered or quailed so incessantly.
Wherever, you Trojan women, can I find Helenus,
the inspired prophet, and Cassandra,*
so that they can interpret my dreams for me?

[For I saw a dappled hind being torn pitilessly from my lap   90
and slaughtered by a wolf's bloody jaws.
And this is my fear:
the ghost of Achilles arose above the topmost crest
of his tomb. And he demanded as his gift of honour
one of the hard-suffering Trojan women.
Turn aside this fate, you gods,
from my daughter, from my daughter, I beseech you.]

Enter the CHORUS *of Trojan women.*

CHORUS (*chants*). Hecuba, I have slipped away to you in haste,
  leaving the tent of my master
  where the lot had assigned me   100
  as a slave. I have been driven out of my city
  of Ilium, a war-captive
  at the Achaeans' spear-point,
  and I have not come to make your sufferings lighter.
  No, I am weighed down with my heavy burden of news
  as I bring you, lady, tidings of woe.
  For at a full assembly of the Achaeans
  it is said that they decided to make your daughter
  a sacrifice to Achilles. You remember when
  he appeared in his golden armour above his tomb   110
  and held back the ships from their sea voyage
  as their sails billowed against the forestays.*
  These were the words he cried aloud: 'Where are you set-
    ting out to, Danaans,*
  leaving my tomb
  without its gift of honour?'
  A mighty quarrel surged* and clashed,
  with two opinions splitting the army of Greek spearsmen.
  Some decided for making the sacrifice at the tomb,
  some for the opposite.
  And one man who eagerly pursued your cause   120
  was Agamemnon, in his loyalty to his bedfellow,
  the prophetess with her wild inspiration.*
  However, Theseus' two boys,*
  those two sons of Athens,
  each gave a speech, and the two joined
  in the single view—that they should crown Achilles' tomb
    with fresh young blood.*
  They said that they would never put
  a liaison with Cassandra
  before Achilles' spear.
  The passions roused by these hotly contested arguments   130
  were nearly equal on both sides—until Laertes' son,
  that cunning-hearted,
  logic-chopping, sweet-tongued courtier of the people,*

persuaded the army
not to reject the best of all the Danaans
to avoid sacrificing a mere slave.
None of the dead, he urged, must stand beside Persephone*
    and say
that as they left Troy's plains,
the Danaans showed no gratitude
to their brothers who had died for the sake of Greeks.   140
And Odysseus will come almost at once
to drag your girl* from your breast,
to tear her away from an old woman's arms.
But go to the temples, go to the altars,*
[crouch as a suppliant at Agamemnon's knees,]*
cry out to the gods in heaven
and those beneath the earth. For either your prayers
will keep your poor child alive and you will have her still,
or you must look upon the girl
as she lies where she has fallen before the tomb   150
in a welter of red blood while it streams
from her gold-decked throat in a darkly gleaming flood.*

HECUBA (*sings*). O my sorrow! What shall I cry out?
    What echoing lament?—
I, Hecuba, miserable in my miserable old age
and my slavery too hard to bear,
too hard to endure? My woe, my woe!
Who can help me? What child,
what city? Old Priam is gone,   160
my sons are gone.
Where can I turn? This way—
or that? Where can I find safety,
where a god or power divine to help me?
O you women of Troy, who have brought me bitter tidings,
brought me bitter sorrows,
you have destroyed me, destroyed me utterly.
Life in the daylight brings me happiness no longer.
O my wretched feet, lead me,   170
old crone that I am,
to this tent.* O my child, daughter
of the unhappiest of mothers, come out,
come out of the house, hear what your mother has to say!

You there, my daughter! [You must know what news,
what news* I have heard about your fate.]

Enter POLYXENA *from the tent.*

POLYXENA (*sings*). Mother, mother, what are you shouting?
What news do you bring, that you have startled me
from the tent like a frightened bird!

HECUBA (*sings*). Alas, my daughter!   180

POLYXENA (*sings*). Why these ill-omened words? They are a
    prelude to sorrows, I think.

HECUBA (*sings*). I cry alas for your life!

POLYXENA (*sings*). Tell me. Do not keep it hidden any longer.
I am afraid, mother,
afraid of what provokes your laments.

HECUBA (*sings*). My child, child of a wretched mother . . .

POLYXENA (*sings*). What is it that you have to tell me?

HECUBA (*sings*). The Argives* have taken the collective
    decision
to slaughter you at the tomb
of the son of Peleus.*   190

POLYXENA (*sings*). Alas, my mother, what are you saying?
Tell me the worst, mother,
the dreadful worst.

HECUBA (*sings*). I shall tell you, my child, the ominous tidings
    I have heard,
tell you that the Argives
have voted decisively about your fate.

POLYXENA (*sings*). O my mother, you victim of terrible suffer-
    ings,*
utterly wretched in your life,
what, what is this new outrage,
accursed, unspeakable,   200
that some power has roused up against you?
No longer, no longer shall I, your pitiable child,
share the servitude of your pitiable old age.
Pitiable woman, you will see me, your pitiable whelp,*
like a heifer bred in the mountains,*
torn from your arms
and sent down to Hades with my throat cut,
to the darkness under the earth, where I,

unhappy Polyxena,
shall lie among the dead.   210
[And I weep for you, my mother, and your misery
with unceasing laments,
but for my own life, its outrage and its shame,
I shed not a tear. No, in dying
I have met with the happier fortune.]*
CHORUS. But look, Odysseus is striding eagerly towards us,
    Hecuba, to bring you new tidings.

ODYSSEUS enters.

ODYSSEUS. Lady, I think that you know the army's intention
    and the vote which it has passed, but I shall tell you never-
    theless. The Achaeans have decided to slaughter your child   220
    Polyxena on the tall mound of Achilles' tomb. They have
    appointed us to fetch and escort the girl.* And the son of
    Achilles* will be the priest who presides over the sacrifice.
    You know what you have to do. Do not make us tear her
    away from you by force, and do not get involved in any
    fisticuffs with me. Rather you must recognize how powerless
    you are and how your misfortunes overwhelm you. In my
    view it is sensible, even amid misfortune, to show good
    judgement.
HECUBA. Alas! I am faced with a great contest,* I think, one
    laden with lamentation and not free from tears. I now real-   230
    ize that I was not to die where I should have died. No, Zeus
    did not destroy me, but kept me alive so that I, Hecuba the
    wretched, could see new and greater agonies piled on ago-
    nies. Yet if a slave may put questions to the free which do
    not bring them sorrow or gnaw at their hearts, then it is
    right that †now that you have had your say† I should ask
    you these things and listen to your answers.
ODYSSEUS. Of course. Ask away. I do not begrudge you the
    time.
HECUBA. Do you remember when you came into Troy as a
    spy?* You were dressed in vile, shapeless rags and gouts of   240
    blood dripped down the chin from your eyes.
ODYSSEUS. I remember. It stabbed me to the quick.*
HECUBA. And Helen recognized you and told only me?
ODYSSEUS. I recollect that I came into great danger.

HECUBA. And you touched my knees in all humility?*

ODYSSEUS. Yes, and clasped your robes so tightly that my hand grew numb.

HECUBA. So tell me what you said then, when you were my slave.

ODYSSEUS. All the arguments I could think up. I wanted to 250 survive.

HECUBA. Did I keep you safe then and send you out of the land?

ODYSSEUS. Yes. Thanks to that, I can look upon this sunlight.

HECUBA. Then are you not degraded by this scheme of yours? You admit that I treated you like this and yet you show me no gratitude. No, you do me all the harm you can. There are no thanks to be won from your breed—all you who seek a politician's fame.* May you be no friends of mine! You care nothing about hurting your friends if only what you say wins favour with the mob. Yet what did they think politic in the death of this girl? Why did they pass that vote? Was it necessity that persuaded them to slaughter a human* at a 260 tomb where oxen are the fitter sacrifice? Or if Achilles wants to take revenge by killing those that killed him, is it just that he should aim at this girl's death? She at least has done him no harm. He should have asked for Helen to be slaughtered at his grave. She brought him to his destruction at Troy. But if one of the captives must be picked out for her surpassing beauty and be killed, this is nothing to do with us. Yes, the daughter of Tyndareus* is the most beautiful woman in the world and she has been found far guiltier than we have. On 270 the score of justice then, that is the contention I urge. But as for myself, hear how you should repay me as I advance my claim to your gratitude. You touched my hand, as you admit—this aged chin too,* when you fell before me. Now I touch your hand and your chin in return, and I ask you to pay back my old favour to you. I beseech you not to tear my daughter from my arms. Do not kill her. We have dead bodies enough. This girl is my delight. In her I forget my sorrows. She is my comfort and takes the place of many things. 280 She is my city, my nurse, my staff, my guide.*

It is wrong for those with power to use it where they should not*—wrong for those who have met with success to think that they will always enjoy it. For once I existed, but that is over now. A single day took from me all my prosperity.

By your chin, dear friend, show me respect, pity me. Go to the Achaean army and advise them to reverse their decision. Tell them that it rouses the anger of the gods to kill women whom you used not to drag from the altars and murder. No, you took pity on them.* For when it comes to 290 bloodshed you Greeks observe the same custom for free men and slaves alike.*

Your reputation will win the day even if you argue poorly. For the same argument does not carry the same weight when it comes from nonentities as it does on the lips of famous men.

CHORUS. No man's nature is so harsh that, if he heard your threnody of long lamentation, he would not let fall a tear.

ODYSSEUS. Hecuba, learn a lesson and do not let your heart's passion lead you to regard a man who gives you good coun- 300 sel as your enemy. Because I met with good treatment at your hands, I am ready to keep you safe—and I mean what I say. But I shall not go back on what I recommended to the whole assembly—that, now that Troy is taken, we should give your daughter as a victim to the first man of our army since he was demanding her. This is where most cities come to grief, when a good and eager patriot wins no more than inferior men. In our eyes Achilles is deserving of honour, lady, for he died most nobly for the land of Greece. Does it 310 not bring us shame if we make use of a man while he is alive but no longer treat him as our friend when he is dead? Well then, what will men say if an army has to be levied, a war to be fought in the future? 'Shall we fight or shall we play the coward when we see that the dead win no honour?' Speaking for myself, in my lifetime I would be utterly content if I had even a little from day to day, but I should like to see my tomb thought worthy of honour. That is an expression of gratitude that truly lasts. 320

If you say that your sufferings are pitiable, listen to what I tell you in reply. On our side we have ancient women and old men no less wretched than yourself. Our girls have lost excellent bridegrooms whose bodies lie hidden beneath this

soil of Ida.* You must endure this. If our custom of honour-
ing the brave is a bad one, we shall happily incur the charge
of folly. You barbarians! I hope that you will not regard your
friends as friends nor give your admiration to those who
have died bravely. This will cause Greece to prosper and you   330
to win a fortune appropriate to your policy.

CHORUS. Alas! What a terrible thing it is to be a slave! This
always holds true. What indignities we endure under the
tyranny of force!

HECUBA. O my daughter, I have cast my words about your
murder into thin air. They have vanished and are nothing.
But if you have some power greater than your mother's, use
every effort, utter every sound that comes from the nightin-
gale's throat, to beg that you may stay alive. Fall a pitiable
suppliant here at Odysseus' knee and try to persuade him—   340
you have your plea, for he has children too*—so that he
may pity your fate.

POLYXENA. I see you, Odysseus, hiding your right hand under
your cloak and turning your head aside in case I touch your
beard. Do not be afraid. You have escaped the Zeus, the god
of suppliants, that lies in me.* Yes, I shall follow you, not only
through necessity but also because I want to die. If I prove
unwilling to do so, I shall be seen as a coward, a woman too
much in love with life. For why should I go on living? My
father was the king of all the Phrygians. This was how my life   350
began. Then I was nourished by fair hopes as a bride for kings,
and many were the rivals who competed to take me off to their
hearth and home as their wife. I—now so unfortunate—was
a mistress to the women of Ida.* Among those women, both
young and old, it was I who attracted all men's gaze. Mortality
apart, I was the equal of the gods. But now I am a slave. First
of all, the strangeness of that name makes me long to die.
Then I may perhaps have a cruel-hearted master who will buy   360
me for silver, me the sister of Hector and of many others, force
on me the task of making bread in his home, and impose the
daily drudgery of sweeping the house and standing by the
loom. And a slave bought from I know not where will defile
my bed, which was once thought worthy of princes.

No, it cannot be. I consign my body to Hades and take my
last look on this daylight with eyes that are free. So take me

off, Odysseus, take me off and kill me. I can see nothing in
our circumstances to encourage any hope or belief that I 370
shall ever find happiness. Mother, I beg you, do not do or
say anything to stop them. No, you must join me in wishing for my death before I suffer shame and degradation. For
those who are not accustomed to the taste of calamity may
endure it, but they grieve as they put their neck beneath the
yoke. Death would be far happier for them than life. It is a
great ordeal to live without honour.

CHORUS. The stamp* of royal birth is a wonderful thing. It
marks people out and its glory grows greater when they 380
prove worthy of it.

HECUBA. You have spoken noble words, my daughter, but
your nobility brings sorrow too. If this favour must be
granted to the son of Peleus, and if you Greeks, Odysseus,
have to avoid the charge of ingratitude, do not kill the girl,
but take *me* off to Achilles' pyre and stab me without mercy.
It was I who gave birth to Paris who shot the son of Thetis
with his bow and destroyed him.*

ODYSSEUS. It was not you, old woman, that the ghost of
Achilles asked the Achaeans to kill, but this girl. 390

HECUBA. But at least kill me together with my daughter, and
the earth and the corpse that are demanding this will receive
a double draught of blood.

ODYSSEUS. The death of your daughter is enough. We must
not add one death to another. If only we did not have to go
through with hers!

HECUBA. I *must* die with my daughter.*

ODYSSEUS. Why? I am not aware that anyone is in a position
to dictate to me.

HECUBA. It is all the same. I shall cling fast to her like ivy to
an oak.

ODYSSEUS. No—that is if you will obey those wiser than yourself.

HECUBA. You can be sure that I shall never let go of this child 400
willingly.

ODYSSEUS. But I shall not leave here without her.

POLYXENA. Do what I tell you, mother. Son of Laertes, you
must be gentle with a parent's understandable passion,
while you, unhappy woman, must stop fighting with our

masters. Do you want to be flung to the ground, to bruise
your old woman's skin as they manhandle you, and to lose
your dignity* when you are torn from my young arms? That
is what you will suffer. You must not. It is not proper. No,
my dear mother, give me your sweet hand, and let me press   410
my cheek to yours. For never again shall I look upon the
radiant circle of the sun. This is the final time. You are listening to my last words. O my mother who gave me birth, I
am going away to the Underworld.

HECUBA. Yours is a pitiable fate, my child, and I am a
wretched woman.*

POLYXENA. There in Hades I shall lie, away from you.

HECUBA. Alas, what can I do? How can I reach the end of my
life?

POLYXENA. I shall die a slave, though I am the child of a free   420
father . . .

HECUBA. O my daughter, I shall live a slave's life under the
sun.

POLYXENA. die without a husband, without the wedding-
song. I should have experienced that.

HECUBA. And I have lost my fifty children.

POLYXENA. What message shall I take from you to Hector or
your old husband?

HECUBA. Tell them that I am the most wretched of all women.

POLYXENA. O bosom, O breasts, how sweetly you suckled me!

HECUBA. O my daughter, wretched in your untimely fate!

POLYXENA. Farewell, my mother, and say farewell to
Cassandra for me . . .

HECUBA. Others fare well. This is not your mother's destiny.

POLYXENA. and to my brother Polydorus among the horse-
loving Thracians.

HECUBA. Yes, if he is alive. But I have no confidence in this,
such misfortunes crowd about me.

POLYXENA. He is alive and he will close your eyes when you   430
are dead.

HECUBA. But I am dead already, though I am still alive.
Calamity has killed me.*

POLYXENA. Odysseus, put this mantle round my head and
lead me off, for my heart has melted with my mother's songs
of woe even before my slaughter, and I am melting hers with

lamentation. O light of day!—I can invoke your name, but
my share in your brightness lasts no longer than my journey to Achilles' pyre where the sword awaits me.

ODYSSEUS starts to lead POLYXENA off.

HECUBA. O my sorrow! I am fainting and my limbs are giving
way. My daughter, touch your mother, stretch out your
hand, give it to me! Do not leave me without my child. All   440
is over for me, my friends. [If only I could see that Spartan,
Helen, the sister of the Dioscuri,* in such a plight! For with
her lovely eyes she brought hellish ruin* upon happy Troy.]

HECUBA faints.

CHORUS (*sings*). Breeze,* ocean breeze,
who carry sea-faring ships
swiftly over the surging waters,
where will you take me
in my misery? Whose house shall I come to,
a purchased slave?
Will it be to an anchorage in the Dorian land   450
or in Phthia where they say
that Apidanus, father of loveliest waters,
enriches the plains,*

or on one of the islands,
carried in my sorrow by the oar that sweeps the sea
to live a pitiable life indoors
where the first-born of all palm-trees
and the bay tree lifted their sacred branches
in loving pride for Leto   460
as she bore Zeus' children?*
Shall I sing with the maidens of Delos
in praise of the golden headband
and the bow of the goddess Artemis?

Or will it be in the city of Pallas*
that I shall yoke her young mares to their lovely chariot
on her saffron robe,*
embroidering them
in the finely-worked threads   470
with all their colours,

or weaving the race of the Titans
which Zeus, son of Cronos, lulls to sleep
with the double blaze of his thunderbolt?*

I cry alas for my children,
alas for my parents and for my country
which smoulders with smoke
as it lies in ruins,
mastered by the Argives' spear.
And I am called a slave in a foreign land,   480
now that I have left Asia
and exchanged the chambers of Hades
for a dwelling in Europe.

Enter TALTHYBIUS.

TALTHYBIUS. Where can I find Hecuba, you Trojan girls, the
woman who was recently the queen of Troy?
CHORUS. She is near you, lying with her back on the ground,
Talthybius. Her robes hide her huddled body.
TALTHYBIUS. O Zeus, what am I to say? That you have regard
for men or that you have merely won this reputation which
has no substance to it? [It is false, and the race of gods   490
merely appears to exist.] Is it fortune that oversees all
human affairs? Was not this the queen of the Phrygians
with all their gold? Was not she the wife of Priam, a man so
blest by fortune? And now her city has been utterly
destroyed by the spear and she herself is lying on the
ground—a slave, an old woman, all her children gone—cak-
ing her wretched head with dust. Alas, alas! I am an old
man, but even so* I pray that I may die before I meet with
the shame of such a fate.

      Stand up, you wretched woman, lift your side upright—   500
and your poor white head.
HECUBA. What! Who is this that will not let my body lie here?
Why do you disturb me, whoever you are, in my grief?
TALTHYBIUS. It is I, Talthybius, who have come here, an
adjutant* of the Greeks. [Agamemnon has sent me to fetch
you, lady.]
HECUBA. O my dearest friend, have the Achaeans decided to
slaughter me on the grave as well? Is that why you are

here? How welcome that news would be! Let us make all the haste we can. Lead the way, old man.*

TALTHYBIUS. I have come to fetch you, lady, so that you may bury your dead daughter. The two sons of Atreus* and the 510 Achaean host have sent me.

HECUBA. Alas, what are you going to tell me? Are you here then not to take me off to die but to bring bad news? You are dead, my child. You have been snatched from your mother and I have lost another child in you. O what sorrow! How did you finish her off? Did you show her respect? Or did you tackle the terrible business, old man, by killing her like an enemy? Tell me, though I shall take no pleasure in your words.

TALTHYBIUS. You would have me win a prize* of tears a second time, lady, in my pity for your child. For telling the grim story now, I shall wet these eyes of mine with weeping 520 just as I did at the tomb where she was killed.

The whole crowd of the Achaean army was there *en masse* before the tomb for the slaughter of your girl. The son of Achilles then took Polyxena by the hand and made her stand on the top of the mound. And I was near by. Picked young men selected from the Achaeans attended, to hold down your poor girl* if she struggled. Then Achilles' son took a full goblet all of gold in his hands and raised on high the libation for his dead father. He signalled to me to call for 530 silence from the whole Achaean army. And I stood up in the middle and said these words: 'Silence, Achaeans, let the whole host be silent! Silence! Not a word!' And I hushed the crowd to stillness. And he said, 'O son of Peleus, my father, receive from me this libation which summons up the dead,* and be appeased. Come, so that you may drink a virgin's pure dark blood which the army and I give to you. Show yourself well disposed towards us and grant that we may untie the ropes which hold our ships' sterns fast,* meet with 540 a favourable return from Troy and, all of us, reach our native land.' That was what he said, and the whole army prayed after him.

Then, seizing his sword of solid gold by the hilt, he started to draw it from its sheath, and with a nod he signalled to the young men picked from the Greek army to take hold of

the girl. But when she saw this, she spoke out these words:
'Argives, you who have sacked my city, I am happy to die.*
Let no one lay a hand on my body. I shall offer my neck with
good courage. By the gods, leave me free when you kill me   550
so that I can die a free woman! I am a princess and it would
shame me to bear the name of slave among the dead.'

The host roared their approval and king Agamemnon told
the young men to let the maiden go. [And they let her go
the moment they heard what the man with the supreme
power had just said.] When she heard this order of the master, she took hold of her dress and tore it from the top of her
shoulder to the middle of her waist by the navel. Her lovely   560
breasts and bosom were revealed like a statue's, and sinking
to her knees upon the ground she spoke the most heart-
rending words of all: 'Look at me! If you are eager to strike
this bosom, young Neoptolemus, strike it now—or if you
want to cut into my neck, here is my throat all ready.' In
his pity for the girl he wavered between reluctance and
eagerness,* but then he cut her windpipe with his sword.
Springs of blood welled forth. But even though she was
dying, she none the less took great care to fall modestly, hiding what should be hidden from men's eyes.*   570

When she had breathed her last in this deadly sacrifice,
all the Achaeans started on different tasks. Some of them
threw leaves on the dead girl,* others heaped up the funeral
pyre bringing logs of pinewood, and anyone who did not join
in would be abused by his fellows with words like this: 'Are
you standing idle, you wretch? Why aren't you carrying a
robe or an ornament for the young girl? Go and give something to this noble-hearted woman whose courage knew no
bounds.'

As I say such words about your dead daughter, I see that   580
you have the best children and the unhappiest fortune of all
women.

CHORUS. This is a terrible agony which has burst boiling upon
Priam's children and my city. It comes from the gods and
there is no escape.

HECUBA. O my daughter, there are so many woes and I do not
know which I should look to. For when I lay hold on one,
here is another that will not let me be, and another grief

calls me away from that one too, as woe follows endlessly
on woe. And now I cannot erase what you have suffered 590
from my mind. No, I must mourn it. But the story of your
nobility has set a limit on my sorrow. Is it not strange that
poor soil bears a good crop if the gods send it a good season
and good soil produces a bad one when it fails to get what
it needs, while in the case of human beings the rotten man
is never anything but bad, and the good are always good?
Misfortune does not change their nature. They are always
admirable. [Is it the parents who make the difference, or the
upbringing? Yet even a good upbringing involves the teach- 600
ing of what is good. And if someone knows this well, he
knows what is dishonourable too because he can measure it
by the yardstick of what is noble.]

But there is nothing to be gained by these idle specula-
tions. (*To* TALTHYBIUS) You must go and take this message
to the Argives. No one must touch my child. The mob must
be kept away from her. In a vast army the mob is hard to
control, the sailors' indiscipline blazes fiercer than fire,* and
the man who commits no crime is seen as a criminal. (*To her*
SERVING WOMAN) And you, my old* servant, take an urn, 610
dip it in the sea and bring it here so that I may wash my
child for the very last time and lay her out, the bride that
never was a bride, the maiden who is a maiden no longer.*

But how can I perform these rituals as she deserves? It is
impossible. But as I can, I shall. What else am I to do? I shall
gather ornaments from the prisoners who live inside these
tents along with me—if any of them have stolen something
from their own homes and escaped detection from our new
masters.

O stately halls, O my once happy home, O Priam who had 620
so much and was so blessed with children, myself here too,
the ancient mother of my children, how we have come to
nothing! We have been stripped of our former pride. So why
do we mortals swell with conceit, one of us over the wealth
of his house, another over his reputation for honour among
the citizens? Wealth and honour are nothing, nothing but
ambitions for the heart and boasting for the tongue. The
truly happy man is the one who meets with nothing bad
from day to day.

The SERVING WOMAN *goes out to the sea.* HECUBA *goes into the*
tent.

CHORUS (*sings*). For me was fated disaster,
  for me was fated woe,   630
  when first Alexandros*
  cut the fir tree's wood on Ida
  to sail across the surge of the salt sea
  to marry Helen, the most beautiful woman
  lit by the bright rays
  of the golden sun.

For troubles and torments worse than troubles
  circle me round.
  From one man's folly came evil for all,   640
  bringing destruction on the land of Simois*
  with disaster for others too,
  and the rivalry was settled
  when the herdsman judged
  the three daughters of the blessed ones on Ida,*

settled with war, with blood and the ruin of my home.
  And by the fair-flowing Eurotas   650
  a Spartan girl* laments at home, with many a tear,
  and a mother beats her grey head with her hand
  and tears her cheek, rending it with bloody nails,
  for her children are dead.

The SERVING WOMAN *re-enters, with attendants carrying the*
veiled corpse of POLYDORUS.*

SERVING WOMAN. Women, where is Hecuba, who surpasses
  all men and her own sex too in sorrows? She is supreme in
  misery and no one will dispute her possession of that crown.   660
CHORUS. What's this, you wretch crying out your ominous
  words? Your messages of woe never rest.
SERVING WOMAN. It is to Hecuba, not you, that I bring this
  sorrow. Calamity does not make it easy for mortals to have
  words of good omen on their lips.
CHORUS. Look. Here she is coming out from the tent. She
  appears opportunely for your message.

HECUBA *re-enters.*

SERVING WOMAN. O my mistress, most unhappy woman, unhappier even than my words can express, all is over with you. You no longer exist though you see the light of day. You have been destroyed. Children, husband, city—all are gone.

HECUBA. You are telling me nothing new. You are throwing 670 these words in the teeth of one who knows it all. But why have you brought the body of Polyxena here to me?* I was told that all the Achaeans were busily seeing to her burial.

SERVING WOMAN (*aside*). She knows nothing. I see it is Polyxena that she is mourning. Her latest woe has not touched her yet.

HECUBA. O my sorrow! It can't be my dear Cassandra, the frantic prophetess, that you have brought here?

SERVING WOMAN. The girl whose name you cry is alive. But you do not mourn yet for the one who lies here dead. Let us uncover the corpse. Look at it and see if the sight fills you with wonder and dashes your hopes. 680

HECUBA. O my agony! I see my son—dead—Polydorus, whom the Thracian was protecting for me in his house. All is over for unhappy Hecuba—I no longer exist.

(*Sings*) O my child, my child,*
  alas! I start a frenzied melody. I have only now
  learnt of this evil from an avenging demon.

CHORUS. Then you have taken in your son's grim fate, you poor woman?

HECUBA (*sings*). I cannot believe, no I cannot believe, this new
    horror which I see.
  New disasters are born from the old ones, 690
  and no day shall ever linger
  without my groans and tears.

CHORUS. Terrible, terrible are the calamities we suffer, wretched woman.

HECUBA (*sings*). O my child, child of a wretched mother,
  by what blow of fate did you die? How did you come to lie
    there in death?
  What man killed you?

SERVING WOMAN. I do not know. I came upon him on the seashore.

HECUBA (*sings*). Had he been cast up on the level sand
  or fallen there beneath the bloody spear?

SERVING WOMAN. The surging water carried him up from 700
the sea.

HECUBA (*sings*). Alas, alas!
I understand the dream
which I saw in my sleep*
(the black-winged vision did not escape me),
the dream I had about you,
O my child, no longer alive under Zeus' daylight.

CHORUS. Who killed him then? Does your dream-wisdom give
you the knowledge to tell me that?

HECUBA (*sings*). It was my own guest-friend, yes, my own, 710
the Thracian horseman, with whom his father had hidden
him.

CHORUS. Alas, what do you mean? So that after the murder
he could keep the gold?

HECUBA. I cannot find the words for it. It is a deed without a
name, beyond amazement.
(*Sings*) It is unholy, unendurable. Where is just dealing
between guest-friends now?
O you most accursed of men, see how you have butchered
this boy's flesh,
hacking his limbs with your iron sword.
There was no pity in you. 720

CHORUS. You wretched woman, whatever power it is that
presses so heavily on you has made you supreme in suffering among mortals. But look, I see here the grand figure of
our master Agamemnon—so let's be silent, friends.

AGAMEMNON enters.

AGAMEMNON. Hecuba, why are you so slow to bury your
daughter in her grave? Why haven't you come on the terms
which Talthybius made known to me, that none of the
Argives should lay a hand on your girl? Well then, we left
her alone, we did not touch her. But you are taking your 730
time, and that surprises me. So I have come to fetch you. For
things there have been well managed—if there is anything
that is good about this situation.
(*With a start*) But who is this man I see by the tent, this
dead Trojan? I can tell that he is not an Argive by the
clothes his body is dressed in.

HECUBA (*turning away and speaking to herself*).* Wretched Hecuba—yes, I am speaking to myself when I speak to you—what shall I do? Should I fall here at Agamemnon's knee* or should I bear my sufferings in silence?

AGAMEMNON. Why have you turned your back on me as you lament? Look at me and tell me what happened. Who is this?   740

HECUBA. But if he were to regard me as a mere slave and his enemy, and push me away from his knees, I would simply add to my sorrow.

AGAMEMNON. I am not a prophet. I cannot search out the path of your intentions unless you tell me.

HECUBA. Am I judging his feelings too much as if we were enemies? Perhaps he is not ill-disposed to me.

AGAMEMNON. If you want me to know nothing about what is going on, we are of one mind. For I have no wish to hear it either.

HECUBA. I could not take revenge for my children* without this man's help. Why do I keep turning the matter over? I   750 must summon up my courage, whether I succeed or fail.

(*Kneeling before* AGAMEMNON) Agamemnon, I supplicate you by your knees and your chin and your triumphant right hand.

AGAMEMNON. What is your request? That I should give you your freedom? That is an easy thing to grant you.

HECUBA. [No, not that. If I can take revenge on evil men, I shall gladly be a slave my whole life long.] I am not begging you for any of the things you suppose.*

AGAMEMNON. So what help *are* you asking me to give you?

HECUBA. You see this dead body over which I shed my tears?   760

AGAMEMNON. I do. But I do not know what this will lead to.

HECUBA. I carried him in my womb and gave him birth long ago.

AGAMEMNON. Which of your children is this, you poor woman?

HECUBA. Not one of those sons of Priam who died beneath the walls of Ilium.

AGAMEMNON. Why, did you bear another son as well as them, lady?

HECUBA. Yet, but to no avail, it seems—this boy you see before you.

AGAMEMNON. Where was he when your city was destroyed?

HECUBA. His father sent him away, fearing that he would be killed.

AGAMEMNON. He was the only one he picked out from all of his children who were alive then? Where did he send him?

HECUBA. To this land, where his corpse has been found.   770

AGAMEMNON. To the man who rules this country, Polymestor?

HECUBA. He was sent here to guard the gold that has cost him so dear.

AGAMEMNON. Who killed him? What fate did he meet with?

HECUBA. Who else could it be? Our Thracian guest-friend murdered him.

AGAMEMNON. Cruel man! I suppose he lusted for the gold.

HECUBA. Yes, after he knew that Troy had fallen.

AGAMEMNON. Where did you find him? Or did someone bring the body here? Who?

HECUBA. This woman. She chanced upon it on the seashore.

AGAMEMNON. Was she looking for him, or about some other task?

HECUBA. She had gone to fetch water from the sea to wash   780
Polyxena.

AGAMEMNON. It looks as if your guest-friend killed him and threw the body out.

HECUBA. Yes, to drift upon the sea. And he had hacked his flesh like this.

AGAMEMNON. Wretched woman! Your sufferings are beyond number.

HECUBA. I am destroyed, and there is no agony left for me to suffer.

AGAMEMNON. Alas, alas! What woman ever met with such misfortune?

HECUBA. There is no one—unless you speak of Lady Fortune herself. But hear the reason that I fall at your knees. If your judgement is that what I have suffered is holy, I shall be content. But if you feel the opposite, you must become the   790
instrument of revenge upon a man who has violated the most holy bonds of guest-friendship. Showing no fear for those below the earth or those above it, he has done a most unholy deed [though he often shared my hospitality and by

the measure of guest-friendship was counted first among my friends. He received all that he should, was given all consideration*—and he killed him. Even if we grant that he had his reasons for wishing to kill him, he didn't judge him worthy of a tomb but flung him into the sea.]

Well then, we are slaves and perhaps we are weak. But the gods and the principle of law that rules them are strong. It is because of this law that we believe in the gods and we can base our lives on a clear distinction between wrong and right. If you corrupt this when it is referred to you, and those who kill their guests and dare to violate what the gods hold sacred are not punished, nothing in our human life is safe. 800

So you must regard these things as shameful and show me respect. Pity me, and standing back from me like a painter look at me and see the miseries I suffer. I was once a queen, but now I am your slave. I once had splendid children, but now I am an old woman and childless too. I have no city, I am utterly alone, the most wretched of mortals. 810

Alas, where are you slinking off to to avoid your miserable suppliant? It seems that I shall achieve nothing. O misery! Why do we mortals toil away—as we should—in pursuit of all the other branches of knowledge, but when it comes to Persuasion, the only sovereign for mankind, we make no special effort to perfect our knowledge by laying out money so that sometimes we might have been able to persuade people to do what we want and thus achieve our ends? So why should one still hope to succeed? The sons who once were mine are mine no longer. I have come to ruin, a war-captive in degraded slavery, and I see the smoke as it leaps here above the city. 820

Another point—and to make Cypris* part of my plea may perhaps seem strange, but nevertheless it shall be spoken— at your side sleeps my daughter, Phoebus' prophetess, whom the Phrygians call Cassandra. What value, my lord, will you set on your nights of love? Will my daughter have any benefit from her loving embraces in your bed—and I from her? [It is in the love-charms of night's darkness that men find their greatest delight.] Listen to me then. You see this dead boy here. If you do good to him, you will be doing well by your brother-in-law. 830

I still have one thing more to say. I wish I had a voice in
my arms and hands and hair,* and in the feet on which I
walk, whether by the skills of Daedalus* or one of the gods,
so that they could all weep together and clasp your knees,
urging arguments of every kind. O my master, O supreme   840
light of the Greeks, be persuaded, give this old woman your
avenging hand. She may be nothing, but even so. For it is
the mark of a good man to serve justice and never fail to
treat bad men badly.

CHORUS. It is strange how everything conspires together in
human life and the laws of necessity determine men's relationships, making friends of bitter enemies and enemies of
those who once were friends.

AGAMEMNON. Hecuba, I feel pity for you and your boy and   850
your fortunes, for your suppliant hand too, and I want the
impious guest-friend to pay you a just penalty for this, both
for the gods' sake and for that of justice—if I can find some
way for you to get what you want and for me to avoid
appearing to have planned this death for the king of Thrace
to gratify Cassandra. For there is an aspect of the situation
that nonplusses me: the troops regard this man as their
friend and the dead boy as their enemy; if he is loved by you,
that is a private matter and the army has no share in it. So   860
think the situation over. For in me you have a man who
wants to be with you in your suffering. I could prove quick
to help you—or slow, if my assistance will lead the
Achaeans to speak ill of me.

HECUBA. Ha! There is no mortal who is free. Either he is the
slave of money or of fortune, or the city mob or the written
laws prevent him from behaving as his judgement suggests.
Since you are afraid and allow too much importance to the
common people, I shall set you free from this fear. Yes, if I
plot some evil against the man who killed this boy, share in   870
the knowledge but not in the deed. But if any disturbance
arises among the Achaeans or they make any move to help
the Thracian when he suffers what he shall suffer, stop it
without appearing to do so, for my sake. As for the rest—
have no fear—I shall see that all turns out well.*

AGAMEMNON. But how? What will you do? Will you take a
sword in your old woman's hand and kill the barbarous

man, or will you use poison—or what other means? Whose
hands will support you? Where will you find friends?

HECUBA. These tents conceal a number of Trojan women.* 880

AGAMEMNON. You mean the prisoners, the spoil of the
Greeks?

HECUBA. With them to help me, I shall take vengeance on the
killer of my son.

AGAMEMNON. And how will women be able to overcome
men?

HECUBA. Women in numbers are formidable, and when allied
with trickery, hard to fight against.

AGAMEMNON. Formidable indeed. Yet I have a poor opinion
of women's strength.

HECUBA. But why? Was it not women who killed Aegyptus'
sons and depopulated Lemnos of all its males?* But so be it.*
Let's stop this line of talk. Please give this woman safe conduct through the army. (*To the* SERVING WOMAN) And when 890
you reach the Thracian guest-friend, say, 'Hecuba, the former queen of Ilium, is calling you on a matter that concerns
you no less than herself. She invites your sons as well, since
the children must hear what she has to say too.'

Agamemnon, postpone Polyxena's funeral so that these
two, brother and sister, burnt side by side on a single pyre,
a double source of grief for their mother, may find burial
together in the earth.

AGAMEMNON. It shall be so. If the army had been able to sail,
I could not grant you this favour. But as things stand—for 900
the god does not send us favourable winds*—we have to
stay here doing nothing as we watch out for a chance to sail.

I hope that things turn out well. For all men, both as private individuals and as citizens, share the wish that evil men
should suffer evil and that good men should meet with success.

AGAMEMNON goes out.

CHORUS (*sings*). O Ilium, my country, no longer
will you be called one of the unsacked cities,
such a cloud of Greeks covers you round,
and has ravaged you with the spear, yes the spear.
You have been shorn of your crown of towers; 910

a most lamentable stain of smoky fire
has blackened you.
Unhappy city, I shall tread your streets no longer.

It was at midnight that my doom began,
when dinner is over and sweet sleep
spreads over the eyes; and my husband
had ceased from his songs and his choral sacrifices
and was lying in the bedroom,
his spear on its peg,   920
watching no more for the throng of sailors—
that had set its foot in Trojan Ilium.

I was arranging my hair
in the cap that binds it up,*
gazing down the gleaming perspective of my golden mirror,
about to fall on my bed's coverlet.*
But a shout rang up through the city,
and all along Troy's streets this was the cry:
'O sons of the Greeks, when, O when   930
will you sack Ilium's citadel
and reach your homes?'

And I left my bed of love
in a single robe like a Spartan girl,* and crouched
uselessly—O my misery!—at Artemis' shrine.
I saw my husband dead
and was led off to the salt sea.
And while I looked back at the city
when the ship set its homeward course
and parted me from the land of Ilium,   940
I fainted in my agony of grief,

as I laid my curses on Helen, the sister of the Dioscuri,*
and on the herdsman of Ida
Paris, our destruction,
since his marriage—no marriage
but a sorrow sent by some demon of vengeance—
lost me my native land
and drove me into exile from my home.
May the salt sea never carry her back!   950
May she never come to the house of her fathers!

POLYMESTOR comes on with his two sons and armed attendants.

POLYMESTOR. O Priam, dearest of men,* and Hecuba, dearest
lady, I weep as I look upon you and your city and your
daughter who has just been killed.* Alas, there is nothing in
which we can find security, nothing—neither in good reputation nor in prosperity, for the prosperous man may fall
upon hard times. The gods mix everything together in a
topsy-turvy muddle, and the reason they cause this confusion is to make us worship them out of ignorance. However, 960
what is the point of lamenting these things when we cannot
run ahead* of our miseries?

But you, Hecuba, if you have any criticism to make of my
late arrival, hold it back. For it happened that I was away in
the central area of Thrace when you came here, and after I
got back, I was just setting out from home when this serving woman of yours met me. She told me your message. I
heard it and have come here.

HECUBA. I am ashamed to look you in the face, Polymestor,
so abject is my situation. Now that fate has given me my
present fortunes, I feel shame before a man who saw me in 970
my palmy days. I could not look him straight in the eye.
But do not interpret this as any ill-feeling towards you
[, Polymestor. And besides, part of the cause is the custom
that women do not look directly at men.]

POLYMESTOR. And no wonder! But what do you want from
me? Why have you sent for me from my house?

HECUBA. I want to tell you and your sons some private business of my own. Please instruct your attendants to stand at
a distance from these tents. 980

POLYMESTOR (*to his attendants*). Off with you! It is safe to
leave me alone here. You are my friend and this army of the
Achaeans is friendly towards me.

The attendants go out.

But you must let me know how I in my good fortune must
help my friends in their distress. For I am at your disposal.*

HECUBA. First of all, about my son Polydorus whom you
received from my hands and are keeping in your house. Is
he alive? I shall ask you the rest later.

POLYMESTOR. Certainly he is. So far as he is concerned, you are truly fortunate.*

HECUBA. O dearest friend, what good words you speak! They 990 are just what I would expect from you.

POLYMESTOR. Then what is the second thing that you want to learn from me?

HECUBA. If he has any memories of his mother here.

POLYMESTOR. He does, and he even tried to come to you here in secret.

HECUBA. Is the gold which he brought with him from Troy still safe?

POLYMESTOR. Indeed it is. I am guarding it in my house.

HECUBA. Keep it safe then, and do not covet what belongs to your neighbour.

POLYMESTOR. Certainly not. I hope to enjoy what I have at present.

HECUBA. So do you know what I want to say to you and your boys?

POLYMESTOR. I do not. You will tell me this information yourself.

HECUBA. There exist, O my friend, loved by me as I love you 1000 now . . .

POLYMESTOR. What is this that I and my children should know?

HECUBA. ancient caverns where the gold of Priam's sons is stored.

POLYMESTOR. Is this what you want to communicate to your son?

HECUBA. Very much so—and through you, for you are a pious man.

POLYMESTOR. Then why do these children need to be here?

HECUBA. It is better for them to know, in case you die.

POLYMESTOR. Those are sensible words. That is the wiser course.

HECUBA. So do you know where Trojan Athena's treasure-caves* are?

POLYMESTOR. Is that where the gold is? What is the marker?

HECUBA. A black rock rising high above the ground. 1010

POLYMESTOR. So is there anything else you wish to tell me about things there?

HECUBA. I want you to look after the money I came away with.

POLYMESTOR. Where is it then? Inside your robes, or have you hidden it away?

HECUBA. We keep it safely in the mass of plunder in these tents.

POLYMESTOR. Where? This is the stockade that encloses the Achaean fleet.

HECUBA. The tents of the female prisoners are private.

POLYMESTOR. Is everything quite safe inside? Are there no men?

HECUBA. None of the Greeks is in the tents, only us women. But come inside—for the Argives are eager to set sail from Troy*—so that you get everything you should and go back 1020 with your boys to the home you have given my child.

> POLYMESTOR *and* HECUBA *go into the tent.*

CHORUS (*sings*). You have not yet paid the penalty but perhaps you will.
Like a man who has fallen into the sea where there is no harbour in sight,
you will tumble with a sideways lurch from your heart's desire
and lose your life. For where liability
to Justice and to the gods coincides,
there comes a deadly, deadly doom.   1030
Your hopes for this journey will cheat you, for it has led you to death, to Hades, you wretched man,
and it is not a warrior's hand that will take your life from you.

POLYMESTOR (*from within*). O agony! I am being blinded, cruelly robbed of my eyes' light!*

CHORUS. Did you hear the wailing of the Thracian man, my friends?

POLYMESTOR (*from within*). O agony—I cry it again, my children—for this grim butchery!

CHORUS. Friends, they have done deeds of unheard of horror in the tent.

POLYMESTOR (*from within*). You shall not escape, however nimbly you run! No, I shall burst open the innermost 1040

corners of these tents with my fists. Look! I am launching a
blow from my mighty hand.

CHORUS. Do you think we should rush in there? This is the
critical moment that summons us to stand shoulder to
shoulder with Hecuba and the Trojan women.

HECUBA comes out of the tent.

HECUBA. Flail away, hold nothing back as you tear out the
doors, since you will never put bright vision back into your
eyes, you will not see your children alive—for I have killed
them.

CHORUS. Have you really mastered your Thracian guest-friend
and destroyed him, mistress? Have you actually done what
you say?

HECUBA. In a moment you will see him in front of the tents,   1050
a blind man reeling madly with blind steps*—the bodies of
his two children as well, whom I and these admirable Trojan
women have killed. He has paid me the just penalty.

But here he is coming out of the tent, as you can see. I
shall get out of the way and put a distance between myself
and this formidable Thracian as he boils with rage.

*POLYMESTOR crawls out on all fours. His children are brought
out on the ekkyklēma.**

POLYDORUS (*sings*).
O my agony! Where can I go, where stop, where find safe
   haven,
as I support myself on my hands and feet
crawling like a four-footed beast of the mountain?
Shall I change my direction—this way or that?—   1060
in my longing to seize
the man-slaying* women of Ilium
who have destroyed me?
Those cruel daughters of the Phrygians—
my curse on their cruelty!—
where have they fled? In which corners are they cowering?
O you Sun god,* if only you could heal the vision
in my bloody eyes,
heal it and rid them of this blindness! Give me light!
Ah, ah,

quiet!* I sense the stealthy movement of women here.   1070
Where should I rush to glut myself with their flesh and
   bones,
feasting on these savage beasts,
to win requital for this brutal outrage
on my wretched self?
Where, O where am I being carried, leaving my children
   defenceless,
to be butchered by these hellish Bacchants,*
torn limb from limb, and flung out on the mountain
as a cruel and bloody banquet for the dogs.*
Where can I stop, where rest, [where go,]
gathering up my flax-woven robe as a ship   1080
furls its sails* with its sea-going rigging,
rushing upon this lair of deadly beasts to protect my children?
CHORUS. Wretched man, the evils that have been inflicted on
   you are certainly hard to bear, but a man who has done
   shameful things must pay a terrible reckoning. [A god who
   presses hard upon you has given you this.]
POLYMESTOR (*sings*).
   Aiai!* You Thracians, you warrior race of spearmen,
   horse-loving subjects of Ares!   1090
   Hey, Achaeans, hey you sons of Atreus!
   I am crying for help. Help! Help!
   For the gods' sake, come here, come!
   Does anybody hear me? Or will no one help me? Why so
      slow?
   Women have destroyed me,
   captive women!
   We have suffered terribly, yes terribly.
   O this outrage against me!
   Where can I turn to? Where can I make for?
   Shall I fly up to the aerial halls of heaven   1100
   where Orion or Sirius* shoots forth flaming rays of fire
   from his eyes, or shall I rush in my misery
   to the black-hued ferry which sails to Hades?
CHORUS. When someone suffers misfortunes too heavy to
   bear, he can be forgiven if he rids himself of his wretched
   life.

AGAMEMNON enters.

AGAMEMNON. I came when I heard shouting. For Echo, child 1110 of the mountain rock, was far from silent as she cried out, causing uproar through the army.* If we didn't know that the Phrygians' towers had fallen to the Greek spear, this din would have caused considerable alarm.

POLYMESTOR. O my dearest friend—yes, Agamemnon, I recognized your voice when I heard it—do you see what I suffer?

AGAMEMNON (*with a start*). Wretched Polymestor, who has brought you to this ruin? Who has bloodied your eyes and made them blind? And who has killed these boys, your sons? He must have felt great anger against you and your children, whoever he was.

POLYMESTOR. Hecuba has destroyed me, together with the 1120 captive women—no, not destroyed me, but worse.

AGAMEMNON. What are you saying? Did you do this deed,* as he says? Did you steel yourself, Hecuba, to this impossible undertaking?

POLYMESTOR. Ah! What are you saying? Does this mean she is somewhere near by? Let me know where she is, tell me, so that I can seize her with these two hands, tear her to pieces and make her flesh all bloody!

AGAMEMNON (*catching old of him*). Hey! What's the matter?

POLYMESTOR. By the gods I beseech you, let me go so that I can attack her with these raging hands.

AGAMEMNON. Control yourself! Empty your heart of its savagery and state your case, so that I can hear each of you in 1130 turn and form a fair judgement about why you have suffered this treatment.

POLYMESTOR. I shall do so gladly. There was one of Priam's sons, the youngest, Polydorus, Hecuba's child, whom Priam his father sent from Troy and gave me to bring up in my house, suspecting, I suppose, that Troy would be taken. I killed him. And now you must hear why I killed him and what excellent judgement and foresight I showed in doing so. I was afraid that if the boy were left alive as your enemy, he would rally Troy and colonize it again, and the Achaeans 1140 would realize that one of Priam's sons was still living and launch a new expedition against the Phrygians' land. Then they would plunder and lay waste these plains of Thrace, and we, the Trojans' neighbours, would suffer the misery which we endured a short while ago.*

Hecuba found out about her son's deadly fate and brought me here on some such pretext as this—she would tell me about chests of gold hidden in Ilium, belonging to Priam's sons. She led me into the tent on my own with my children, to prevent anyone else knowing about this. I sat down on the 1150 middle of the couch to rest my legs. And many Trojan maidens sat beside me, for all the world as if I were their friend, some on my left, others on my right, and they praised the Edonian* weave of these robes of mine, holding them up to the beams of light to look at them, while others inspected my two Thracian spears and so stripped me of my pair of weapons. And all the women who were mothers kept admiring my children, dandling them in their hands and passing them from one to the other to get them away from their father. And then— 1160 can you believe it after their soothing chatter?—some of them suddenly snatched swords from somewhere in their robes and stabbed my boys, while others grabbed my hands and limbs and clung on to them like octopuses.*

I wanted to help my children but whenever I tried to lift my face, they held me down by the hair, and whenever I attempted to move my hands, I got nowhere as they crowded round their wretched victim. In the end—O agony greater than agony!—they did their terrible work. They took 1170 hold of clasps* and stabbed at the wretched pupils of my eyes, making them all bloody. Then they ran off through the tents in flight. Out I leapt like a wild beast in pursuit of these murderous dogs,* and I searched every wall, beating, pounding like a huntsman.

I have suffered all this to further your interest—because I killed your enemy, Agamemnon. But to put the matter briefly, if any man has spoken ill of women in times gone by,* if any man speaks in this vein now or will do so in the future, I shall sum up the whole matter in these words: nei- 1180 ther the earth nor the sea has produced a race like them, and anyone who has ever come into contact with them knows this well.*

CHORUS. Do not be so insolent and don't classify us all together and level such criticisms at the female sex simply because of your sufferings. [For there are many of us. Some are ⟨unjustly⟩* hated, while others do fall into the category of bad women.]

HECUBA. Agamemnon, the tongue should never have more influence among men than deeds. On the contrary, if a man has acted rightly, his words should have the ring of truth, while if he has acted badly, his words should sound a false 1190 note. And injustice should never be able to speak well. There are clever men who have mastered this subtle art but they cannot stay clever all the time. No, they come to a bad end. Not one of them has yet avoided this.

I have begun my speech with these words addressed to you, Agamemnon. Now I shall turn to him and reply to what he has said. You claim that you killed my son to save the Achaeans from a second ordeal* and to help Agamemnon. But in the first place, you monstrous wretch, barbarian races would never become friends with Greeks. It 1200 would be impossible. And besides, what interest of Agamemnon's were you so keen to further? Were you planning to make a marriage alliance with some Greek? Or are you a relative of his? Or was there some other reason? Were they really going to sail here again and cut down the crops of your land? Whom do you think you will persuade of that? It was the gold that killed my son, if you were willing to speak the truth—the gold and your greed. For tell me this. How was it that when Troy prospered and our towering wall still embraced our city, when Priam was alive and Hector's 1210 spear triumphant, how was it that you did not kill the boy, or keep him alive and bring him with you to the Argives— that is if you had really wanted to do this man a favour? After all, you were bringing him up, you had him in your house. But when we were no longer in the light and the smoke signalled that the city was in enemy hands, you killed the guest-friend who had come to your hearth.

And now let me tell you something else which makes it plain how vile you appear. If you were a friend to the Achaeans, you ought to have taken the gold you are keeping, which you say is not your own but his,* and given it to 1220

them. After all, they were in need and had long been
strangers to their native country. But you cannot bear to let
it out of your hands even now. No, you still persist in keeping it in your house.

Another point. If you had brought up my child and protected him as you should have, you would now have a name
for goodness. For while prosperity never lacks fair-weather
friends, in bad times it is the good men who show true
friendship. If you were short of money and my son was living happily, he would be proving a great treasure to you.
But as things stand now, you do not have that man* as your 1230
friend, any benefit from the gold has vanished, your children
are dead, and you have been reduced to this!

I tell you, Agamemnon, if you help him, you will be seen
as a bad man. You will be doing a favour to one who is neither pious nor loyal to those to whom he should have been,
to a guest-friend who is neither holy nor just. We shall say
that you take pleasure in bad men because you are like them
yourself. But I shall not speak ill of my masters.

CHORUS. Splendid! How true it is that goods deed always give
men the basis for a good speech!

AGAMEMNON. I find it a troublesome task to pronounce 1240
judgement upon evil deeds that concern other people, but I
have to do so none the less. For it is a shameful business to
take this matter in hand and then push it aside. To be plain
with you, I do not think that it was for my sake or indeed
that of the Achaeans that you killed a man who was your
guest-friend. No, you wanted to keep the gold in your house.
But you are using the arguments that suit your purpose in
your calamity. So perhaps it may be a light matter among
you people to kill a guest-friend, but it is shameful for us
Greeks to act in this way. So how can I escape criticism if I
judge that you are innocent?* It is impossible. Since you 1250
have the hardiness to do ignoble deeds, you must put up
with disagreeable treatment.

POLYMESTOR. Alas, I have been defeated by a woman, a slave
too. I must accept a punishment from my inferiors.

HECUBA. Isn't this just, if you have done evil deeds?*

POLYMESTOR. I cry out in my sorrow for my children here
and my poor eyes!

HECUBA. Are you in pain? What of it? Don't you think that I
feel pain for my boy?

POLYMESTOR. You rejoice in your brutality to me. You will
stop at nothing.

HECUBA. Why shouldn't I rejoice as I take my vengeance on
you?

POLYMESTOR. But perhaps you will not be happy when the
sea-water . . .

HECUBA. carries me to the shores of Greece? Do you mean 1260
that?

POLYMESTOR. No, when it closes over you after you have
fallen from the masthead.*

HECUBA. Who will force me to leap?

POLYMESTOR. You will climb up the ship's mast on your own.

HECUBA. With wings on my back? Or some other way? Tell
me.

POLYMESTOR. You will become a dog with fire-red eyes.*

HECUBA. How do you know about my transformation?

POLYMESTOR. The Thracian prophet Dionysus* told me this.

HECUBA. And didn't he prophesy any of your present calamities to you?

POLYMESTOR. No. If he had, you would never have caught
me with your tricks like this.

HECUBA. Shall I die where I fall or survive and live out †my 1270
life† there?*

POLYMESTOR. You will die. And your tomb will be called by
the name . . .

HECUBA. You don't mean a name that conjures up my
changed shape?

POLYMESTOR. Poor Dog's Tomb,* a landmark for sailors.

HECUBA. I don't care, for you have paid me the just penalty.

POLYMESTOR. And fate decrees that your daughter Cassandra
must die.

HECUBA. I spit out your words.* That is the fate I wish on you.

POLYMESTOR. This man's wife, that bitter keeper of his house,
will kill her.

HECUBA. I pray that the daughter of Tyndareus may never run
so mad.*

POLYMESTOR. She will kill this man too, lifting an axe on
high.

AGAMEMNON. You there, are you mad? Are you in love with 1280
suffering?

POLYMESTOR. Kill me if you like. Whatever you do to me, a
bloody bath is still waiting for you in Argos.*

AGAMEMNON. Drag him off, servants! Use force.

POLYMESTOR. Does it give you pain to hear me?

AGAMEMNON. Stop his mouth!

POLYMESTOR. Yes, gag me. I have said my say.

AGAMEMNON. Throw him out on some desert island—and be
quick about it! This effrontery is unendurable.

POLYMESTOR *is dragged off.*

And you, poor Hecuba, go and bury the bodies of both your
children.

HECUBA *goes out.*

You must come near the tents of your masters, Trojan
women. For I see the winds are here now to escort us home.* 1290
May we have a happy voyage to our fatherland, may we discover that all is happy in our houses, and find release from
our troubles!*

AGAMEMNON *goes out.*

CHORUS (*chants*). On to the harbours and the tents, my friends.
We are about to taste the grim labours of slavery.
Yes. Necessity is harsh.

The CHORUS *goes out.*

THE TROJAN WOMEN

Characters

HECUBA, formerly queen of Troy
POSEIDON
ATHENA
TALTHYBIUS, a Greek herald
CASSANDRA, a daughter of Hecuba
ANDROMACHE, a daughter-in-law of Hecuba
MENELAUS, king of Sparta
HELEN, formerly the wife of Menelaus
CHORUS of Trojan captive women

The action is set before the city of Troy in front of the tents where the captive Trojan women have been quartered. HECUBA *lies on the ground.**

Enter POSEIDON.

POSEIDON. I am Poseidon. I have come, leaving the salt depths of the Aegean sea where the dancing Nereids twirl their steps so gracefully.* For since the time when Phoebus and I set up the stone circle of towers around this land of Troy with our straight rules, good will towards the city of the Phrygians has never left my heart.* Now it is smoking. Sacked by the Argive* spear, it lies in ruins. For through Pallas' schemes, Epeius, a Phocian from Parnassus,* fash-   10
ioned a horse pregnant with arms and sent its deadly weight inside the towers. [As a result it will be called by future gen-erations the Wooden Horse, fraught with hidden spears of wood.]* The sacred groves are desolate and the sanctuaries of the gods are awash with blood. And Priam has fallen in death near the steps below the altar of Zeus the Protector of the Hearth.* Massy gold and Trojan spoils are being sent to the ships of the Achaeans. They are waiting for a fair wind   20
to blow from the stern so that after ten long years they can have the joy of looking upon their wives and children—the Greeks who made war upon this city.

I am abandoning famous Ilium and my altars, since I
have been worsted by the Argive goddess Hera and by
Athena, who joined forces to destroy the Phrygians.* For
whenever the curse of desolation lays hold on a city, religion
grows sickly and there is no will to honour the gods.
Scamander* echoes with many a howl from female captives
as they are allotted their masters. And some the Arcadian   30
people have won, some the Thessalians, some the Athenian
chiefs, descendants of Theseus. But all the Trojan women
who have not been allotted are in these tents. They have
been picked out for the foremost men of the army, and with
them is the Spartan daughter of Tyndareus, Helen, rightly
classed as a prisoner.

And if anyone wishes to look upon this unhappy woman
(POSEIDON *points to* HECUBA), here is Hecuba lying in front
of the entrance, shedding many a tear for many reasons. She
is unaware that her daughter Polyxena has been killed in a   40
pitiable sacrifice at Achilles' tomb. Priam and her children
are no more. As for the virgin Cassandra whom lord Apollo
left mad,* Agamemnon will abandon piety and the wish of
the god and bed her by force in an unlawful marriage.

Well then, dear city with your finely squared towers, you
that were once so happy, fare you well. If Pallas, the daughter of Zeus, had not destroyed you, you would still be standing on your foundations.

Enter ATHENA.

ATHENA. Am I permitted to speak to one who is so closely
related to my father, a great divinity honoured among the
gods, now that I have laid aside my former enmity?   50
POSEIDON. You are. After all, family ties, lady Athena, work
no small magic on the heart.
ATHENA. I am grateful to you for your kindly attitude. And I
propose for discussion, lord, a subject of common interest to
us both.
POSEIDON. Can it be that you are bringing some new word
from one of the gods, either from Zeus or some other deity?
ATHENA. No. It is because of Troy—where we are treading
now—that I have come to you to ally your power with
mine.

POSEIDON. Surely you have not cast out your former enmity
    and come to pity Troy now that the fire has burnt it to   60
    ashes?

ATHENA. Return to the point at issue before we discuss that.
    Will you talk matters over with me and join me in wanting
    what I want to do?

POSEIDON. Certainly. But I want to find out your precise inter-
    est in the matter. Have you come to help the Achaeans or
    the Phrygians?

ATHENA. I want to bring joy to the Trojans who were previ-
    ously my enemies and to give the Achaean army a bitter
    journey home.

POSEIDON. Why do your feelings chop and change like this?
    You shift between excessive hate and love, as chance dic-
    tates.*

ATHENA. Do you not know that I have been outrageously
    insulted—I, and my temples too?*

POSEIDON. Yes, I do know. It was when Ajax dragged off   70
    Cassandra by force.*

ATHENA. And he was neither punished nor reprimanded by
    the Achaeans.

POSEIDON. Yet it was by your power that Ilium was actually
    sacked.

ATHENA. That is the very reason why I wish to join you and
    do them harm.

POSEIDON. For my part, I am ready to help with what you
    want. What will you do?

ATHENA. I want to blight their journey home.

POSEIDON. While they are still here on land or on the salt sea?

ATHENA. When they are sailing off home from Troy. And Zeus
    will send rain and vast hailstones and dark gusting blasts of
    wind. He says that he will give me the fire of his thunder-   80
    bolt to strike the Achaeans and burn their ships with its
    flames. And you for your part must make the Aegean sea
    roar with huge waves and whirlpools and fill the hollow bay
    of Euboea with corpses so that for the future the Achaeans
    may learn to revere my sanctuaries and respect the other
    gods.

POSEIDON. It shall be so. The favour does not call for many
    words. I shall whip up the Aegean sea. The shores of

Myconos and the rocks of Delos, and Scyros and Lemnos and   90
the promontories of Caphareus will hold the corpses of many
dead men.*

Go to Olympus, take the thunderbolts from your father's
hands and watch for the time when the Argive army is
under full sail. The mortal who sacks cities and temples and
tombs, the holy places of the dead, is a fool. Having given
them to desolation, he himself meets destruction in time to
come.

POSEIDON *and* ATHENA *go out.*

HECUBA (*chants*). Up, unhappy woman! Lift your head
and your neck from the ground! This is no longer Troy,
we are no longer Troy's queen.   100
Fortune has veered round. Endure it.
Sail* on a sensible course. Sail as fits your fortune,
and do not set the prow of life's ship
against the swell, as chance steers your voyage.
Alas! alas!
What is there here that I do not mourn in my misery?
Country, children, husband—all are gone.
O the surpassing grandeur of my ancestors
now cast down*—so you were nothing then!
Why should I be silent? Why should I not be silent?   110
Why should I lament?
How wretched I am in this heavy fate
which makes me lie here as I do, my limbs spread low,
stretched out on my back on the ground's hard bed.
Alas for my face, alas for my forehead
and my ribs, how I long
to twist and turn my back and my spine
now to one side of my body, now to the other,
as I endlessly weep and lament.
But even this is music to the wretched—   120
to sing of their joyless woes.

(*Sings*) You ships' prows which went
on swift oars over the purple sea
to holy Ilium
by way of the harbours of Greece with their good anchorage
to the accompaniment of the flutes' hated paean*

and the voice of the melodious pipes,
and hung your Egyptian ropes
from your sterns,*
alas, in the bays of Troy   130
in your quest for the hateful wife of Menelaus,
that foul disgrace to Castor*
and shame to the Eurotas,*
the murderer of Priam, the father
who sowed fifty children,
the woman who has run me, Hecuba the wretched,
aground on this ruin.
Alas, look at where I sit here in degradation
near the tents of Agamemnon.
I am being led away from my house,   140
a poor old slave-woman,
my head pitifully ravaged as I lament in my mourning.
But O you sorrowful wives
and ill-wedded daughters
of the bronze-speared Trojans,
Ilium is smouldering, let us bewail it.
Just as the mother-bird raises the cry
for its nestlings, so shall I begin the chant,
a very different measure from that which once I led
to honour the Phrygians' gods   150
as I led the dance with the loud-ringing stamp of my foot
while Priam leant on his sceptre.

The FIRST HALF-CHORUS *enters.*

FIRST HALF-CHORUS (*sings*).
  Hecuba, what are you saying, what are you crying out?
  What do your words refer to? I heard your pitiful lamentations
  from inside the tents.
  Fear darts through the hearts of the Trojan women,
  who bewail their slavery
  inside these dwellings.
HECUBA (*sings*). Children, the Achaean oarsmen
  are already moving towards the ships.   160
FIRST HALF-CHORUS (*sings*).
  Alas, what are they planning? Are they now
  about to take me off over the sea from my fatherland?

HECUBA (*sings*). I do not know. I assume it means our ruin.
FIRST HALF-CHORUS (*sings*). Oh, oh!
 You wretched Trojan women, come out of the tents
 to hear of your troubles.
 The Argives are getting ready for their journey home.
HECUBA (*sings*). Ah, ah!
 I beg you not to send
 the frenzied Cassandra* outside   170
 to be shamed before the Argives in her madness.
 Do not add this distress to my griefs.
 Oh, oh!
 Troy, unhappy Troy, you no longer exist.*
 Unhappy too are those who leave you,
 both the living and the dead.

The SECOND HALF-CHORUS *enters.*

SECOND HALF-CHORUS (*sings*). Alas, I have come trembling
   out of these tents of Agamemnon
 to hear you,
 my queen. Surely the Argives
 have not made the decision to kill me, their wretched victim?
 Or are the sailors at the stern   180
 now getting ready to ply their oars?
HECUBA (*sings*). My child, I have come, my heart
 ashiver with panic since I woke at dawn.
SECOND HALF-CHORUS (*sings*).
 Has a herald of the Greeks come already?
 To whom have I been allocated as a wretched slave?
HECUBA (*sings*). I think that the drawing of your lots will be
   soon.
SECOND HALF-CHORUS (*sings*). Oh, oh!
 Which Argive, which Phthian*
 or islander will lead my unhappy self
 away from Troy to his land.
HECUBA (*sings*). Alas, alas!   190
 And who will own me, miserable old woman that I am,
 where, where* on earth shall I live as a slave
 like a drone,* Hecuba the wretched,
 corpse-like,

the image of the fleeting dead—
alas, alas!—
as I keep guard at a front door
or nanny children,
I who held the privileges in Troy?
CHORUS (*sings*). Alas, alas, in what sorrowful strains
could you cry out at this degradation!
No longer shall I move the whirling shuttle
back and forth on Trojan looms.   200
For the final time I look upon the house of my parents,
the final time. I shall endure greater hardships
as I go to a Greek man's bed—
a curse on that night and the fortune that brings me to it!—
or draw water from the sacred waters of Pirene,*
a pitiful servant.
If only we could go to the famous
and blessed land of Theseus*—
but not, no, not to the swirling waters of the Eurotas   210
and Helen's hateful dwelling
where I shall encounter Menelaus as his slave,
the man who sacked Troy.

I have heard it said that the holy land of Peneus,*
the lovely plain at Olympus' base,
abounds in wealth
and generous fertility.
To go there is my second choice
after the sacred and holy land of Theseus.
And I hear that Hephaestus' land,   220
mother of the mountains of Sicily,
the land of Etna across the sea from Carthage,
is famous for its garlands of excellence,*
as is the land
near †the Ionian sea†
that Crathis, loveliest of rivers,
which stains the hair to redness,
waters with its sacred streams,
nurturing and giving its blessings to a country of fine men.*

(*Chants*) But look, here comes a herald   230
from the army of the Greeks, a dispenser of fresh news.*

How quickly he walks!
What news does he bring? What will he say?
Now we are slaves of the Dorian land.

Enter TALTHYBIUS.

TALTHYBIUS. Hecuba—yes, you know me for I made frequent 240
journeys to Troy as a herald from the Achaean army. I am
Talthybius. You got to know me in those former times, lady,
and now I have come to bring you fresh information.

HECUBA (*sings*). It was this, this, dear women, that I feared
long ago.*

TALTHYBIUS. You have now been allocated, all of you, if that
was what made you afraid.

HECUBA (*sings*). Alas, what city of Phthian Thessaly
or Cadmus' land* is it?
Tell us.

TALTHYBIUS. Each woman was assigned to a different man.
You were not allocated all together.

HECUBA (*sings*). Who has been assigned to whom? For which
of the Trojan women
does a happy fate lie in store?

TALTHYBIUS. I have the information. But ask about each individual, not everyone together.

HECUBA (*sings*). Who has been allotted my daughter,
wretched Cassandra? Tell me.

TALTHYBIUS. King Agamemnon took her. There was no ballot for her.*

HECUBA (*sings*). To be a slave to his Spartan wife?   250
I cry alas!

TALTHYBIUS. No, as a bride in a clandestine union.

HECUBA (*sings*). What, the maiden of Phoebus, to whom the
golden-haired god
gave as her gift a life free from marriage?

TALTHYBIUS. Love for the god-inspired girl pierced Agamemnon's heart.

HECUBA (*sings*). My child, throw down the holy branches
and fling from your body
the sacred garlands which bedeck you.

TALTHYBIUS (*blithely unresponsive*). Indeed. After all, isn't it a
great thing for her to win a royal bed?

HECUBA (*sings*). What of my youngest child, whom you took   260
    from me?
  Where is she?

TALTHYBIUS. Are you asking about Polyxena, or who else do
    you mean?

HECUBA (*sings*). Yes, Polyxena. To whom has the lot joined
    her?

TALTHYBIUS. She has been assigned to Achilles' tomb as an
    attendant.*

HECUBA (*sings*). O my sorrow! So I bore her to attend a grave!
  But what is this custom,
  or what rite of the Greeks is this, my friend?

TALTHYBIUS. Count your daughter happy. All is well with
    her.

HECUBA (*sings*). What is this you say?
  Tell me, does she look upon the light of day?   270

TALTHYBIUS. Her fate has laid hold on her. She has found
    relief from trouble.

HECUBA (*sings*). And what of the wife of Hector, skilled in
    arms,
  wretched Andromache, what is happening to her?

TALTHYBIUS. There was no ballot for her either. The son of
    Achilles has taken her.

HECUBA (*sings*). And I who need a stick for my aged hand as
    a third leg,
  who am I to serve?

TALTHYBIUS. Odysseus, king of Ithaca, has taken you as his
    slave in the lot.

HECUBA (*sings*). Ah, ah!
  Beat your shorn head!
  Tear your two cheeks with your nails!   280
  Ah, woe is me!
  The lot has assigned me
  as a slave to a foul man of trickery,
  an enemy of justice, a lawless monster
  who turns everything inside out
  and then back again
  with his double tongue,
  transforming men to hatred of what they once held dear.*
  Weep for me, Trojan women.

An evil fate has destroyed me. All is over for me,   290
a wretched woman who has met
with the most unhappy allocation of all.

CHORUS. You know your fate, my queen. But which of the
Achaeans or Greeks is master of my fortunes?*

TALTHYBIUS. Off with you, slaves, you must bring Cassandra
out as quickly as you can, so that I may first hand her over
to the general and then take to the others the female captives who have been allocated to them.

But look! What is this torch blaze burning inside? Are the
Trojan women firing their quarters because their trans-   300
portation from this land to Argos is imminent, and are they
setting fire to their bodies in a suicide bid? Or is it something
else? Certainly, in such circumstances freedom finds the
yoke of misfortune hard to bear. Open up, open up! I must
not allow these women to do what suits them and find that
the Achaeans cast the blame, and the odium, on me.

HECUBA. It is not that. They are not burning the tents. No, my
frenzied daughter Cassandra is darting this way at a run.

CASSANDRA rushes on, brandishing a torch in either hand.

CASSANDRA (*sings*). Hold up the fire, display it, bring it here!
I pay reverence—look upon me, look!—
to this temple with my torches. O lord Hymenaeus,*   310
happy is the bridegroom,
happy am I in my coming marriage
to a king in Argos.
Hymen, O Hymenaeus, lord!
For you, mother, go on mourning my dead father
and dear fatherland
with tears and laments,
while I light up the blaze of my torch
to a gleaming radiance   320
for my marriage,
giving light to you, O Hymenaeus,
giving light to you, O Hecate,*
as is the custom
when maidens wed.

Swing your foot high, lead the dance, lead it—
Euan, euoi!*—

as for my father's happiest fortunes.
Holy is the dance.
Lead it, Phoebus. It is in your temple
that I make sacrifice, crowned with a garland of bay.   330
Hymen, o Hymenaeus, Hymen!
Dance, mother, lead the dance,
twirl your feet this way and that,
join with me happily as I move mine!
Oh, sound out the wedding song
in honour of the bride
with songs and shouts of blessing.
Come, O daughters of the Phrygians
with your lovely dresses,*
sing of the husband   340
who is fated to share my marriage bed.

CHORUS. My queen, won't you take hold of your frenzied
daughter in case her nimble dancing takes her among the
Argive soldiers?

HECUBA. Hephaestus, you hold up the torch when mortals
marry, but it is a torch of woe that you kindle here, and far
from what my high hopes pictured. Alas, my child, I never
thought that you would be married at the spearpoint, least
of all an Argive one. Give me a torch.* It is wrong that you
should carry them as you dart about in your frenzy, and you
have not been brought to sanity by your misfortunes, my
child, but are just the same as before. Take the torches   350
inside, you Trojan women, and give your tears in place of
this girl's wedding songs.

CASSANDRA. Mother, deck my victorious head with garlands
and rejoice in my marriage to a king. Escort me, and if I
seem less than eager to you, push me along by force. For if
Loxias* exists, Agamemnon, the famous lord of the
Achaeans, will marry me in a union more disastrous than
Helen's. Yes, for I shall kill him,* and I shall lay waste to his
house in revenge for my brothers and my father.   360

But I shall say no more of that. I shall not sing of the
axe which will cut into my neck and others' necks as well,
and the agonies of matricide to which my marriage will
lead, and the ruin of the house of Atreus.* No, I shall show
that our city here is happier than the Achaeans. I may

have the god in me, but nevertheless I shall stand outside
my frenzy to say this much. In their hunt for Helen, the
Greeks lost countless men—because of one woman, one
love affair. In a hateful cause, their clever general killed 370
what was dearest to him, sacrificing for his brother his
delight in children in his house, for the sake of a woman—
and that a woman who had not been carried off by force.
No, she went willingly.*

Then, after they came to the banks of Scamander, they
died one by one, though they were being stripped of no
boundary lands nor their native country with its high towers. And those whom the war god took never saw their children again. They were not shrouded in robes by their wives'
hands but they lie in a foreign land. And it was a similar
story back at home. The wives died as widows, the fathers 380
with no sons in their houses—they had brought up their
children in vain.* And there is no one who can let fall an
offering of blood upon the earth at their graves.* [Yes, this
is the praise* their army deserves. It is better to say nothing
of the shameful deeds.* May my inspiration not prove a
songstress who sings of evil.]

As for the Trojans, first of all—and this is the noblest
fame—they died for their fatherland, and the corpses of any
whom the spear took were carried to their homes by their
friends. The earth of their native land embraced them and
they were shrouded by the hands of their families, as was 390
proper. And all the Phrygians who did not die in battle lived
with their wives and their children day after day. These were
pleasures which the Achaeans missed,

And listen to the truth about Hector, whose story seems
so tragic to you. He has departed this life with the reputation of the noblest of men, and it was the coming of the
Achaeans that caused this. If they had stayed at home, who
would have known of his courage? Paris too—he married
Zeus' daughter. If he had not married her, he would have
had in his house a wife whom no one talked of.

Yes, anyone who is sane should avoid war. But if it comes 400
to that, it is no shameful garland for his city if a man dies
nobly, while if he dies ignobly, it brings disgrace. For these
reasons, mother, you must not feel pity for our land or for

my marriage. For by this union I shall destroy my bitterest
enemies and yours.

CHORUS. How happily you smile at your family's catastrophe!
You sing of things which you will perhaps show to be less
obscure than when you sang them.

TALTHYBIUS. If Apollo had not driven you out of your wits
and into this frenzy, you would not be sending my generals
on their way from this land with such ill-omened utterances. 410
No, you would pay the price for them. I see that the grand
and great and those with a reputation for wisdom are not a
bit better than the insignificant. For the supreme king of all
the Greeks, the beloved son of Atreus, has submitted to the
power of love which made him choose this frantic woman.
I am a poor man, but I would never have sought to bed her.

You are out of your mind, and so I cast your insults of
the Argives and eulogies of the Phrygians to the winds to
carry away. Follow me to the ships. You are a good match 420
for our general.

(*To Hecuba*) And you follow when the son of Laertes wants
to lead you off. You will be the servant of a good woman,*
as those who came to Ilium tell us.

CASSANDRA. What a fine fellow this lackey is! Whyever do we
dignify these men with the name of herald when all join in
loathing them, these attendants at the beck and call of kings
and cities?* You say that my mother will come to the palace
of Odysseus? What about the words which Apollo commu-
nicated to me? He says that she will die here. I shall not 430
bring reproach upon her by telling the rest.* Poor Odysseus,
he does not know what sufferings are in store for him. He
will look back on my troubles and those of Troy and they
will seem to him to shine like gold. He will live through ten
years on top of the ten here and come alone to his fatherland. ⟨He will go⟩ where terrible Charybdis †has her
dwelling, on the rocks of a narrow strait,†* and the moun-
tain-ranging Cyclops who eats raw flesh and Ligurian Circe
who transforms men to pigs. ⟨He will meet with⟩ shipwreck
on the salt sea, and longing for the lotus, and the holy cat-
tle of the sun, whose bloody flesh will one day send forth a 440
sound that will prove bitter for Odysseus. To cut short my
account, he will go to Hades while he is still alive, he will

escape the sea's waters, and when he reaches his house, he will find countless troubles there.*

But why do I shoot out these prophecies of Odysseus' sufferings like darts?*

(*To Talthybius*) Go quickly on your way.

Let me marry my bridegroom in the house of Hades. Yes, you ignoble man,* you will be ignobly buried by dark, not in the light of day, you commander-in-chief of the Danaans,* who think your achievements so grand. As for me, they will fling out my naked corpse, and the ravines flowing with winter water will give me to the animals to feast on near my husband's grave, me, Apollo's servant! O garlands of the god who is dearest to me,* you joyful emblems of his worship, fare you well. I have left the festivals in which I once found joy. Away with you! I tear you from my body—so that while my flesh is still pure, I may give them to the winds to carry to you, O lord of prophecy.* Where is the general's ship? Where must I get on board? You cannot be too quick as you watch out for a wind to swell your sails, since in me you will be taking one of three Furies from this land.* 450

Farewell, my mother. Do not shed a tear. O my dear fatherland and my brothers beneath the ground and our father who begat us, it will not be long before you greet me. 460 I shall come among the dead as a victor. I shall have laid waste the house of the sons of Atreus, the men who destroyed us.

HECUBA *faints.* CASSANDRA *is led out by* TALTHYBIUS.

CHORUS. Attendants of ancient Hecuba, can't you see how our mistress has fallen flat on the ground without a word? Won't you take hold of her? Will you really leave an old woman lying there, you wretches? Help her up onto her feet.

HECUBA. Let me lie where I have fallen. Unwanted actions are far from welcome, girls. For in the face of all I suffer, all I have suffered and shall go on to suffer, what can I do but 470 fall? O you gods! I know that I am invoking fickle allies, but even so it makes some sense to call upon the gods whenever one of us meets with misfortune. So first of all I wish to sing my swan-song over the blessings of my life. In this way I shall enhance the pathos of my sufferings. I was of royal

blood,* I married into a royal house, and there I gave birth
to the best of children—yes, they were no mere ciphers but
the foremost men of the Phrygians. No Trojan woman, no
Greek or barbarian could boast that she had borne such children. And I saw them fall beneath the Greek spear and had
this hair of mine shorn at their corpses' graves.* As for   480
Priam, the father who begat them, I had not heard of his fate
from others when I mourned him. No, it was with these very
eyes that I saw him butchered at the household altar, with
these same eyes that I saw my city captured. And as for the
girls whom I brought up to marry the pick of noble bridegrooms, they have been snatched from my hands. It was for
others that I brought them up. I have no hope that they will
ever see me again or that I shall see them myself. Last of all,
to crown my miserable woes, I shall come to Greece as an   490
old slave-woman. And they will put me to the tasks that
least befit this old age of mine—either to keep the keys as a
porteress—I, the mother of Hector!—or to make bread and
to lay my shrivelled body on the ground to sleep—I who
slumbered on a queen's bed—my battered skin clothed in
tattered rags. What degradation for one who was formerly
so prosperous! Alas, how wretched I am. What sufferings
have I met with, what sufferings lie in store for me—and all
because of one marriage and one woman!

O my child, O Cassandra, you who share your inspiration   500
with the gods, what troubles attend the loss of your virginity! And you, my unhappy Polyxena, where are you? No,
none of the sons or daughters whom I bore brings me help
in my suffering, though I had many children.* So why do
you lift me up? With what hopes? Guide me on these feet
that once trod so delicately in Troy—but now they are a
slave's—take me to my straw pallet on the ground with its
pillow of stone* so that I may collapse and die, harrowed by
my tears. Consider no prosperous man to have good fortune   510
until he is dead.*

HECUBA collapses.

CHORUS (*sings*) Sing, O Muse,
a new song about Ilium,
a funeral dirge accompanied by tears.

For now I shall cry out a song for Troy,
a song of how I was destroyed,
became a wretched captive of the spear,
victim of the four-wheeled Wooden Horse of the Greeks
when the Achaeans left it at the gates   520
as it clattered to the heaven,
bedecked with gold, crammed with arms.*
Standing on the Trojan rock, the people cried out:
'Go, Trojans, now that your toils are over,
take this holy image up to the citadel
for the Trojan goddess, the daughter of Zeus!'*
Which of the young women, which old man
did not come from their houses?
Delighting in their songs,
they embraced the trick that was their ruin.   530

All of the race of the Phrygians
rushed to the gates,
to present to the goddess the polished structure of mountain
     pinewood,
the Argives' ambush pregnant with Troy's ruin,
a gift to the maiden with immortal steeds.
Flinging round it ropes of spun flax,
they dragged it like a ship's black hull
onto the floor of the stone temple of the goddess Pallas,   540
to bring death to our country.
And when the darkness of night fell
upon our joyous toil,
the Libyan pipe and Phrygian songs
rang out, and the maidens
raised and tapped their feet
as they sang a happy song,
and in the houses the radiant gleam of the fires
shed a dark half-light
for those who slept.*   550

And I was dancing in the palace then and singing
to the maiden daughter of Zeus
who dwells on the mountains.*
A bloody cry
rang through the city
and filled Pergamum.*

And much-loved children flung their arms, fluttering in
    panic,
round their mothers' robes.
The war god came forth from his ambush—   560
it was the maiden Pallas' handiwork.*
The Trojans were slaughtered at their altars,
heads hacked off
widowed the young women in their beds
and brought to Greece a garland of victory
in the children they bore it,*
but sorrow to the native land of the Phrygians.

ANDROMACHE *is carried in on a wagon on which are Hector's
weapons and other spoils of the Trojans. She holds* ASTYANAX* *in
her arms.*

(*chants*). Hecuba, do you see Andromache
carried here in our enemies' wagon?
With her, close to her heaving breast,   570
comes her beloved Astyanax, Hector's son.
Where are they taking you on the wagon's back,
unhappy woman,
as you sit by Hector's brazen arms
and the spoils of the Phrygians won by the spear from Troy,
with which Achilles' son, Neoptolemus,
will crown his Phthian temples?*

(ANDROMACHE *and* HECUBA *sing till* 607)

ANDROMACHE. My Achaean masters lead me off.
HECUBA. O my sorrow!
ANDROMACHE.   Why do you cry a dirge that belongs
    to me?
HECUBA. Alas . . .
ANDROMACHE.   for these my woes . . .
HECUBA. O Zeus . . .
ANDROMACHE.   and for my ruin!   580
HECUBA. my children . . .
ANDROMACHE.   we were your children once!*
HECUBA. Our happiness is no more, Troy is no more . . .
ANDROMACHE. unhappy Troy.
HECUBA   and my noble children.
ANDROMACHE. Woe, woe . . .

HECUBA.   Yes, and woe for my . . .

ANDROMACHE. agonies.

HECUBA.   How lamentable the fate . . .

ANDROMACHE. of our city . . .

HECUBA.   which lies smouldering.

ANDROMACHE. May you come, O my husband . . .

HECUBA. You call upon my son down in Hades,*
  wretched girl.

ANDROMACHE. to protect your wife!   590
  And you, O scourge of the Achaeans . . .

HECUBA. yes, the eldest-born of the sons who once were mine,
  Priam's sons!

ANDROMACHE. lull me to sleep in Hades.
  Great is this longing . . .

HECUBA.   Unhappy girl, these are the sorrows
  we suffer . . .

ANDROMACHE. for our city in ruins . . .

HECUBA.   Sorrows are piled on
  sorrows.

ANDROMACHE. through the gods' malevolence, when your
  son eluded death,*
  the son who brought low Troy's citadel to win a loathsome
  marriage.
  Bloody bodies of the dead lie stretched before the temple of
  Pallas
  for the vultures to carry off. He won the yoke of slavery for   600
  Troy.

HECUBA. O my fatherland, my poor fatherland . . .

ANDROMACHE.   I weep for
  you as I leave you . . .

HECUBA. Now you behold its pitiful end.

ANDROMACHE.   and for my house
  where I bore my child.

HECUBA. O my children, your mother in her desolate city is
  robbed of you.
  †What lamentations, what sorrows,†
  what tears upon tears are poured forth
  over our homes. Those who die forget their sorrows.

CHORUS. When misfortunes come, how sweet are tears and
  sorrowful songs and grief-laden music!

ANDROMACHE (*gesturing to herself, Astyanax and the wagon with its load*). O mother of Hector, the man that once 610 destroyed so many of the Argives with his spear, do you see this?

HECUBA. I see how the gods work, how they raise on high what is nothing, and bring to ruin what seems to be something.

ANDROMACHE. I am being led off as plunder with my son. Nobility has been utterly transformed and has turned to slavery.

HECUBA. Necessity is a fearful thing. Just now Cassandra was torn from me by force. She no longer exists.

ANDROMACHE. Alas, alas! It seems that a second Ajax has appeared to torment your daughter.* But you are plagued in another way too.

HECUBA. There is no limit to my misfortunes. They are beyond 620 number. One woe treads on another's heels.

ANDROMACHE. Your daughter Polyxena is dead. She was butchered at Achilles' tomb, a gift to a lifeless corpse.

HECUBA. What misery for me! So it was this that Talthybius really meant when he spoke to me earlier in riddling hints.

ANDROMACHE. I saw her myself, and I got down from this wagon, covered her corpse with robes, and beat my breast for her.

HECUBA. Alas, my child, for your unholy sacrifice. Again I cry alas! What a foul murder!

ANDROMACHE. She is dead, yes. That is that. But even so, in 630 dying she has met with a happier fate than I have in continuing to live.

HECUBA. Dying and living are very different things, my child. The former is nothing, but while there's life, there's hope.

ANDROMACHE. [Mother, my mother, listen to what I have to say. My words have the stamp of nobility and will bring pleasure to your heart.] I tell you that not to be born is the same as being dead, and that it is better to die than to live in misery. †The dead have experienced the miseries of life but feel its pain no more,† while those who have fallen from good fortune into misery are heart-sore because of the pros- 640 perity they have lost.

Polyxena is dead. It is just as if she had never looked upon

the light of day. She knows nothing of her misfortunes. But
I, a woman who was ambitious for good reputation and won
it in generous measure, failed to find good fortune. In
Hector's home I tried to practise all the virtues that are considered the mark of a good wife. First of all, in the matter of
leaving the house—something that, whether a woman
already attracts criticism or not, automatically gives her a
bad reputation—I put aside my longing for that. Yes, I   650
stayed at home. And I would not allow any smart female
gossip inside that home, but found there an admirable
teacher in my own cast of mind, and was content with that.
Before my husband, I always kept my tongue quiet and my
expression calm. I knew in what spheres I should rule my
husband, in what spheres I should concede victory to him.
My reputation for these things reached the Greek army, and
has proved my ruin. For when I was captured, the son of
Achilles wanted to take me as his wife. I shall be a slave in   660
the house of a murderer.* And if I lay aside my love for
Hector and open up my heart to my present husband, I shall
appear to be a traitor to the one who is dead. Then again, if
I show my new husband loathing, I shall be hated by my
masters. And yet they say that a single night breaks down a
woman's distaste for a man's bed. I detest the wife who
throws off her loyalty to her former husband when she
makes a new marriage, and loves another. Not even a filly
will happily bear the yoke when separated from her fellow.   670
Yet animals are dumb and have no powers of reasoning. In
their nature they are inferior to humans.

O my dear Hector, in you I had a husband good enough
for me, a man great in understanding, birth, wealth and
courage.* You took me from my father's house as a virgin.
You were the first to share my maiden bed. And now you
are dead and I am going over the sea to Greece—to the yoke
of slavery, a prisoner of war. Surely the death of Polyxena   680
whom you mourn is not more appalling than my fate? I do
not even have what is a refuge for all mankind—hope. No,
I do not delude myself that I shall meet with good fortune.
Yet even delusions are pleasant.

CHORUS. Your tragedy is the same as ours. As you lament
your own fate, you teach me where I stand in my woes.

HECUBA. I have not yet been on a ship myself but I know
about them from pictures and from hearsay,* and I am
aware that, if a storm is mild enough for the sailors to
endure it, they are all eagerness to find safety from their
troubles, one standing by the tiller, another at the sails,   690
another keeping bilge-water out of the ship. However, if the
sea is stirred up to violence and overwhelms them, they give
in to their fortune and surrender to the run of the waves. So
I too have many woes, but I let them be. I keep my peace
and say nothing, for this sea of troubles from the gods over-
powers me. No, my dear child, forget about Hector's tragedy.
Your tears will never save him. Honour your new master,
seduce your husband into loving you for the way you   700
behave.* And if you do this, you will give pleasure to all your
friends and you may bring up this son of my son to prove
Troy's greatest support, so that the children one day to be
born from your blood may found Ilium anew and the city
can still exist.*

But another subject takes us away from this one. Who is
this Greek lackey I see coming here to tell us more new decisions?

Enter TALTHYBIUS *with attendants.*

TALTHYBIUS. Wife of Hector, the best of of the Phrygians in   710
days gone by, do not hate me. It is with great reluctance that
I have to announce the common decision of the Danaans*
and the grandsons of Pelops.*

ANDROMACHE. What is it? Your first words hint at bad news
to come.*

TALTHYBIUS. It has been decided that this boy . . . How can
I bring myself to say it?

ANDROMACHE. will have a different master from me? No!

TALTHYBIUS. None of the Achaeans will ever be his master.

ANDROMACHE. Then is he to be left here, a last trace of the
Phrygians?

TALTHYBIUS. I do not know how I can easily tell you my bad
news.

ANDROMACHE. I thank you for your consideration—unless
you are bringing bad tidings.

TALTHYBIUS. They are going to kill your boy. There, you know the worst.

ANDROMACHE. Alas. You bring me word of something even 720 more appalling than my marriage.

TALTHYBIUS. Odysseus* prevailed as he spoke among all the Greeks . . .

ANDROMACHE. O sorrow, sorrow! Our sufferings are beyond all measure!

TALTHYBIUS. saying that they should not bring the son of a noble father to manhood . . .

ANDROMACHE. I pray that such views may win the day when it comes to his children.

TALTHYBIUS. and that they must throw him from the towers of Troy. But let this happen and you will appear the wiser. Do not cling on to the child but grieve over your woes with a noble heart. You have no power—so do not delude yourself that you have. There is nowhere you can turn for help. No, you must think about your situation. Your city and your 730 husband are no more. You are conquered, and we are capable of fighting against a single woman. In view of all of this, I hope you will not fall in love with conflict, or do something which will bring shame on yourself or rouse hostility, or fling curses at the Achaeans. For if you say anything which will anger the army, this boy of yours will not be buried or meet with compassion, while if you keep quiet and bear your fortunes with a good grace, you will not leave his body behind unburied and you will find the Achaeans more sympathetic.

ANDROMACHE. O my dearest one, my child so extravagantly 740 honoured,* you will leave your wretched mother and die at your enemies' hands. [A father's nobility, the source of salvation to all others, will kill you, and] your father's courage has done you no good service. O my unhappy marriage bed, the wedding for which I came to Hector's halls long ago! It was not to bear a son to be slaughtered by the Danaans* as a sacrificial victim. No, he was to become the king of fertile Asia. O my child, are you weeping? Are you conscious of your misfortunes? Why have you grasped me with your 750 hands, clinging to my dress, falling under my protecting wings like a young bird? Hector will not come to bring you safety. He will not seize his famous spear and rise up from the ground. None of your father's kinsmen will come, none of the mighty Phrygians. A deadly fall from a great height will break your neck and stop your breath. There will be no pity for you. O my baby whom I hold in my arms, so dear to your mother, O the sweet fragrance of your skin!* It was for nothing then that this breast suckled you in your swad-dling-clothes! All my labour was in vain, all the tasks that 760 wore me down. Now you must embrace your mother. You never will again. Cling to the woman who gave you birth. Wind your arms around my back. Fasten your lips to mine.

O you Greeks, you who have devised atrocities worthy of barbarians,* why are you killing this innocent boy? You daughter of Tyndareus, you were never born from Zeus.* I say that you are the child of many fathers, first of all the Avenging Spirit, then of Envy and Murder and Death and all the evils that the earth breeds. I am certain that Zeus never 770 fathered you, you minister of death to barbarians and Greeks. My curse on you! With your lovely eyes* you brought shameful destruction on the famous plains of the Phrygians.

Take him, carry him off, fling him down, if that is what you have decided! Feast on his flesh. For it is the gods who are destroying us and we can find no way to ward off death from the boy. Hide away my wretched body. Fling it onto the ships. Yes, I am off to make a fine marriage, I who have lost my son.

CHORUS. Unhappy Troy, you have lost countless men because 780 of one woman and her hateful marriage.

ANDROMACHE goes off in the wagon.

TALTHYBIUS (*chants*). Come, boy, leave the loving embrace
of your wretched mother, and come off to the top of the
towers
that crown the city of your fathers,
where the vote decrees that you must breathe your last.
Take him.
Such words befit a messenger
whose nature is made of sterner stuff
and more inclined to heartlessness than mine.

HECUBA (*chants*). O my child, O son of my wretched son,   790
    your mother and I are being robbed of your life.
    There is no justice here. What am I to do?
    What service can I perform for you, ill-fated boy? I can give
        you
    these blows to my head, these hands pounding my breast.
    I have the power to do that. Woe for the city!
    I cry woe for you! What suffering remains for us to endure?
    What is there to stand in the way
    of our total destruction here and now?
            TALTHYBIUS *and his attendants lead off* ASTYANAX.

CHORUS (*sings*). O Telamon, king of Salamis, nurse of bees,*
    you who have your dwelling on the sea-girt island   800
    which faces the holy hill,*
    where Athena first revealed the branch of the grey olive,
    a goddess's gift, a crown and glory to gleaming Athens,*
    you came, you came from Greece,
    with Alcmena's son, the bowman,*
    your partner in noble deeds,
    to sack Troy,
    Troy, the city that once was ours,
    when, cheated of the mares,* he led the finest flower of Greece,
    and checked his sea-voyaging oar   810
    by the fair-flowing Simois,* and fastened the cables from the
        sterns,
    and from the ships he took his trusty bow
    which brought death to Laomedon. He destroyed
    the walls of stone, Phoebus' fine handiwork,* in a red blast
        of flame
    and sacked the city of Troy.
    Twice, yes in two onslaughts, the bloody spear-point
    wrought destruction on the Trojans around their walls.

    It was in vain, then, O son of Laomedon*   820
    who move so daintily amid the golden wine jugs,
    in vain that you fill Zeus' cups in glorious servitude.
    The city that gave you birth blazes with fire.
    Like a bird keening for its young,
    its seashores cry out,
    here for husbands, here for children,   830

here for aged mothers.
Your dewy bathing pools
and the training places where you ran
are gone. But you keep your youthful face
lovely in its calm
as you pay your graceful service by the throne of Zeus.
Yet the Greek spear
has destroyed the land of Priam.

Love, Love, you once came to the halls of Dardanus,   840
you who touch the hearts of the heavenly ones,
to what great heights did you exalt Troy then,
joining her to the gods in a close bond!
I shall level this reproach at Zeus no more.
The light of the white-winged Day,*
friendly to mortals,
looked on the destruction of our land,   850
looked on the ruin of Pergamum,
though she had in her bedroom
a husband from this land to give her children,*
the man whom the starry four-horsed chariot of gold,
snatched up and took away
to be a great hope for his fatherland.
But Troy's love charms over the gods are no more.

Enter MENELAUS *with attendants.*

MENELAUS. This day's sun—with what splendid radiance it   860
shines!—this day on which I shall take possession of my wife
[Helen. Yes, I am Menelaus, who went through many toils
with the Achaean army.]* I came to Troy not for a woman's
sake, as people think I did, but in pursuit of a man who
cheated me, his host, when he stole my wife as plunder from
my palace. Now the gods have ensured that he has paid the
penalty, he and his land, which has fallen to the Greek
spear. I have come to take off the Spartan woman. I call her
that since I cannot bring myself to speak the name of my for-   870
mer wife. Here are the prisoners' tents where she is numbered with the rest of the women from Troy. Those who
laboured to win her with the spear have given her to me to
kill—or, if I wish, to spare her life and take her back to the
land of Argos.

I have decided not to trouble myself here in Troy about Helen's fate, but to take her on my ship across the sea to Greek soil and to hand her over there to be killed in retribution for all those whose loved ones died at Ilium.

But come now, off with you, my servants, into the tents. 880 Bring her out here. Drag her by her hair, the murderess. And when the winds blow favourably, we shall take her to Greece.

HECUBA. O you who support the earth and have your dwelling upon it, whoever you are, hard to guess at, hard to understand, Zeus, whether you are the necessity imposed by nature, or human intelligence,* I offer you my prayers. For as you move with silent tread, you dispose all human affairs according to justice.

MENELAUS. What is this? What strange new prayers you make to the gods!

HECUBA. I praise you, Menelaus, if you are going to kill your 890 wife. But avoid seeing her in case she traps* you with desire. She traps the eyes of men, she destroys cities, she burns homes. She casts such spells. I know her. So do you and those who have suffered.

HELEN is dragged out, splendidly dressed.

HELEN. Menelaus, this is an alarming start to things. I have been haled out here before the tents by your brutal attendants. I am fairly sure that you hate me, but still I want to put my question to you. What decisions have you and the Greeks made about whether I am to live? 900

MENELAUS. There was no precise decision over you. No, the whole army handed you over to me, the man you wronged, to be killed.

HELEN. In that case, can I respond to this and explain that if I die, my death will be unjust?

MENELAUS. I did not come to bandy words with you but to kill you.

HECUBA. Listen to her, Menelaus. Don't let her die without this. And let me speak in opposition to her. For you know nothing of her wickedness in Troy. When you put together 910 both sides of the debate, her death is inevitable. There will be no escape for her.

MENELAUS. To grant this will cost us time. However, if she
wishes to speak, she may. But you can be sure that I shall
make this concession to her because of what *you* have said,
not out of any consideration for her.

HELEN. Perhaps you will not reply to me, irrespective of
whether I speak well or badly, because you think of me as
an enemy. I shall reply with opposing arguments to the
charges which I think you will level against me in debate [as
I respond to your accusations].

My first point is that this woman gave birth to the start
of our misfortunes when she gave birth to Paris. Secondly,   920
old Priam brought destruction on Troy and on me when he
failed to kill his son then and there, that deadly semblance
of the firebrand, Alexandros.* Listen to the truth about what
happened next. This Alexandros judged the trio of three
goddesses* and for her gift Pallas told him that as general of
the Phrygians he should destroy Greece. Hera promised that
Paris should hold sway over Asia and all Europe if he put
her first. Cypris* expressed her admiration for my loveliness
and promised to give me to him if she outdid the rival god-   930
desses in beauty. Consider what happened then. Cypris
defeated the other goddesses, and to this extent my marriage
was a benefit to Greece. You are not ruled by barbarians,
either as a result of military conquest or the domination of
a tyrant. But what brought Greece good fortune proved my
ruin. I was ruined by my beauty, and I am damned by those
who should have given me a garland to crown my head.

You will say that I have not yet discussed the point at
issue, how I suddenly stole away from your house. There
came the evil genius of the woman who stands before you—
whether you wish to call him Alexandros or Paris. He had
no insignificant goddess* with him. And you, you idiot, took   940
off on your ship for the land of Crete and left him in your
house in Sparta.

So much for that. I shall ask the next question not of you
but of myself. What was in my mind when I went from my
home with the stranger, betraying that home and my fatherland too? Punish the goddess* and become superior to Zeus,   950
who has power over all the other gods but is a slave to her.
However, you must pardon me.

But to come to a point where you could still make a spe-
cious case against me, when Alexandros had died* and gone
down to the underworld and the marriage struck by the goddess had come to an end, I should have left my house and
gone to the Argives' ships. But that is just what I tried to do,
and my witnesses are the guards of the towers and the look-
outs on the walls who often caught me secretly lowering
myself from the battlements to the ground on a rope. [And
that new husband of mine, Deiphobus, who had seized me
by force, held on to his wife against the Phrygians' will.]* In   960
view of this, my husband, cannot you see now how utterly
wrong it would be to kill me? Paris married me by force, and
in my home in Troy I suffered a bitter slavery. No victor's
prize for me! Do you want to be superior to the gods? Only
a fool would wish for that.

CHORUS. My queen, defend your children and your fatherland.
Prove that her arguments, however persuasive, are simply
false, since her fine words come from a criminal's lips, and
that is a terrible thing.

HECUBA. First of all I shall ally myself with the goddesses and
show that there is no justice in her words. I do not believe   970
that Hera and the maiden Pallas sank to such depths of folly
that the former tried to sell off Argos to barbarians, and that
Pallas would ever barter Athens into slavery to the
Phrygians. They did not come to Ida for the childish glam-
our of a beauty contest. After all, why should the goddess
Hera have conceived so great a desire to be beautiful? Was
it so that she could win a better husband than Zeus? Was
Athena in eager pursuit of a match with one of the gods?
But she shunned marriage and asked her father to let her
stay a virgin.* Don't try to give respectability to your crime   980
by making the goddesses out to be fools. You will certainly
not convince intelligent people of this.

You said that Cypris—and what a ridiculous idea this
is!—came with my son to Menelaus' house. Couldn't she
have taken you to Troy, you and Amyclae* and everything
else, while staying quietly in heaven? My son was out-
standingly beautiful and when you saw him your mind was
utterly possessed by sexual passion. Every time men commit
actions of uncontrolled immorality, that is Aphrodite, and it

is appropriate that the name of the goddess begins with folly.* When you looked upon him as he glittered with gold 990 in his oriental raiment,* you went raving mad. For it was a little world you inhabited in Argos, and you hoped that when you had left Sparta behind, you would overwhelm the city of the Phrygians, awash with its gold, with your extravagance. Menelaus' palace did not give you sufficient scope for your riotous luxury.

Enough of that. You say that my son took you off by force. Which of the Spartans witnessed this? Did anyone hear you shouting out for help? And young Castor and his 1000 brother were still there, not yet amid the stars.* Then when you came to Troy with the Achaeans hot on your track, and the deadly struggle of war broke out, if news reached you that Menelaus' side was winning, you used to praise him, to make my son grieve that he had a great rival for your love. But if the Trojans met with success, Menelaus was nothing to you. You kept your eye fixed firmly on events and led your life following the tides of fortune. You had no wish to keep company with virtue.

And then you say that you tried to steal away by let- 1010 ting yourself down from the towers by a rope, since you were in Troy against your will. Tell me, where were you caught stringing yourself up in a noose or sharpening a sword—the courses that a noble woman would take in her misery over the loss of her former husband? Yet I was constantly giving you this advice: 'Daughter, leave the city. My sons will marry other women, and I shall smuggle you off to the Achaean ships. Put an end to the fighting both for the Greeks and for us.' But this was a bitter medicine for you to swallow, since you were running riot 1020 in the house of Alexandros and wanted the barbarians to prostrate themselves before you.* These things were important to you.

After all this you have come out here in your fine attire and you have breathed the same air* as your husband, you hateful creature. You should have come humbly in rags, shuddering with fear, your head shaved bare, showing a sense of shame over your former sins rather than this impudent flaunting.

Menelaus, let me leave you in no doubt about my conclusion. Crown Greece with honour by an act worthy of you. 1030
Kill this woman. Set up this law for the rest of the female
sex, that whoever betrays her husband must die.

CHORUS. Menelaus, take vengeance on your wife in a manner
worthy of your ancestors and your house. Rebut the charge
of cowardice that the Greeks level at you* and appear noble
even in the sight of your enemies.

MENELAUS. You have come to the same conclusion as myself.
Yes, this woman went willingly from my house to share a
foreigner's bed, and her introduction of Cypris into her
speech is mere rodomontade. Off with her! Let them stone
her!* Let the quick moment of your death atone for the long 1040
toils of the Achaeans. In that way you will learn not to dishonour me.

HELEN. I beg you by your knees, do not blame me for the madness of the gods* and kill me for that. Pardon me.

HECUBA. Do not betray your friends whom she killed. I
beseech you for their sake and their children's too.

MENELAUS. No more, old woman. I am paying no attention
to her. No, I command my attendants to take her away to
the ships in which she will be carried over the sea.

HECUBA. Don't put her on the same ship as yourself.

MENELAUS. Why? Has she put on weight since I saw her 1050
last?*

HECUBA. Once a lover, always a lover.*

MENELAUS. That depends on the attitude the lover adopts. But
it shall be as you wish. She will not go onto the same ship
as us. For in fact your advice is rather good. And once she
has reached Argos, the wretched woman will meet the
wretched death that she deserves. Her fate will give the
whole female sex a lesson in chastity. This is by no means
an easy thing to teach. Even so, her destruction will strike
fear into their lack of self-control, even if they are still more
shameful than her.

MENELAUS *and the attendants go out with* HELEN.

CHORUS (*sings*). Did you then, O Zeus, betray to the Achaeans 1060
your temple in Troy
and your altar, fragrant with incense,

and the flame of its sacrificial offerings*
and the smoke of myrrh ascending into the air,
and the holy city of Troy
and the ivy-clad glades of Ida, of Ida,
which flow with torrents of melted snow,
and the end of the land which is struck first by the dawn,*
that gleaming and holy region?   1070

Gone are the sacrifices we made to you in vain,
and the lovely singing of the dancers,
and, in the darkness, the night-long festivals of the gods,
and the images wrought from gold,
and the Phrygians' holy moon-cakes,*
twelve in number.
It concerns me, lord Zeus, it concerns me
whether, as you sit on your throne in the remote air of heaven,
you take thought for the conflagration of our ruined city
which a flaming onrush of fire has dissolved.   1080

O my love, my husband,
you wander in death,
unburied, unwashed,* and a ship
darting over the sea on the wings of its oars
will carry me to Argos, that land grazed by horses,
where men dwell in the heaven-high Cyclopean walls of
    stone.*
Countless children at the gates †clinging to their mothers'
    necks†
groan through their tears, shouting, shouting: 1090
'Mother, alas, the Achaeans
are taking me off from your sight,
all alone onto a dark ship
with oars that skim the sea,
to sail to holy Salamis
or the Isthmian peak
between two seas
where the home of Pelops has its gateway.'*

While Menelaus' boat is sailing   1100
on the high sea,
may a sacred flash of blazing Aegean lightning be flung with
    mighty force

and fall the whole length of the ship,
for he takes me weeping into exile,
away from Ilium, from my country, to be a slave to Greece,
while the daughter of Zeus has the golden mirrors
in which maidens delight.*
May he never come to Sparta, his native land,   1110
and to the hearth and home of his fathers,
and the district of Pitane
and the temple of the goddess with its bronze gates,*
after capturing that woman who shamed great Greece
by her hellish* marriage
and brought grim sufferings
for the streams of Simois.

*TALTHYBIUS enters with attendants carrying the corpse of
ASTYANAX on his father Hector's shield.*

(*chants*) Oh, oh,
how fresh misfortunes for our country
tread on one another's heels! Wretched wives of the Trojans,
look upon this corpse,   1120
Astyanax, whom the Danaans have killed,
throwing him from the towers, in a grim game of quoits.
TALTHYBIUS. Hecuba, one ship is left here and it is fretting at
its oars. It will carry the remainder of the spoils of the son
of Achilles to the shores of Phthia. Neoptolemus himself has
set sail. He had heard of some fresh misfortunes which have
struck Peleus. Apparently Acastus, the son of Pelias, has
driven him from his country.* This is why Neoptolemus has
resolved not to delay and gone off so fast. With him went 1130
Andromache, who drew many a tear from me as she
lamented the fatherland she was leaving and bade farewell
to Hector's tomb. And she begged him to allow this corpse
to be buried, the body of your Hector's son who was flung
to his death from the walls. As for this bronze-backed shield
which struck fear into the Achaeans when the boy's father
held it before his body, she begged him not to take it to the
hearth of Peleus or to that same bedroom where she will be
his bride, [the mother of this corpse, Andromache—and the 1140
sight of it would bring pain.] No, she pleaded that the boy
should be buried not in a cedarwood coffin and a stone tomb

but upon this. He should be given into your arms, so that you can wrap the body round with robes and garlands so far as your strength and circumstances allow. For she has gone, and her master's haste has stopped her giving the child burial herself. As for us, when you have adorned the body, we shall cover it in the earth and set sail. You must carry out Andromache's instructions as quickly as you can.

I have saved you one labour. As I crossed the streams of 1150 the river Scamander I bathed the corpse and washed the blood from the wounds. Now I shall go to break the ground open and dig him a grave. If we both play our parts in this task, we can get it finished quickly and set out on our journey home.*

TALTHYBIUS goes out.

HECUBA. Set the round shield of Hector on the ground. It gives me no joy to look upon this painful sight. You Achaeans, who swell with greater pride in your spears than your wits, why were you so frightened of this boy that you committed a murder that has no precedent? Was it in case he might 1160 some day restore our fallen city?* Your strength amounted to nothing then. Even when Hector and our numberless army triumphed with the spear, we used to fall in battle. But now that the city has been taken and the Phrygians are wiped out, you are still frightened of this little boy. I cannot praise a man when his fear is irrational.

O my dear child, how cruelly your death came upon you. For if you had reached manhood, taken a wife and held the royal power that makes men the equals of the gods and then died for your city, you would have been happy, if there is any 1170 happiness in all of this. But as it is, you have no memories of seeing these things and understanding them in your heart, my child. They were a heritage which did not come down to you. Unhappy boy, how pitiably the walls of your father's city, the towers that Phoebus built, have shorn the locks of your head which your mother tended like a garden, smothering them with her kisses! Amid them the blood laughs out where the bone is broken. I cannot conceal the horror of this.

O these hands, lying all broken at the joints, such sweet remembrances of your father's hands! This dear mouth was 1180 once so free with braggart promises, but it is silent now. You deceived me when you clung tight to my robes and said, 'O mother,* when you are dead, I shall cut a big lock of my hair and I shall bring troops of friends to your grave and address you with loving words.' But it is not you who will bury me. No it is I who shall bury your pitiable corpse, an old woman, who has lost her city and her children, giving burial to a mere boy.

Alas! All those embraces, all the care I lavished on you, all those broken nights—gone, gone! What could a poet write about you on your grave? 'The Argives once killed this 1190 child because they feared him'? An epitaph to bring shame on Greece!

Even so, though you take no share in your father's heritage, you *shall* have his bronze-backed shield—you will be buried upon it.

(*To the shield*) O you protector of Hector's noble arm, you have lost the man who looked after you so well. How sweet the imprint that lies on your handle, and the mark of sweat on your rounded rim, the sweat which so often dripped from Hector's forehead as he pressed you against his beard amid the toil of battle!

Bring, bring* adornments for this pitiable corpse, as far as 1200 our circumstances allow. My fortune allows me no opportunity for display. But you shall take what I have. A mortal who rejoices because he thinks his prosperity is secure is a fool, for fortune, like an unstable man, has a way of jumping this way and that, †and no one is ever happy simply in himself†.

CHORUS. Look, these women are carrying ornaments from the Trojan spoils in their hands to lay on the body.

HECUBA. My child, your father's mother places adornments upon you from the things that once were yours. But you have won no victory over your companions with horse or bow— 1210 those sports which the Phrygians duly observe, †though they do not pursue them to excess†.* As it is, god-hated Helen has taken* all this away from you. She has destroyed your life too, and brought your whole house to ruin.

CHORUS (*sings*). Ah, ah! You have stabbed me, stabbed me
to the heart, you who were once
a great lord in my city.*

HECUBA. The Phrygian finery in which you should have dressed
   yourself for your wedding with the most royal of Asian
   princesses—I now place it on your body. And you, Hector's 1220
   beloved shield, once the victorious mother of countless tro-
   phies, receive this adornment.* In dying with this body, you
   will win immortality. You are far more worthy of honour than
   the arms of that monster of cleverness, Odysseus.*

CHORUS (*sings*). Alas, alas!
   The earth will receive you, dear child
   whom we lament so bitterly.
   Groan, mother . . .

HECUBA (*sings*).   Alas!

CHORUS (*sings*). groan a dirge for the dead.

HECUBA (*sings*).   O my sorrow!   1230

CHORUS (*sings*). Yes, sorrow for your woes that cannot be for-
      gotten.

HECUBA. I shall heal your wounds with bandages, unhappy
   doctor that I am. Yet, though I call myself that, I cannot do
   a doctor's work. And your father will see to what must be
   done among the dead.

CHORUS (*sings*). Strike, strike your head
   with your hands beating their oar-strokes.
   O misery, misery!

HECUBA. You dearest women!

CHORUS (*sings*). †Hecuba, speak to us. We are your friends.†
      What does your cry betoken?

HECUBA. So my suffering was all that concerned the gods— 1240
   that, and Troy too, the city they picked out for their hatred.
   All our ox-sacrifices were in vain. Yet if god had not turned
   the world upside down, we would vanish into obscurity. We
   would never have given men to come the inspiration to sing
   of us in their song.*

   Go, bury the corpse in a wretched tomb. For he has the
   ornaments the dead should have. I think it makes little difference to them if they are given rich funeral honours. It is
   merely a vainglorious display for the living.   1250

                 The body of ASTYANAX *is carried off.*

CHORUS (*sings*). Oh, oh!
   Wretched is the mother whose great hopes for her life

have been mangled in this boy!
(*Of Astyanax*) You were greatly blessed,
you were born from royal parents,
yet how terrible the death that has destroyed you!
(*In sudden alarm*) Ah, ah!
Who are these men I see on the heights of Troy
brandishing* fiery torches in their hands?
A new disaster
is about to be added to Troy's tally of woe.

TALTHYBIUS re-enters.

TALTHYBIUS. I tell you captains who have been ordered to 1260
burn this city of Priam to let the flame lie idle in your hands
no longer but to set it to work, so that we can raze Ilium to
the ground and start our journey home from Troy with gladness in our hearts.* But let my single order have two effects.*
So you, you girls of Troy, go off to the ships of the Achaeans
when the leaders of the army raise the trumpet's blare. Then
you can be sent off from this land.

And you, you most wretched of old women, follow these
men. They have come from Odysseus to fetch you. The lot 1270
that assigns you to him as his slave is sending you from your
native land.

HECUBA. O my sorrow! This is now the be-all and the end-all
here of all my woes. I shall leave my fatherland, my city is
being torched. Come, old legs, make what haste you can,
however difficult it may prove, so that I can salute my
wretched city.

O Troy, city that breathed forth greatness once among
barbarians, soon you will be stripped of your famous name.
They are burning you and leading us off from the land as
slaves. O you gods! And yet why do I call upon the gods? 1280
They did not hear me in the past when I called to them.
Come, let us run into the pyre.* For it is best for me to die
together with this my country as it burns.

TALTHYBIUS. Your woes have driven you mad, wretched
woman. (*To Odysseus' men*) But take her off, do not delay.
You must bring Odysseus his prize and give Hecuba here
into his hands.*

TALTHYBIUS goes off.

(The rest of the play is sung.)

HECUBA. Otototototoi!*

    Son of Cronus, lord of Phrygia,* father,
    do you see these things that we suffer?
    The race of Dardanus does not deserve all this.   1290

CHORUS. He has seen it. The great city of Troy
    is destroyed. It is a city no more. It is a thing of the past.

HECUBA. Otototototoi!

    Troy blazes.
    The buildings of Pergamum and the city
    and the tops of its walls are consumed with fire.

CHORUS. Like smoke on the wings of the breezes,
    our land, laid low in war, now vanishes into nothingness.
    [Our halls are overrun by the devouring fire,   1300
    and by the enemy's arms.]*

HECUBA. O land that nursed my children!

CHORUS. Ah, ah!

HECUBA. O children, hear me, listen to your mother's cry!

CHORUS. You call on the dead with your wailings.

HECUBA. Yes, and I set my aged limbs upon the ground
    and beat the earth with my two hands.

CHORUS. We join you in kneeling on the ground,
    and call our wretched husbands
    from the shades below.*

HECUBA. We are being led, dragged off . . .

CHORUS.   Pain, you shout 1310
    pain!

HECUBA. to a house of slavery.

CHORUS.   and away from my fatherland.

HECUBA. Oh, oh, Priam, Priam,
    you are dead, unburied,* without a friend.
    You know nothing of my dreadful fate.

CHORUS. Black death veiled his eyes,
    holy amid unholy slaughter.*

HECUBA. O halls of the gods and my dear city!

CHORUS. Ah, ah!

HECUBA. The flame of destruction and the spearpoint have
    you in their power.

CHORUS. You will soon fall upon the dear earth into
    anonymity.

HECUBA. The dust winging its way to the sky like smoke   1320
  will mask the house which I shall see no more.
CHORUS. The name of our land will go into oblivion.
  All is scattered and gone,
  and unhappy Troy is no more.
HECUBA. Did you understand? Did you hear?
CHORUS.   Yes, the crash-
      ing as the citadel tumbles.
HECUBA. An earthquake over all of Troy, an earthquake . . .
CHORUS.
      overwhelms the city.*
                        The trumpet sounds. The women move off.*

HECUBA. Oh, oh, my trembling, trembling limbs,
  support my steps. (*To the women*) Go forward
  to the day when your life of slavery begins.   1330
CHORUS. O unhappy Troy. (*To* HECUBA). Even so,
  move on to the ships of the Achaeans.*
                        The women leave the stage.

ANDROMACHE

Characters

ANDROMACHE, Neoptolemus' slave, formerly wife of Hector,
    prince of Troy
SERVING WOMAN of Neoptolemus' house
HERMIONE, daughter of Menelaus and wife of Neoptolemus
MENELAUS, king of Sparta
BOY, son of Neoptolemus and Andromache
PELEUS, grandfather of Neoptolemus
NURSE of Hermione
ORESTES, cousin of Hermione
MESSENGER
THETIS, sea-goddess and former wife of Peleus
CHORUS of women of Phthia

The play is set at Thetideion in Phthia in Thessaly in front of the
palace of Neoptolemus. ANDROMACHE *sits at a shrine of Thetis*
which contains an altar and a statue of the goddess.

ANDROMACHE. O Asian land, O city of Thebe,* from which I
came long ago with a lavish dowry of rich gold* to Priam's
royal hearth when I was given to Hector to be his wife and
bear his child,* I, Andromache, in days gone by a woman to
be envied, but now the most wretched of all of them. [Has
there been or will there ever be a woman as wretched as
myself?] Yes, I saw my husband Hector killed by Achilles,
and Astyanax, the son I bore to my husband, flung from our   10
sheer towers after the Greeks took the land of Troy. I myself,
born in a home once counted the freest of all, have arrived
in Greece as a slave, given to the islander* Neoptolemus as
a choice spear-prize from the spoils of Troy. And I live in the
grassy plains which skirt this land of Phthia and the city of
Pharsalus. Here the sea-goddess Thetis found a refuge from
humans and lived in privacy with Peleus.* The people of
Thessaly call this place Thetideion because of the marriage   20
with the goddess. And the son of Achilles took possession of
this house, allowing Peleus to rule the Pharsalian land, since

he refused to hold the sceptre himself while the old man was
still alive.* I slept with Achilles' son, now my master, and
have borne a male child for this house.

And until now, despite my evil lot, I was kept going by
the hope that, if my son stayed alive, I would find some help
and protection amid my misfortunes. However, after my
master married the Spartan girl Hermione* and stopped
sleeping with me, his slave, I have been hounded by her   30
cruel reproaches. For she says that I am using secret drugs
to make her childless and hateful to her husband,* and that
I want to supplant her with myself as mistress of this house
and will resort to anything to break up her marriage. In fact,
I never wanted a relationship with Neoptolemus,* and now
it is all over. May great Zeus be my witness that I went to
bed with him against my will! But I can make no impression
on her. She wants to kill me, and her father Menelaus is
abetting his daughter in this. And now he is in the house.   40
He has travelled from Sparta for this very purpose. I am
frightened and have come to sit at this shrine of Thetis beside
the palace in the hope that the goddess can save me from
death. For Peleus and the descendants of Peleus revere it as
a monument to his marriage with the Nereid.* As for my
only child, I have smuggled him away to another house
since I am afraid that he may be killed. For his father is not
here to help me and is of no use to the boy. No, he is away   50
in the land of Delphi where he is paying Loxias* the penalty
for the madness which had previously caused him to go to
Pytho* and demand satisfaction from Phoebus for the murder of his father.* He hoped that by asking for pardon for his
former transgressions, he could somehow get the god to
show him goodwill in the future.

Enter a SERVING WOMAN.

SERVING WOMAN. Mistress—I address you by this title with
no hesitation since I thought it right to do so in your own
home too when we lived on Trojan soil, and I was loyal
there to you and your husband when he was alive—now I   60
have come to tell you some news. Even though I am afraid
in case one of my masters notices, I feel pity for you. For
Menelaus and his daughter are plotting terrible things

against you and you must protect yourself from their schemes.

ANDROMACHE. O my dearest fellow-slave—yes, you are the fellow-slave of one who was once a princess but is now the unfortunate woman you see before you—what are they doing? What new plots are they weaving in their bid to kill unhappy, yes unhappy Andromache?

SERVING WOMAN. It is your son, you poor woman, whom you smuggled away from home to safety. They are going to kill him. Menelaus has gone off from the house to get him.

ANDROMACHE. O my sorrow! Has he discovered that I sent   70
my son away? However did he find out that? How wretched I am! All is over with me.

SERVING WOMAN. I don't know. I heard this from them.

ANDROMACHE. So it is all over. O my child, the pair of vultures will take you and kill you, while the man they call your father is still lingering in Delphi.*

SERVING WOMAN. Yes, I think you would not be in such a sorry plight if he were here. But as things stand, you have no friends to help you.

ANDROMACHE. Is there any news about Peleus? Won't he be coming?*

SERVING WOMAN. He's too old to help you if he does come.   80

ANDROMACHE. I assure you, I have sent for him more than once.

SERVING WOMAN. Do you really think that any of the messengers cared about you?

ANDROMACHE. Of course not! Are *you* willing to go as my messenger then?

SERVING WOMAN. What excuses shall I make if I am away from the house for a long time?

ANDROMACHE. You will find no shortage of pretexts. After all, you are a woman.*

SERVING WOMAN. The situation is dangerous. It is no small matter that Hermione is on the watch.

ANDROMACHE. You see? You disown your friends in their need.

SERVING WOMAN. No, no, do not reproach me with that. Yes, I will go, even if I suffer for it. After all, people do not pay much attention to what happens in a slave woman's   90
life.

ANDROMACHE. Off with you then!

The SERVING WOMAN *goes out.*

I shall go on keening to the sky the tearful dirges and
laments on which my heart is always brooding. For women
by their nature find delight if they can for ever cry out and
give voice to the sorrows that surround them. And I have
not one thing but many things to mourn, the city of my
fathers, Hector who is dead, and the hard lot to which I am
yoked now that I have fallen into a life of slavery against all
deserving. No mortal should be called happy before he has   100
died and you see how he passes his final day and goes
below.*

(*Sings*)* It was no marriage but a curse that Paris brought
   to Troy on its rocky height
    when he led Helen to sleep with him there in his bed-
    room.
It was because of her, O Troy, that Greek warriors sailing
   swiftly
    on a thousand ships* caught you and took you with fire
    and the spear,
took Hector too, the husband of my wretched self—whom
   the son of the sea-goddess Thetis
    dragged as he drove his chariot around our walls.*
I myself was led away from my bedroom to the seashore,
   casting the hateful garb of slavery over my head.*   110
And many tears flowed down over my flesh when I was
   leaving
    my city and my bedroom and my husband in the dust.*
I cry out in my wretchedness. Why did I have to go on living in the light
    as Hermione's slave? Because of her oppression
I have come as a suppliant to this statue of the goddess and
   casting my arms around it
    I melt away in tears like a trickle dripping from the
    rocks.*

Enter the CHORUS *of women of Phthia.*

CHORUS (*sings*). O lady, you have been sitting so long
   on the floor of the shrine of Thetis which you will not leave.

Even though I am a Phthian I have still come to you, an
    Asian by birth,
in the hope that I may find* some cure for you   120
from the troubles, so hard to unloose,
which have locked you and Hermione in hateful strife,
you poor woman, over the marriage bed you share
since you have a husband in common,
the son of Achilles.

Acknowledge your fortune. Consider the evil plight into
    which you have fallen now.
Will you struggle against your masters—
you, a girl from Troy, while they are Spartans born and
    bred?
Leave the dwelling of the sea-goddess
where she receives the sacrificial sheep.   130
How does it profit you in your numbing sorrow
to waste your body to disfigurement under your masters'
    harsh control?
Force will overcome you. You are nothing.
Why do you put up this struggle?

No, come, leave the splendid shrine of the Nereid goddess,
and recognize that you, a slave-girl
from a foreign city,
are in a strange land, where you cannot see
any of your friends, you unhappiest of women,
the most wretched bride of all.   140

I at least felt the deepest pity for you, woman of Troy,
when you came to the house of my masters. But fear
makes me hold my peace
(even though I do pity your plight)—
in case the child of Zeus' daughter*
realizes that I feel goodwill towards you.

Enter HERMIONE.*

HERMIONE. The glittering gold diadem that crowns my head
    and this embroidered robe that swathes my body in which I
    have come here are no mere offerings from the possessions
    of Achilles or the house of Peleus, but they were given to me 150
    by my father Menelaus from the Laconian land of Sparta

with many bridal gifts. So I have the right to speak freely [and I make my answer to all of you with these words].

Though you are a slave, a woman captured in war, it is your wish to throw me out of this palace and possess it for yourself. Your drugs have made me hateful to my husband and it is you who are causing my womb to waste away in barrenness.* Yes, the nature of Asiatic women gives them expertise in such matters. I shall make you stop all this. This 160 dwelling of the Nereid with its altar and shrine will be of no avail to you. No, you shall die. And supposing that some mortal or god is willing to save you, you will have to give up the pride of your former prosperity and cower in grovelling humility at my knees. You will have to sweep my house,* sprinkling the water of Achelous* from golden pitchers with your own hands. You will learn what country you are in now. There is no Hector here, no Priam, no gold, simply a Greek city. You have fallen to such depths of blind 170 insensitivity, you wretched woman, that you have the hardihood to share a bed with the son of the father who killed your husband and to bear children to murderers.

This is what all barbarians are like. Fathers have sex with daughters, sons with mothers, sisters with brothers, those bound by the closest ties of family love kill each other, and the law prevents none of these things.* Don't bring these ways of yours among us. It is not decent for one man to keep two women in the reins of marriage. No, the man who wishes to live with propriety is content if he looks to a single 180 loved one in his bed.

CHORUS. A woman's heart is a jealous thing and always bitter towards rivals in marriage.

ANDROMACHE. Alas, alas! Youth is a curse for mankind, especially when people add injustice to their youth. I am fearful in case the fact that I am your slave may debar me from speech when I have many just points to urge. And then again, if I win the argument, I am afraid that my servile status may do me harm. For the high and mighty take superior arguments badly when they are spoken by inferiors. 190 Nevertheless I shall not betray myself and let my cause go by default.

Tell me, young lady, what valid reason could have
induced me to try to undermine your lawful wedlock? Is it
that the Phrygians' city is greater than Sparta and outruns
it in prosperity? Is it that you see me at liberty? Or is it that
my youthful and vigorous body, the greatness of my city,
and my friends inspire me with such confidence that I wish
to possess your house in your place? Or is it so that I can
bear children in your place, to be slaves and a wretched
encumbrance* to myself? Or will they let *my* children be the   200
rulers of Phthia if you have none of your own? Do the
Greeks love me, and all for Hector's sake? Was I unknown
and not the Phrygians' princess? It is not through any drugs
of mine that your husband hates you. It is because you are
not a pleasant woman to live with. Herein lies the love
charm—it is not beauty, lady, but virtue which delights
one's bedfellow. If you are irritated at anything, you say that
the city of Sparta is great and you speak dismissively of   210
Scyros, you are a wealthy woman in a house of paupers,
and in your opinion Menelaus is a greater man than
Achilles. That is why your husband hates you. Even if a
woman is given to a bad husband, she must live with the
fact and not compete with him in pride. If you had got as
your husband a king in snowy Thrace where one man
shares his bed with many woman in turn,* would you have
killed them? If you had, you would have been convicted of
branding all women with the charge of an insatiable sexual
appetite. How disgusting! Admittedly we women suffer   220
worse from this disease than men,* but we put a virtuous
front on it. For my part, O my dearest Hector, if Aphrodite
caused you to trip at all, I even joined you in loving those
whom you loved for your sake,* and often in times gone by
I have held my breast to your bastards to avoid showing you
any bitterness. And by doing this, I would win my husband
over through my virtue, while you in your fear do not allow
a drop of the dew from heaven to settle on yours. Do not try
to outdo your mother,* lady, in the love of men. All sensible   230
children should steer clear of the ways of bad mothers.

CHORUS. Mistress, let us persuade you to come to terms with
   her, †as far as you can do so without losing face†.

HERMIONE. Why do you speak so arrogantly, engaging me in

a contest of words—for all the world as if *you* were the
decent woman while I am nothing of the kind?

ANDROMACHE. The arguments on which you have taken
your stand prove that I am quite right about that.*

HERMIONE. I pray that your way of thinking may never make
its home with me, woman.

ANDROMACHE. You are young and you speak about shameful things.

HERMIONE. But you do not *speak* about them, no, you *do*
shameful things to me—as far as it lies in your power.

ANDROMACHE. You're at it again! Can't you keep quiet about   240
your sexual problems?

HERMIONE. What! Is not sex always the most important thing
for women?

ANDROMACHE. Yes, for women who manage it well. If they
don't, it brings dishonour.

HERMIONE. We do not govern our city by the ways of barbarians.

ANDROMACHE. Both there and here too shameful deeds win
shame.

HERMIONE. Clever, very clever. But even so you must die.

ANDROMACHE. Do you see the statue of Thetis looking
straight at you?

HERMIONE. Yes—and it hates your fatherland for the murder
of Achilles.

ANDROMACHE. It was Helen who killed him, not I—yes, your
mother.

HERMIONE. What! Will you probe my woes still further?

ANDROMACHE. See, I say nothing. I shut my mouth up tight.   250

HERMIONE. Tell me what I came here to ask you.

ANDROMACHE. I tell you that you do not have as much good
sense as you should have had.

HERMIONE. Will you leave this sacred precinct of the sea-
goddess?

ANDROMACHE. Yes, if I am not to be killed. Otherwise I shall
never leave it.

HERMIONE. Be sure that your death is certain and that I shall
not wait for my husband to come.

ANDROMACHE. But I shall not hand myself over to you either
before he does.

HERMIONE. I shall use fire against you* and shall show you
no respect.

ANDROMACHE. Light your fire then. The gods will be witnesses of this.

HERMIONE. I shall torture your flesh with terrible wounds.

ANDROMACHE. Slaughter me. Stain the altar of the goddess 260
with my blood. She will come after you.

HERMIONE. You barbarian! You stubborn, insolent creature!
Will you outface death then? But I shall soon dislodge you
from where you sit here and you will come away willingly,
such a bait do I have for you. But I shall say no more. My
actions will soon speak for themselves. Go on sitting there as
a suppliant! For even if molten lead were to hold you fast,*
I shall still dislodge you before Achilles' son arrives—the
man in whom you trust.

HERMIONE goes into the house.

ANDROMACHE. Yes, I trust him. It is a strange thing that
some god* established remedies for men against savage 270
snakes while no one has yet discovered a cure for what is
worse than a viper or fire—a woman [who is bad. We are
so terrible a curse for mankind].

CHORUS (*sings*). Great indeed were the woes which he started
when he came to the glen on Ida,*
the son of Zeus and Maia,*
leading the lovely trio
of goddesses*
armed for their hateful beauty contest,
to the cow-stalls   280
and to the solitary young hersdman
and his lonely hearth and home.

When they came to the thickly wooded mountain glen,
they bathed their gleaming bodies
in the streams of the mountain springs
and went to Priam's son, oudoing one another
in the extravagance of their malignant promises,
and Cypris won the day with her deceptive words
which were a joy to hear,   290
but they brought bitter destruction of life
upon the Trojans' wretched city and the citadel of Troy.*

If only his mother had rejected him, casting him over her
    head
to an evil doom,
before he made the upland pastures of rocky Ida his home—
at the time when Cassandra shouted out by the oracular
    bay-tree
to kill him,*
the child fated to bring terrible ruin on Troy's city.
Whom did she fail to approach, which of the elders*
did she fail to beg to kill the baby?   300

Then the yoke of slavery would not have come
to the women of Troy, and you, lady,
would have had a royal palace as your dwelling,
and it would have cut loose from Greece
the grievous troubles †round Troy in which†
the young men wandered* for ten years with their spears,
and their beds would never have been left empty
nor old men been bereaved of their sons.

Enter MENELAUS *with Andromache's* BOY *and attendants.*

MENELAUS. I have come here after getting hold of your son—
yes, the boy you smuggled out to another house behind my   310
daughter's back. You confidently expected that you would
be saved by this image of the goddess, and this child by the
people who hid him. But you have been found to be less
astute, lady, than Menelaus whom you see before you. And
if you do not leave and abandon this precinct, this boy will
have his throat cut instead of you. So think about it—are
you willing to die, or do you want him to be killed because
of the wrong you are doing me and my daughter?

ANDROMACHE. O reputation, reputation, you puff up to greatness the lives of countless men who really amount to noth-   320
ing! [I count those men happy whose glory is truly won, but
as for those who have gained it fraudulently, I shall not
allow it them but grant them only the chance appearance of
wisdom.] Were *you*, such a little man, once the general of
the choice men of Greece? Did *you* take Troy from Priam?
You, whom the words of your daughter, a mere girl, have
inflated with so much rage that you have stooped to a contest with a wretched slave-woman! I no longer consider that

you deserve Troy—or that Troy deserves you. [Outwardly 330
those who have a reputation for sound thinking shine
bright, but inside they are like all men—, though maybe not
in wealth. This carries great influence.

Come now, Menelaus, let's argue the matter out.]
Suppose I die by your daughter's hand. Suppose that she has
killed me. She could not then avoid the pollution of murder.
And at the bar of popular opinion you too will stand trial for
this murder. Yes, your complicity will make this inevitable.
But supposing that I escape death, are you going to kill my
child? In that case, do you really think that his father will
take the murder of his son lightly? Troy does not call him so 340
cowardly a man! No, he will take the necessary steps, by his
actions he will show himself worthy of Peleus and his father
Achilles, and he will drive your daughter from his house. If
you offer her in marriage to someone else, what will you
say? That her virtue is running away from a bad husband?
He will not believe you. Who *will* marry her? Are you going
to keep her in your house without a husband until she
becomes a grey-haired widow? O you foolhardy man, do you
not see how many misfortunes will flood upon you?
Wouldn't you prefer your daughter to find herself wronged 350
in any number of liaisons than suffer what I say? It is not
right to bring about great evils for trivial reasons and, if we
women are a ruinous curse, men should not make their
nature like ours. As for myself, if I am using drugs on your
daughter and making her womb sterile as she says, I will not
crouch at this altar. No, I shall be willing, indeed eager to
stand my trial before your son-in-law in person, for I shall
owe no less a penalty to him if I have made them childless. 360
That is my case. As for your character, there is one thing
that I am afraid of about you. It was because of a quarrel
over a woman that you destroyed the wretched city of the
Trojans too.

CHORUS. You are a woman talking to a man, and so you have
said too much. †You have lost sight of womanly modesty.†

MENELAUS. Woman, this is a petty business and unworthy of
my regal power, as you say, unworthy of Greece too. But be
sure of this. Whatever a man needs at a given moment is
more important to him than taking Troy.* I am standing by

my daughter as her ally—for I judge it a serious matter if 370
her marriage breaks down. Yes, everything else that a
woman can suffer is secondary, but when she loses her husband she loses her life. As for slaves, just as it is right for him
to rule mine, so it is proper for members of my family,*
myself too, to rule his. For with friends, if they are really true
friends, nothing is private—they share their possessions.
And while I wait for the man who is not here, I shall prove
a cowardly and unthinking fellow if I do not settle my affairs
in the best way possible.

No, get up and leave this shrine of the goddess. For if you 380
are killed, this boy of yours escapes his doom, while if you
are unwilling to die, I shall kill him. It is inevitable that one
of the two of you departs this life.

ANDROMACHE. Alas, what a bitter lot in life you set me to
choose! My fate is abject if I win my life, wretched too if I fail
to win it. You who are doing great deeds for a trivial reason,
listen to what I say. Why are you killing me? Because of
what? What city have I betrayed? Which of your children did
I kill? What house did I burn? I was forced to go bed with 390
my master. So will you kill me and not him, the man who is
to blame for this? Will you ignore the original responsibility
and rush to the conclusion which followed later?

I cry alas for these sorrows. O my unhappy fatherland,
what terrible sufferings I endure! Why did I have to be a
mother too and add this second agony to the agony of Troy's
destruction? [But why do I grieve over the past and ignore
the woes that surround me now? Why don't I dwell upon
them?] I saw the butchered Hector dragged behind the chariot* and Troy's pitiful incineration, and I myself was dragged 400
by the hair to the ships of the Argives as their slave. Then
when I came to Phthia, I married Hector's murderer. So
what pleasure does life hold for me? What do I have to look
to? To my present fortunes or those that are past? This one
child was all that was left to me, the most precious thing in
life to me. And those who made the decision on this are
going to kill him. No, they shall not, if my poor life can save
him. For in my death there is hope that he may be saved,
while for me there is only shame if I do not die for my son. 410

ANDROMACHE *leaves the altar.*

Look, I leave the altar and here I am in your power. You can butcher me, murder me, bind me, hang me by the neck. O my child, I who gave you birth am going to Hades so that you may not be killed. If you escape doom, remember how I, your mother, was strong enough to die. Give your father kisses, pour forth tears, wrap your arms around him, and tell him what I did. I see it now, for everyone children are the very breath of life. Those who have no children and raise objections to them have less sorrow but their happiness is an unhappy fortune.*   420

CHORUS. I pity her for what I heard her say. Misfortunes, even when they are a stranger's, win pity from all mortals. You should have brought your daughter to an agreement with this woman, Menelaus, so that she could be freed from her troubles.

MENELAUS. Seize her, attendants, grab her in your arms. For she will not like what she is going to hear. (*MENELAUS' attendants seize ANDROMACHE*) I have you in my grasp.* I held out the threat of death for your son to get you to leave the sacred altar of the goddess. That was my cunning device to bring you into my grip and slaughter you. Understand that this is   430 the way things are for you. As for the fate of this child, my daughter will make the decision, whether she chooses to kill or not to kill him.*

Off with you into the house so that you, a slave, may learn never to show insolence towards the free.

ANDROMACHE. O my sorrow! You trapped me by trickery. I have been deceived.*

MENELAUS. Tell everybody about it. I do not deny it.

ANDROMACHE. Is this what you who live by the Eurotas* mean by political skill?

MENELAUS. Yes, and those at Troy too—that people who have suffered should retaliate.

ANDROMACHE. Do you think that the gods are not gods and do not look after justice?

MENELAUS. When their punishment falls, I shall bear it. But   440 I *will* kill you.

ANDROMACHE. What, and this nestling too, snatching him from under my wings?*

MENELAUS. No. I shall give him to my daughter to kill, if she wants to.

ANDROMACHE. O sorrow! Let me mourn my heart out for you then, my child!

MENELAUS. To be sure, no sturdy hope awaits him.

ANDROMACHE. O you inhabitants of Sparta, most hateful of mortals to all mankind, you cunning schemers, lords of lies, stitching together your evil contrivances, thinking crooked thoughts, none of them healthy but all involved and tortuous,* it is unjust that you have success throughout Greece. What abomination does not dwell with you? Are there not 450 countless murders? Aren't you always shown up as men corrupted by malice, saying one thing with your tongue but thinking another? My curse upon you!* The death which you have decreed is not such a cruel fate for me. After all, I met my end when the wretched city of the Phrygians was destroyed, my famous husband too, whose spear often made you a coward at sea instead of one on land!* And now as you confront a woman, you show yourself a grim-faced warrior* and you want to kill me. Kill away! You can be certain that my tongue will not waste any flattery on you and your 460 daughter. You were born to greatness in Sparta, but so was I in Troy. If my plight is a bad one, don't let that make you too confident. You too could find yourself in the same situation.

MENELAUS *takes* ANDROMACHE *and the* BOY *into the house.*

CHORUS (*sings*). I shall never speak in praise of men who have
        both a wife and a mistress,
nor of brothers born from rival mothers—
the result is strife in the home and grief which springs from
        enmity.
May my husband be content with a single union
and share his marriage bed with no other.   470

In cities too, it is not easier to endure two kingships
than one*—
this leads to sorrow piled on sorrow and to dissension for the
        citizens.
When two craftsmen create a song,*
the Muses' custom is to cause dissension.

And whenever swift breezes sweep the sailors on,
divided counsels at the tiller   480

and a crowd of experts in competition prove weaker
than an inferior intelligence in full charge.
A single individual proves effective both in houses
and in cities, whenever men work
to find an advantage.

The Spartan woman, daughter of the general Menelaus,
has shown this. For she raged like fire against the rival for
     her bed,
and is trying to kill the wretched Trojan girl
and her son out of malignant strife.   490
The murder is godless, lawless, profitless.
There will be a time when retribution for these actions
will come upon you, lady.

ANDROMACHE, *bound, enters from the house with her* BOY *and*
              MENELAUS *with his attendants.*

(*Chants*) But look, I see in front of the house
this pair of captives clinging together—
condemned by the verdict to death.
O you unhappy woman, and you wretched boy
who are dying because of your mother's marriage,
though it is nothing to do with you
and our royal masters do not think you guilty.   500
ANDROMACHE (*sings*). Here I am, being sent down into the
     earth,
     my wrists made bloody
     by the ropes that hold them fast.
BOY* (*sings*). Mother, mother, I am going down there with you
     beneath your wing.*
ANDROMACHE (*sings*). I, a wretched victim, O you first men
     of the land of Phthia.
BOY (*sings*).   O father,
     come to help your loved ones.
ANDROMACHE (*sings*). You will lie, O my dear child,   510
     clasped to your mother's breasts,
     your corpse side by side with hers, beneath the earth.
BOY (*sings*). I cry out in my sorrow. What will become of me?
     I am wretched indeed, mother, and so are you.
MENELAUS (*chants*). Go beneath the earth. For you have come
     from an enemy city, and the two of you

are being killed for two urgent reasons. My vote
destroys you, while my child Hermione
does away with your child here.* Yes, it would be great folly
to leave enemies descended from enemies alive   520
when it is possible to kill them
and free the house from fear.

ANDROMACHE (*sings*). O husband, husband, if only I could have
your hand and your spear to fight for us,
  you son of Priam!

BOY (*sings*). What song can I find, unhappy boy,
  to turn away my fate?

ANDROMACHE (*sings*). Fall close by your master's knees
  and supplicate him, my child.

BOY (*sings*).   O my friend,*   530
  my friend, spare me! Do not kill me!

ANDROMACHE (*sings*). My eyes dissolve in tears,
  dripping like a spring that trickles sunless
  from some smooth crag.* How wretched I am!

BOY (*sings*). I cry out in my sorrow.
  What cure can I find for my woes?

MENELAUS (*chants to* BOY). Why do you fall at my knees? You may as well supplicate
  a rock in the sea or a wave with your prayers.*
  For I am a help to my friends
  while I have no incitement to love you   540
  since I spent a great part of my vital energies
  in taking Troy—and your mother.
  You will have her to thank
  for your journey down to Hades.

CHORUS. But look, I see Peleus near by, walking this way as
  fast as his old age* allows.

Enter PELEUS *with an attendant.*

PELEUS. I ask all of you and the man in charge of the butchery, what's this? What is it all about? For what reason is the
  house infected like this? What are you up to with your plots?
  There has been no trial. Menelaus, stop right there. Do not
  be so hasty to abandon justice. (*To his attendant*) You, lead   550
  me on more quickly. This is a business that brooks no delay,

I think. No, now, if ever, is the time for me to recover the strength of my youth. The first thing then is for me to hearten Andromache here, like a favourable wind breathing upon a ship's sails. (*To* ANDROMACHE) Tell me, by what right are these men haling you and the boy along, your hands tied fast in these bonds? For you are being killed like a ewe with its lamb beneath it—while I and your lord and master are somewhere else.

ANDROMACHE. These fellows, old man, are leading me off to death with my son, just as you see. What can I say to you? 560 For it was not with a single summons that I sent for you so urgently. No, I dispatched countless messengers. You must have heard all about the domestic strife caused by this man's daughter—and the reasons why I am being killed. And now they are leading me off, after dragging me from the altar of Thetis who bore you your noble son and whom you honour and revere. They have not passed judgement on me in any trial, they have not waited for those away from home.* No, they realized that I was all alone with my son here whom 570 they are going to kill along with unhappy Andromache, though he has done nothing wrong.

But I beg you, old man, falling before your knees—it is not possible for me to touch your beloved chin with my hand*—save me, by the gods! If you do not, we shall die, and this will bring shame on your house and tragedy on me, old man.

PELEUS (*to* MENELAUS' *attendants*). I order you to untie these ropes before someone gets hurt for this—and to free her two hands from their bonds.

MENELAUS. And I forbid it. I am not inferior to you, and the key point is that I have much greater authority over her. 580

PELEUS. What are you saying? Will you run our household now that you are here? Is it not enough for you to rule the people of Sparta?

MENELAUS. It was I who took her as a captive from Troy.

PELEUS. Yes, but my grandson won her as his prize.

MENELAUS. Are not my possessions his, and his mine?

PELEUS. Yes, to treat well, not badly—and not to kill brutally.

MENELAUS. Rest assured that you shall never take her from my hands.

PELEUS. Yes, I will—after giving you a bloody head with this staff of mine.

MENELAUS. Come close to me and lay your hands on me then. You'll see!*

PELEUS. How do *you* belong with men, you utter degenerate 590 from degenerate stock? What right have you to be reckoned a man? You are the fellow who lost your wife to a man from Phrygia when you left †your hearth and home without slaves,† without locks,* for all the world as if you had a chaste wife in your house—though she was in fact the most promiscuous woman alive. Spartan girls could not be chaste even if they wanted.* With naked thighs and loose dresses, they abandon their homes and share the running-tracks and the wrestling-schools—I find this intolerable—with the boys. Ought we to be surprised then if you fail to educate your 600 women to chastity? You should ask Helen about this. After all, she abandoned the ties of her marriage and rushed off revelling from home to another country with a young man. And was it because of her that you then gathered together so great a host of Greeks and led them to Ilium? Once you had discovered her to be promiscuous, far from going to war, you ought to have spat her out and let her stay there, paying Paris to keep her and never taking her back to your house. But the wind of your thought did not blow that way. 610 No, you destroyed many souls* of good men, you made old women childless in their houses and robbed grey-haired fathers of their noble sons. I am one of those wretched men. I look upon you as the murderer of Achilles, as a source of pollution. You alone returned from Troy without a single wound* and you brought back your lovely armour in its lovely cases, as pristine as when you took it there. And for my part, when my grandson was about to marry, I kept on saying to him that he should not ally himself to you in this 620 way or take the daughter* of a promiscuous woman into his house. For the faults of mothers come out in their daughters. I ask you, suitors, to take care and be sure to marry the daughter of a virtuous mother.

On top of that, how outrageously you treated your brother when you ordered him, the simple-minded fool, to cut his daughter's throat.* Were you so afraid that you

would lose your promiscuous wife? And after you had captured Troy—yes, I shall move on to that point too as I argue
with you—you did not kill your wife once you had taken her
in your grasp,* but when you saw her breast, you dropped
your sword* and welcomed her kiss, fawning on the treach-   630
erous bitch, a slave to love, you utter weakling!

And then you came to this house when my son was
away, and now you are laying it waste. Deaf to honour, you
are trying to kill an unfortunate woman and her son, a boy
who will make you and your daughter in the house cry for
it, even if he is three times a bastard.* Just as poor soil often
produces a better crop than rich earth, many bastards are
superior to the legitimate.

No, take your daughter back to Sparta. It brings more
honour to mortals to have as a father-in-law and friend a
man who is poor but good rather than one who is rich and   640
bad. You are a nobody.

CHORUS. Men's tongues can lead them on from a trivial beginning to a great feud. Mortals who are wise keep careful
guard not to cause quarrels with friends.

MENELAUS. Why on earth do people attribute wisdom to old
men and those who once had a good reputation among the
Greeks for good sense?—when you, Peleus, the son of a
famous father,* made a marriage alliance with me, yet you
now say things that bring shame to you and reproaches
upon us because of this barbarian woman, whom you   650
should have driven beyond the waters of the Nile, beyond
the Phasis,* and you should have always been calling on me
to help you to do so. She is from Asia, where countless sons
of Hellas fell to the ground, slaughtered by the spear, and
she played a part in the shedding of your son's blood. For
Paris, who slew your son Achilles, was the brother of
Hector, and she was Hector's wife. And you go in under the
same roof as her and think it proper to live with her and
share the same table, and you allow her to bear her hateful
children in the house. And when I take thought for your   660
interest and for mine, old man, and want to kill her, I have
her snatched from my hands. Yet think of this—for there is
no disgrace in touching on the subject—if my daughter
proves infertile while this woman has children, will you

make them rulers of the land of Phthia and will men of barbarian birth rule over Greeks? Then am *I* mad because I hate
what is unjust, and are *you* sane?

[And now consider this as well. If you had given your
daughter to one of the citizens and then she were suffering
like this, would you be taking it calmly? I do not think so, 670
Yet why do you scream out this abuse against your relatives
in support of a foreigner? And then again, a man and a
woman wronged by her husband feel equal grief. Likewise a
man who has a promiscuous wife in his house. He has great
power at his disposal, but for her matters are in the hands
of her parents and friends. So is it not right that I should help
my own?]*

You are an old, old man. You would help me more by
talking of my generalship than by saying nothing about it.
Helen's troubles were not of her own choosing. The gods 680
sent them, and that proved of the greatest assistance to the
Greeks. Though they knew nothing of arms and warfare,*
they took the step to courage. Familiarity teaches mortals
everything. And if I held back from killing my wife when I
came face to face with her, I showed good sense. I would
rather you had not killed either, in the case of Phocus.*

I have made this attack on you out of goodwill towards
you, not out of anger. If you are quick-tempered, it simply
makes you speak at more painful length, while my fore- 690
thought actually gets me somewhere.

CHORUS. Both of you, stop this futile debate at once—this is
by far the best thing to do—or else the two of you will take
a fall together.

PELEUS. Oh, how wrong the custom is in Greece! Whenever
an army triumphs over the enemy, it is not considered the
achievement of those who struggled. No, the general wins
the reputation. He has wielded the spear as just one man
among countless others, yet though he has done no more
than any one individual, he gets greater credit. [The arro- 700
gant men who sit in office in cities look down upon the
people, though they are nobodies. But the people will prove
infinitely wiser than they are, supposing they are ever
endowed with daring and with it a common sense of purpose.] And so you and your brother sit back, puffed up with

Troy and your generalship there, although it was the laborious efforts of others that exalted you.

I shall teach you never to reckon Paris of Mount Ida* a greater enemy to you than Peleus, if you do not get yourself quickly away from this house—and good riddance to you!— you and your childless daughter; the son I fathered will drag 710 her by the hair through this palace and drive her out of it. Since the girl* is barren, she cannot endure it if others bear children while she has none of her own. But must our family produce no offspring just because she is unfortunate in this respect?

(*Indicating* ANDROMACHE) Leave this woman alone, you attendants, and good riddance to you! Let me discover if anyone is going to stop me untying her hands. (*To* ANDRO-MACHE) Up with you! For despite my trembling,* I shall untie the knotted ropes that bind you myself.

You utter coward, look how you have galled her hands! Did you imagine that you were tying up an ox or a lion? 720 These knots are so tight. Or were you afraid that she might take a sword and defend herself against you?

(*To the* BOY) Come over here into my arms, boy, and help me to untie your mother's bonds. I shall bring you up in Phthia to be a great enemy to these people. Except for the fact that you Spartans have the glory that you win by the spear in battle, you can be sure that in all other respects you are no better than anyone else.*

CHORUS. Old men are naturally uncontrolled. Their quick temper makes them hard to guard against.

MENELAUS. You are all too prone to rush into such abusive talk. I did not come into Phthia of my own accord and I shall 730 neither do nor suffer anything that degrades me. And now— for I don't have unlimited time to spare—I shall go off home. There is a city not far from Sparta which was previously friendly but is now behaving aggressively towards us.* I want to lead an expedition against this city and get it in my power. But when I have settled matters there as I intend, I shall return. And when I stand before my son-in-law face to face, I shall give and take instruction. If he punishes 740 Andromache here and behaves reasonably towards us in the future, he shall meet with reasonable treatment from me, but if he gives way to anger, he shall encounter *my* anger. [Yes, the treatment he receives will arise naturally from the treatment he gives.]

Your talk doesn't worry me. You are like a shadow, an empty reflection of reality. You have a voice, but mere words are the only power you possess.

MENELAUS and his attendants go off.

PELEUS (*to the* BOY). Stand here, my child, where I can put both my hands on your shoulders, and lead me off. (*To* ANDRO-MACHE) And you as well, unhappy woman. Though you encountered a wild storm, you have reached a calm harbour.

ANDROMACHE. Old man, may the gods reward you and your 750 family for saving the boy and my unlucky self. But be careful that these men (*pointing after* MENELAUS' *attendants*) don't crouch in ambush for the two of us where the road is deserted to take me off by force when they realize how old you are, how weak I am, and what a child this boy is.* Watch out for this in case we have escaped now only to be captured later.

PELEUS. Don't start talking like a cowardly woman! Go on your way! Who will lay a hand on the two of you? He'll be sorry if he does. By the grace of the gods and thanks to our cavalry* and our large army, we hold the power in Phthia. 760 I'm not the dodderer you think I am.* No, I still stand tall and when it comes to someone like him, I shall defeat him with a single glance, aged though I may be. Even an old man, if he is courageous, can be mightier than many young-sters. After all, what's the use of being fit and strong if you're a coward?

ANDROMACHE, with the BOY, and PELEUS go out.

CHORUS (*sings*). May I have no being, unless of a noble family and with a share of a wealthy house.
For if someone suffers something which has no remedy, 770
those who are nobly born find no lack of resources,
yes, there is honour and renown for those
who are proclaimed as the sons of goodly houses.*
Time does not take away what good men leave behind them.*
Even when they are dead, their virtue shines bright.

It is better not to win an ignoble victory
than to bring down justice by the invidious use of power.   780
This is sweet for mortals in the short term,
but as time goes by it turns to ashes,
and disgrace engulfs the house.
The life I praise is this, this is the life I wish to win—
to use power within the confines of justice
both in marriage and in politics.

O you ancient son of Aeacus,*   790
I can well believe that you joined with the Lapiths
to fight against the Centaurs with your famous spear,
and that on the Argo's deck you passed through
the Clashing Rocks by the Black Sea
to its inhospitable waters on your famous voyage,
and that when the son of Zeus in days gone by
encircled the famous city of Ilium with slaughter,
you shared the glory with him   800
when you came back to Europe.*

The NURSE comes out of the house.

NURSE. O dearest women, what a terrible succession of disasters has befallen us today! Now that my mistress in the
house, I mean Hermione, has been abandoned by her father
and is at the same time conscious of what she did when she
planned to kill Andromache and the boy, she wants to die.
She is afraid that as payment for her actions her husband
may send her from the house in dishonour [or kill her since 810
she tried to kill those she had no right to]. She wants to hang
herself by the neck and her attendant guards have difficulty
in stopping her, difficulty too in snatching weapons away
from her right hand. She feels such remorse and she recog-
nizes that her previous actions were far from good. I am
worn out with preventing my mistress hanging herself, my
friends. You go inside the palace* and stop her committing
suicide. For when new friends arrive they have more influence than the same old ones.

CHORUS. Listen, we can hear servants shouting in the house   820
over what you came here to tell us. It looks as if the
unhappy woman is going to reveal to us how much she
regrets the terrible things she has done. For she is coming

out of the palace, trying to escape from the hands of her servants in her eagerness for death.

HERMIONE (*sings*). O my agony!*
  I shall tear my hair and rend my skin
  with these cruel nails!
NURSE. My girl, what are you going to do? Will you disfigure
  yourself?
HERMIONE (*sings*). Alas, alas!
  Off with you from my hair into the sky,   830
  my finely woven veil!*
NURSE. My child, cover your breasts, fasten your robes.
HERMIONE (*sings*). Why must I cover my breasts with my
    robes*
  when I have treated my husband in ways
  that cannot be concealed but are plain for all to see?
NURSE. Do you grieve that you plotted death for the rival wife?
HERMIONE (*sings*). I lament the destructive recklessness
  of what I did—a woman accursed in the eyes of men,
  accursed.
NURSE. Your husband will pardon you for your mistake.   840
HERMIONE (*sings*). Why have you torn the sword from my
    hand?
  Give it back to me, my friend,* give it back
  so that I can strike fully home. Why do you stop me hang-
    ing myself?
NURSE. But what if I were to release you in your frenzy, and
  so let you die?
HERMIONE (*sings*). I cry out against my fate.
  Tell me, where is the fire's welcome flame?*
  Where can I climb to a rocky height
  either by the sea or in the wooded mountains,
  so that I can throw myself down and belong to the dead   850
  below?
NURSE. Why do you torment yourself so? The gods send misfortunes to all mortals sooner or later.
HERMIONE (*sings*). You have abandoned me, father, aban-
    doned me on the coast,
  all alone without a sea-dipped oar to save me.*

It is clear that my husband will kill me, yes, kill me.
No longer shall I live in this house
where I was a bride.
What god's statue shall I rush to as a suppliant?
Or shall I fall as a slave at my own slave's knees?   860
If only I were a dark-winged bird
to fly from the land of Phthia
to where the ship of pine-wood
passed through the dark-blue cliffs,*
the first ship ever built!

NURSE. O my child, I did not praise your excessive reactions
before when you blundered in your treatment of the Trojan
woman, and now again I have no good to say of your
extreme transports of terror. Your husband will not break up
his marriage with you as you fear. He will not be won over   870
by the worthless words of a barbarian woman. In you he
possesses no captive from Troy, but the daughter of a king,
whom he took with many bridal gifts—and from a city of no
mean prosperity. And your father will not betray you as you
fear, my child, and allow you to be thrown out of this
palace. No, go inside and don't make yourself conspicuous
in front of the house—otherwise it will bring disgrace on
you [to be seen outside these halls, my girl].

The NURSE *goes into the house.*

CHORUS. Look, here comes some stranger who looks as if he is
from abroad. He is rushing towards us eagerly.   880

Enter ORESTES.

ORESTES. You foreign women, is this the royal palace where
the son of Achilles dwells?*

CHORUS. Yes. But who are you that you ask this question?

ORESTES. I am the son of Agamemnon and Clytemnestra and
my name is Orestes. I am going to the oracle of Zeus at
Dodona.* And since I have come to Phthia, it seems a good
idea to me to find out about my cousin, Hermione the
Spartan, and see if she is alive and well.* For though she
lives on plains distant from us, she is still dear to me.   890

HERMIONE. O son of Agamemnon, your appearance here is
like a haven to sailors in a storm. I beg you by these your

knees,* pity me for the sorry fortune which you see is mine. Suppliant branches are no stronger than my arm, with which I touch your knees.*

ORESTES (*with a start*). What is this? Surely I can't be mistaken? Do I really see the daughter of Menelaus, the mistress of the house, here before me?

HERMIONE. Yes, the only child that the daughter of Tyndareus bore to my father in his house.* You can be sure of my identity.

ORESTES. O Phoebus the Healer, release her from her sorrows. 900 What's going on? Is it gods or mortals who are treating you badly?

HERMIONE. Some of my troubles are self-inflicted, others come from the man who is my husband, and others from a god. I am ruined in every way.

ORESTES. What disaster could befall a woman if she has no children yet—unless something is wrong in her marriage?

HERMIONE. Yes, that is precisely where the sickness lies. How skilfully you have brought me to admit it!*

ORESTES. Does your husband love some other bedfellow instead of you?

HERMIONE. Yes, the captive woman who shared Hector's bed.*

ORESTES. That's a bad thing you speak of—when one man has two bedfellows.

HERMIONE. That's exactly the situation. And then I acted in 910 self-defence.

ORESTES. Did you plot against a woman—as women do?

HERMIONE. Yes, I plotted death for her and her bastard child.

ORESTES. And did you kill them, or did some chance snatch them from you?

HERMIONE. It was the old man Peleus, who showed respect for the inferior side.*

ORESTES. Did you have someone as your accomplice in this murder plan?

HERMIONE. Yes, my father, who came from Sparta for this very purpose.

ORESTES. What, and was he defeated by the old man's strength?

HERMIONE. Yes, by respect for his old age. And he has gone away, leaving me all alone.

ORESTES. I understand.* What you have done makes you
afraid of your husband.

HERMIONE. You have grasped the situation. Yes, he will kill   920
me, and he will have justice on his side. Why talk about it?
But I beg you—and I call on Zeus, protector of kindred*—
escort me as far away from this land as possible, or to my
father's palace. For this house seems to me to have a voice
and to be driving me out, and the land of Phthia hates me.
If my husband leaves Phoebus' oracle and comes back home
before you take me away, he will put me to a shameful
death, or I shall be a slave to his counterfeit wife whose mistress I was before.

Perhaps someone might ask, 'How did you come to commit this wrong?' It was the visits of bad women that proved   930
my undoing.* They played on my vanity as they said these
words: 'Will you tolerate sharing the bed in your house with
that basest of women, the war captive, the slave? By Hera
the queen,* she wouldn't have enjoyed the marriage bed in
my house and stayed alive!' And I, listening to these Siren
words,* [to these clever, criminal and cunning chatter-
boxes,] was puffed up with folly. After all, why did I have to
keep watch on my husband when I had everything I
needed? I was extremely wealthy, I was mistress of the   940
house, my children would have been legitimate,* while her
bastards would have been half-slaves at their beck and call.
But never, never—I say it twice over—should a husband
with any good sense allow women to pay visits to his wife
in his house, for they give lessons in evil. One will help to
destroy a marriage in hope of gain,* a second has sinned
herself and wishes others to share her corruption, while
many behave like this from simple lust. And the result is that
men's homes become diseased. That's how things are—so   950
keep a good guard* on the doors of your houses with bolts
and bars. For women visiting from outside spread the infec-
tion of their many sins.

CHORUS. You have gone too far in your denunciation of your
own sex. I can forgive this in your case, but even so women
have a duty to gloss over female weaknesses.

ORESTES. It was a wise fellow who taught mortals to listen to
tales coming from the opposing side.* For I knew of the con-

fusion in this house and of the quarrel between you and 960
Hector's wife, and I watched and waited to see if you would
stay here or would want to bid good riddance to this house
in your terror over your attempted murder of the captive
woman. I did not come here out of respect for any message
of yours but with the intention—if you gave me a chance to
talk, as you have—of escorting you from this house. You
were once betrothed to me and you live with this man
because of the baseness of your father who gave you to me
as my wife before he invaded Troy's borders but later
promised you to the man who has you now, if he should 970
sack Troy's city. When the son of Achilles returned here, I
forgave your father,* and I begged Neoptolemus to give up
his marriage to you, telling him of my fortunes and the lot
that holds me now, and saying how I could take a wife from
my friends, but it would not be easy to find one from for-
eigners because of the exile which keeps me from my house.
He responded with insolence, throwing in my teeth the murder of my mother and the goddesses with the bloodshot
eyes.* And I, humbled by the troubles of my house, was sorrowful, yes, sorrowful, but I bore up amid misfortune, and 980
went away reluctantly, stripped of my hopes of marriage
with you.

Now therefore, since your fortunes have met with this
reversal* and you have fallen into this calamity that leaves
you helpless, I shall take you to your home and I shall hand
you over to your father. For there is a strange power in kin-
ship and when one is in trouble there is nothing better than
a friend from one's family.

HERMIONE. My father will take care of my wedding arrange-
ments and it is not up to me to make any decision about
them. But take me off from this palace as quickly as you 990
can in case my husband arrives home and catches me before
you get me away, or the old man Peleus finds out that I have
abandoned the house and comes chasing after me in a
chariot.

ORESTES. Have no fear of an old man's strength. And do not
be frightened of the son of Achilles because of all his insolent treatment of me. Such are the immovable meshes of the
hunting net of death that I have set for him with this my

hand. I shall say no more about this, but later, when it has
all been done, the rock of Delphi* will know, and I, the killer
of my mother, will teach him not to marry one who ought
to have been my wife—if the oaths of my friends and allies
hold firm in Apollo's land. His demand to lord Apollo for sat- 1000
isfaction for his father's death will have bitter consequences
for him, and his change of heart will be of no help to him as
he now makes amends to the god.* No, he will die a grim
death thanks to that god and my slanders.* He will realize
what it means to be my enemy. God brings the fortunes of
his enemies to ruin and has no truck with pride.

                    ORESTES *and* HERMIONE *go out.**

CHORUS (*sings*). O Phoebus who raised the towering walls of 1010
      Ilium's citadel,
and Poseidon,* lord of the waters, who ride your chariot
with its blue-grey* mares over the surface of the salt sea,
why did you give over to dishonour
the work your hands had crafted
and abandon wretched, wretched Troy
to the raging god of war,
master of the spear?*

Numberless were the chariots with their noble horses which
      you yoked by the banks of Simois*
and you set men against each other in bloody contests   1020
in which no garland was the prize.*
The princes of Ilium
are dead and gone
and fire blazes no longer
with its scented smoke for the gods
on the altars in Troy.

The son of Atreus is gone too, killed by his wife's trickery,
and, in repayment for her act of murder,
she met with death at her children's hands.*   1030
It was a god's prophetic command, yes, a god's,
that turned against her, when Agamemnon's son
left the sanctuary,* journeyed to Argos,
and killed her—proving his mother's murderer.
O divine Phoebus, how am I to believe this?*

Many a groan over wretched children
resounded through the meeting places of the Greeks
and wives left their homes   1040
to share their bed with another man.* Not on you* alone,
not only on your friends has sorrow's agony fallen.
Greece has suffered a pestilence, yes, a pestilence.
It crossed over the sea from Troy, yes, to our fertile fields,
and fell like a thunderbolt, dripping bloodshed on the
    Greeks.

Enter PELEUS.*

PELEUS. Women of Phthia, answer my question. For I heard
    an uncertain report that Menelaus' daughter had left this
    palace and gone away. It is my eagerness to find out if this   1050
    is true that has brought me here. After all, friends at home
    are bound to exert themselves over the fortunes of those who
    are away.*

CHORUS. Peleus, what you heard was correct. It is not right
    for me to keep quiet about the troubles that surround me.
    Yes, the queen has run off from this house.

PELEUS. What was she afraid of? Tell me everything, please.*

CHORUS. She was frightened that her husband might throw
    her out of the house.

PELEUS. What? In revenge for her plot to kill his child?

CHORUS. Yes, and her attempt to murder the captive woman.

PELEUS. Did she leave the palace with her father—or someone   1060
    else? Who was it?

CHORUS. Agamemnon's son has taken her out of this land.

PELEUS. What does he hope to achieve? Does he want to
    marry her?

CHORUS. Yes, and to bring about your grandson's death.

PELEUS. Will he lie in ambush or meet him in open fight?

CHORUS. In the holy temple of Loxias* in co-operation with
    Delphians.

PELEUS. Alas! This is terrible indeed. Won't someone go to
    Apollo's shrine as fast as he can and explain what is hap-
    pening there to our friends in Delphi—and stop Achilles' son
    being killed by his enemies!

Enter MESSENGER.

MESSENGER. O sorrow, sorrow! How wretched I am! What a 1070
tale of disaster I have come to tell you, old man, and my
master's friends as well!

PELEUS. Alas! What forebodings rise in my prophetic heart!

MESSENGER. You have to know, old Peleus, that your grandson is no more, so deadly were the sword blows which the
Delphians and the stranger from Mycenae inflicted on him.

CHORUS. Ah, ah, what is happening to you, old man? Do not
fall! Stand upright.

PELEUS. I am lost. All is over for me. My voice dries up, my
limbs give way beneath me.

MESSENGER. Keep standing and listen to what happened, if
you really want to help your friends.*   1080

PELEUS. O fate, how you have engulfed your miserable victim
as I dwell on the furthest verge of old age! Tell me how he
died, please, my only son's only son. I cannot bear to hear
and yet I want to.

MESSENGER. When we came to Phoebus' famous precinct, we
spent three shining orbits of the sun in sight-seeing and it
appears that this awoke suspicions.* The people who live in
the god's territory began to congregate in groups, and
Agamemnon's son went round the city spreading the poison 1090
of his words in everybody's ears: 'Do you see this man who
is going round the god's sanctuary with its rich supply of
gold, the treasuries of mortals? He is here for the second time
for the same reason that he came before. He wants to sack
the temple of Phoebus.' As a result of this, a surge of resent-
ment began to wash through the town. The civil authorities
flocked to the council chamber, and unofficially* all those in
charge of the god's treasures had guards placed over the
columned temple. We were on our way, leading our sheep
reared on the foliage of Parnassus,* and we didn't yet know 1100
anything about all this. We took our stand at the altar* with
the consuls* and Apollo's prophets. And one of them spoke
the following words: 'Young man, what prayer should we
make to the god for you? Why have you come here?' He
replied, 'I wish to atone to Phoebus for my previous trans-
gression. For I asked him before to give compensation for my
father's death.'* And at this point it became obvious what a
great impact Orestes' words had made. He had convinced

everybody that my master was lying and had come with 1110
shameful intentions.

He went up the steps into the temple so that he could pray
to Phoebus in front of the oracular shrine, and he was busy
with the burnt offerings. But, as he found to his cost, an
ambush of armed men had been set for him in the shadow
of a bay-tree* and the son of Clytemnestra, the contriver of
all these things, was one of the number.* As the son of
Achilles was standing there praying to the god in full sight
of everybody, they used the sharp blades of the swords with
which they were armed to stab him while he was off his
guard and wore no armour. He withdrew, for he was not 1120
wounded in any vital part, and as he staggered back he
grabbed some armour hanging from the pegs on a side wall.
He stood on the altar, the very picture of a grim fighter, and
shouted these questions to the sons of Delphi: 'Why are you
trying to kill me? I came here on a pious pilgrimage. What
is your reason for murdering me?' There were countless
Delphians near by but not one of them said a word. They
simply kept pounding him with stones. Pelted with missiles
coming at him from all directions thick and fast like
snowflakes, he held his weapons in front of him and tried to 1130
protect himself against the onslaught by thrusting his shield
out this way and that.

But they got nowhere. No, the great shower of missiles—
arrows, thonged javelins, spits with two points tugged from
the slaughtered oxen they had pierced—fell together before
his feet. You would have seen a terrible Pyrrhic dance* as
your boy warded off the missiles. But when they had formed
a circle round him and were holding him there giving him
no breathing space, he abandoned the hearth of the altar
where the sheep are received, and leapt the Trojan leap* as
he rushed on them. They, like doves when they spot a 1140
hawk,* turned their backs in flight. Many fell in the crush,
some from wounds, others treading each other underfoot in
the narrow area of the exit. Ill-omened shouting amid the
temple's holy silence re-echoed from the rocks.* My master
stood in a kind of calm, glittering in his bright armour—
until someone* uttered a strange and hair-raising cry from
the middle of the shrine and this roused the army and

renewed their fighting spirit. Then the son of Achilles fell,
pierced in the ribs by the sharp-bladed sword [of the 1150
Delphian who killed him]* in company with many others.
And when he fell to the ground, there was no one who did
not stab him with his sword* or strike him with a stone,
pounding and smashing him. And all of that handsome body
has been wasted by savage wounds. They flung his corpse,
which was lying near the altar, outside the fragrant temple.
And we snatched it up as quickly as we could and are bringing it to you, old man, to weep over and bewail with your
laments and to see to his burial in the earth. Such is the 1160
treatment that the lord who prophesies to others and is the
arbiter of justice to all men, has meted out to the son of
Achilles as he sought atonement. Like a base human being,
he would not forget an ancient feud. How then could he be
wise?*

  The corpse of NEOPTOLEMUS *is carried in on a bier.*

CHORUS (*chants*). Look, here is our king now approaching his
     home
after his journey on a bier from the land of Delphi.
The dead man suffered terrible things, and terrible too
is your suffering, old man. For you receive Achilles' boy
into your house not as you would wish,   1170
and in your sorrows
you have met with the same fate as your grandson.
PELEUS (*sings*). O what sorrow for me! What a horror I see
     here
and receive into my house with a touch of my hand.*
Alas, alas I cry.
O city of Thessaly, all is over for us,
we are ruined. I no longer have a family, no children are left
     in the house.
What afflictions I have to endure! To what friend
can I turn my eyes and find pleasure?   1180
O beloved mouth and cheek and hands,
if only fate had slain you beneath Ilium
by the banks of Simois!*
CHORUS. In that case he would be honoured in his death, old
     man, and so your own lot would be happier.

PELEUS (*sings*). O marriage, marriage,* it is you
  that has destroyed this house and destroyed my city!
  Alas! What sorrow! O my child!
  If only my family had never
  burdened itself—   1190
  in the hope of children for the house—
  with that hateful marriage with Hermione which has
    brought you death!
  If only she had perished before then, struck by a thunderbolt!
  And if only you, a mere mortal, had never fastened upon
    Phoebus, a god,
  the blame for the death of your father, a Zeus-born hero,*
  killed by the archer's skill.*
CHORUS (*sings*). O misery, O misery, I shall begin the lamen-
    tations
  for my dead master with the dirge for the dead.
PELEUS (*sings*). O misery, in my turn I weep for you,   1200
  a wretched, ill-starred old man.
CHORUS. Yes, it was fated by a god, it was a god who brought
  this disaster to fulfilment.
PELEUS (*sings*). O my beloved boy, you have left the house des-
    olate.
  You have abandoned me [wretched me—o sorrow!—]
  to a childless old age.
CHORUS. You should have died before your children, old man.
  Yes, you should have died.
PELEUS (*sings*). Let me tear my hair,
  let me pound my head   1210
  with my hand's brutal beat! O city,
  Phoebus has taken my two children* from me.
CHORUS (*sings*). Ill-starred old man, what sorrows you have
    seen and endured!
  What will your life be now?
PELEUS (*sings*). Desolate, with no children, with no limit to my
    sorrows,
  I shall drain my cup of suffering till I die.
CHORUS. It was for nothing that the gods blessed you in your
  marriage.*
PELEUS (*sings*). All that happiness has flown away and van-
    ished.

There is no cause for proud boasting now.   1220
CHORUS. You dwell all alone in a desolate house.
PELEUS (*sings*). I no longer have a city.
   Away with you, my sceptre!*   (*He flings it to the ground.*)
   And you, you daughter of Nereus in your gloomy caves,*
   will see me tumbling to my destruction.
CHORUS (*chants*). Oh, oh!
   What is it that moves?* What divinity do I see?
   Girls, see, look!
   This is some divine being voyaging through the translucent
     sky
   and coming to the plains
   of horse-rearing Phthia.   1230

      THETIS appears above the stage building.

THETIS. Peleus, I, Thetis, have left the house of Nereus and
   come here in recognition of our former marriage.* First I
   advise you not to take your present miseries too much to
   heart. I too, who should have borne children who would
   bring me no cause for tears—after all, I am a goddess and
   the daughter of a god—have lost the son I gave you, swift-
   footed Achilles,* the first man of Greece.
     I shall tell you why I am here. Listen carefully to me.
   Carry this dead son of Achilles to Apollo's hearth and bury 1240
   him there, so that his grave may declare that he was vio-
   lently murdered by Orestes' agency, and prove a reproach to
   the Delphians. As for the captive woman—Andromache, I
   mean—she must dwell in the land of Molossia,* old man,
   united with Helenus* in the marriage bed, and this boy,*
   now the sole survivor of Aeacus'* line, must go there with
   her. A succession of Molossian kings descended from him
   must pass through life in prosperity. For your race and mine 1250
   must not be so absolutely erased, old man, nor must that of
   Troy. Yes, the gods are concerned about that city too, even
   though it fell by the will of Pallas.*
     As for you—so that you may be grateful for your mar-
   riage with me—I shall put an end to your human sufferings
   and make you immortal, a deathless god.* And after that
   you will dwell with me, one god in company with another,
   in the house of Nereus. From there, you will emerge from

the sea with your feet dry* and see Achilles, the son we both 1260
love so much, as he dwells on his island home by the shore
of Leuce within the inhospitable sea.*

But now off with you to the god-built city of Delphi, tak-
ing this dead man with you, and bury him in the earth.
Then you must go and sit in a hollow cave on Cuttle Reef.*
Wait until I arrive bringing my fifty dancing Nereids from
the sea to escort you. For you must accomplish what is fated,
and this is the desire of Zeus. Grieve no longer for the dead. 1270
After all, this is what the gods have decreed for all mankind.
Death is the debt men have to pay.

PELEUS. O my lady, O my noble bedmate, you daughter of
Nereus, I greet you. What you are doing now is worthy of
yourself and of your children. I now put a stop to my griev-
ing since this is your bidding, goddess, and after I have
buried this my grandson, I shall go to the valleys of Pelion*
where I took your lovely body in my arms.

THETIS disappears.

[And in view of that, should not men of good judgement
marry wives of noble birth and give their daughters in mar- 1280
riage to noble men? They should not set their heart on a
base marriage, even if it will bring a surpassingly rich dowry
to the house. For those who marry the noble will never meet
with suffering from the gods.]*

PELEUS goes off taking the body of Neoptolemus.

CHORUS (*chants*). The divine will manifests itself in many
forms,
and the gods bring many things to pass against our expec-
tation.
What we thought would happen remains unfulfilled,
while the god has found a way to accomplish the unexpected.
And that is what has happened here.*

The CHORUS goes out.

EXPLANATORY NOTES

HECUBA

2   *Hades*: the god of the Underworld.

3   *I am the son of Hecuba, the daughter of Cisseus*: Euripides changes Homer's account. In that poet's work, Polydorus is the son of Priam and Laothoë and is killed by Achilles, while Hecuba is the daughter of Dymas, a Phrygian.

4   *the Phrygians' city*: in tragedy, 'Phrygians' means 'Trojans'. Therefore, this city is Troy.

7   *his Thracian guest-friend*: this is the first use of the key term 'guest-friend' (Greek *xenos*) in the play. For Greeks, guests, hosts, and strangers fell into the same category, since the repayment of hospitality could make a host of a one-time stranger who had become a guest. Zeus was the god who oversaw such relationships, which were defined by the term *xenia* (= hospitality), and anyone who violated them would thus incur the wrath of the most powerful of the deities.

8   *this fertile steppe of the Chersonese*: the Thracian Chersonese is the narrow strip of land which runs along the north of the Hellespont (the modern Dardanelles) across from Troy. 'The characters are in a sort of no man's land between Asia and Greece' (J. Mossman, *Wild Justice: A Study of Euripides' Hecuba* (Oxford, 1995), 23).

9   *by the spear*: this may simply highlight the warlike character of the Thracians, but C. Collard (*Hecuba* (Warminster, 1991), n. at 9) is surely right to suggest that it is also 'an early indication of Polymestor's violent nature'.

11   *Ilium*: i.e. Troy, called Ilium after its founder Ilus. The name of Troy comes from Ilus' father Tros.

13   *I was the youngest of Priam's children*: cf. Homer, *Iliad* 20.408–10: '[Polydorus'] father always forbade him to fight, because he was the youngest of the sons born to him, and the one he loved most.' Cf. n. at 3.

20   *I flourished like a sapling*: one of the editors quotes the Psalms: 'that our sons may grow up as young plants'; and 'his children like the olive-branches round about his table'. The source of Euripides' simile is presumably Homer, *Iliad* 18.56, in which

Achilles' mother Thetis says of him, 'He shot up like a young sapling.'

23   *the god-built altar*: Poseidon and Apollo built Troy.

24   *slaughtered by the blood-polluted hand of Achilles' son*: Achilles' son Neoptolemus killed Priam as he was taking refuge at the altar of Zeus Herkeios ('of the Household', cf. 'hearth' in 22). One of the most memorable illustrations of this grisly episode is on a vase by the Cleophrades Painter from the first quarter of the fifth century BCE in the National Museum of Archaeology, Naples. It shows Priam as he sits on the altar and 'holds his hands to his head in a touching gesture of despair. His head has been cut and is bleeding; the battered and gashed body of his grandson lies sprawled in his lap. A beautiful young warrior [Neoptolemus] puts his hand on the old king's shoulder, not to comfort him, but to steady him before brutally delivering the fatal blow' (Susan Woodford, *An Introduction to Greek Art* (London, 1986), 72).

29   *the constant ebb and flow of the waves*: one meaning of the Greek word here translated 'ebb and flow' is 'a double race-course'. The chariots would speed up one side of it, turn round a post at the end, and come back along the other side. Hence its appropriateness for the toing and froing of Polydorus' body between sea and shore.

35   *the Achaeans*: i.e. the Greeks. Achaea is a region in southern Greece, in the north east of the Peloponnese.

37   *above his tomb*: Achilles had been killed at Troy. In this play, however, Euripides sets his tomb on the Chersonese.

44   *on this day*: like the action of most tragedies, that of this one takes place in a single horrendous day, as was commended by Aristotle (*Poetics* 1449[b]).

47   *can win my burial*: until the corpse was properly buried, the dead person's spirit could not find rest in the Underworld.

49   *those who hold power below*: since Polydorus is dead, it is only the divinities of the Underworld who can grant him favours.

53-4   *the tent of Agamemnon*: in *The Trojan Women* Hecuba is assigned to Odysseus, in this play to Agamemnon.

58   *s.d.*: 'From the moment Hecuba appears supported by women in 59, the community of women is an important theme, and one which becomes increasingly prominent as the play progresses and the women unite against Polymestor' (Mossman, p. 27).

68–72   *O day's bright radiance . . . my vision of the night*: to tell the sun
           a bad dream was viewed as a cure, since the sun was supposed
           to have the power to neutralize the influences of night.

87–8   *Helenus, | the inspired prophet, and Cassandra*: Helenus was the
           son of Priam and Hecuba. In fact, in this play Euripides wishes
           us to believe that Polydorus was their last surviving son. In
           keeping Helenus alive here, he may be reflecting the tradition
           that he survived the war and eventually married Andromache
           in Epirus in north-west Greece.
                Apollo had endowed Cassandra, a daughter of Priam and
           Hecuba, with prophetic powers but accompanied his gift with
           the cruel proviso that no one would believe her until she
           prophesied her own death.

111–12   *held back the ships . . . the forestays*: the forestays were the
           strong ropes on which the sails were hoisted up the mast. I
           take it that the ghost of Achilles caused the wind which was
           billowing in the sails to drop (cf. 37–9).

113   *Danaans*: i.e. Greeks. Danaus is said to have founded the
           citadel of Argos.

116   *surged*: the metaphor picks up the literal surge of the sea in
           which Polydorus' body is being swept to and fro. The setting
           of the play by the seashore is constantly brought to our atten-
           tion.

121   *the prophetess with her wild inspiration*: i.e. Cassandra, the
           daughter of Priam and Hecuba, whom Agamemnon is taking
           back to Greece as his mistress. Cf. n. at 87–8.

122   *Theseus' two boys*: Acamas and Demophon. Though they are
           not at Troy in Homer's *Iliad*, on a cup of the Brygos Painter in
           the Louvre, they are shown taking Polyxena away for sacri-
           fice.

125–6   *they should crown Achilles' tomb with fresh young blood*: the
           dead were regularly 'crowned' with liquid offerings, including
           blood-sacrifices. Human sacrifice was not viewed as an accept-
           able practice by the Greeks. (Achilles' sacrifice of twelve
           Trojans on the pyre of Patroclus (*Iliad* 23.175–6) is the excep-
           tion that proves the rule.)

131–3   *Laertes' son . . . courtier of the people*: Laertes' son is Odysseus.
           Collard remarks (n. at 130–3) that 'Odysseus' sturdy elo-
           quence in Homer and resourcefulness with words become in
           later poets, especially dramatic, a ready glibness and devious
           manipulation of the unsophisticated'. We seem to be in the

world of the so-called demagogues, figures such as Cleon, who in the view of the historian Thucydides (e.g. at 3.36, 4.21, and 6.35) manipulated popular opinion at Athens at the time when *Hecuba* was written.

136   *Persephone*: the wife of Hades (see n. at 2) and hence queen of the Underworld.

142   *your girl*: i.e. Polyxena. The word I have translated as 'girl' in fact means 'filly'. The Greeks frequently used the words for the young of animals to refer to human beings (cf. 'whelp' and 'calf' in 206 and 526). The suggestion seems to be of vulnerability and innocence. Cf. Shakespeare, *As You Like It* (II.vii.128—Orlando speaking of Adam): 'Whiles like a doe, I go to find my fawn.'

144   *go to the temples, go to the altars*: the Chorus' suggestions, on the desolate expanse of the Thracian Chersonese, are totally unreal and may reflect their desperation.

145   *crouch as a suppliant at Agamemnon's knees*: when one was asking a favour, to kneel before the person whom one was asking and touch their knees put strong pressure on them to accede to it.

150–2   *in a welter . . . darkly gleaming flood*: 'The description shows Euripides' fascination with colour' (Collard, n. at 150–3). Cf. n. at 468.

172   *to this tent*: i.e. the tent where Polyxena is.

175–6   *what news,* | *what news*: such repetitions are a notorious mannerism of Euripides and were devastatingly satirized by Aristophanes, e.g. at *Frogs* 1352–5:
    But he to the blue upflew, upflew,
    On the lightliest tips of his wings outspread;
    To me he bequeated but woe, but woe,
    And tears, sad tears, from my eyes o'erflow,
    Which I, the bereaved, must shed, must shed.
        (trans. B. B. Rogers)
    Cf. in *Hecuba* 170–1, 184, 199, 909, 1067, 1097.

188   *The Argives*: the Greeks generally, not simply those from Argos in southern Greece.

190   *the son of Peleus*: i.e. Achilles.

197   *O my mother, you victim of terrible sufferings*: Polyxena breaks what one could almost propose as a convention of Greek dramatic literature—that whoever is talking claims to be the most miserable person on stage. Thus her concern for her mother

comes over with particular force.

205   *whelp*: see n. at 142.

205–6   *like a heifer bred in the mountains*: this adds a poignant note of
           abnormality to the slaughter of Polyxena since sacrificial
           heifers were normally domestic.

211–15   *And I weep . . . happier fortune*: poignant lines which are totally
           in accord with Polyxena's touching reluctance to give her own
           grief primacy. Cf. n. at 197.

218–23   *Lady, I think . . . girl*: the perfunctory brutality with which
           Odysseus makes his chilling pronouncement is surely intended
           to be deeply shocking, an impression confirmed when it tran-
           spires that Odysseus is in fact in no great hurry (238).

224   *the son of Achilles*: i.e. Neoptolemus.

229   *contest*: the Greek word for 'contest' (*agōn*) is used in a the-
           atrical context to indicate a major scene of confrontation
           between two of the protagonists. Just such a scene is launched
           here by this highly apposite word.

239   *Do you remember when you came into Troy as a spy*: Odysseus'
           spying mission and Helen's detection of him are in Homer's
           Odyssey (4.242 ff.), but an ancient critic's comment is not
           without point: 'this fiction is incredible and not Homeric:
           Hecuba would not have kept quiet if she saw an enemy spying
           upon the Trojans' circumstances, but Helen would naturally
           have done so because she was repenting of Aphrodite's folly'
           (trans. Collard).

242–50   *I remember . . . this sunlight*: stichomythia, i.e. a passage in
           which the characters speak in single lines. This device is par-
           ticularly well situated to scenes of confrontation.

245   *And you touched my knees in all humility*: see n. at 145.

254–5   *There are no thanks . . . a politician's fame*: the same ancient
           critic as is quoted above in 239 here remarks acidly, 'Euripides
           is talking about his own city's [Athens'] politics; he's like that,
           confusing the times' (trans. Collard).

260   *to slaughter a human*: cf. n. at 125–6.

269   *the daughter of Tyndareus*: i.e. Helen, actually the daughter of
           Zeus but born from Leda, whose husband was Tyndareus.

274   *this aged chin too*: the knee and the chin were the parts of the
           body most significantly touched in supplication (see n. at 145).
           It may be that the chin was touched to avert words of rejec-

tion, just as the knees may have been touched to prevent one's being kicked away.

281   *She is my city, my nurse, my staff, my guide*: such poignant statements have their root in Andromache's famous words to her husband (*Iliad* 6.429–30): 'But Hector, you are father and honoured mother and brother to me, as well as my strong husband.' Mossman comments (p. 109) that the use of the word 'city' 'is highly resonant in this context: the destruction of the city has dominated the play's opening; it is at the core of all Hecuba's unhappiness; its smoking ruins can just be glimpsed in the background; and yet while Polyxena lives she represents for Hecuba all the advantages of a city: order, protection, companionship, and support.'

282   *It is wrong . . . where they should not*: cf. Shakespeare, *Measure for Measure*, II.ii.117–9:

> O, it is excellent
> To have a giant's strength; but it is tyrannous
> To use it like a giant.

290   *No, you took pity on them*: i.e. even though you dragged them from the altars, you did not proceed to the impiety of killing women who had taken sanctuary.

291–2   *For when it comes . . . slaves alike*: Demosthenes, giving us the law for the violation of rights (21.48–50), states that slaves and free men were protected equally in sanctuary.

325   *Ida*: Ida was the great mountain range near Troy. Here it simply means Troy.

340–1   *for he has children too*: in fact, Odysseus had only one child, a son called Telemachus.

342–5   *I see you, Odysseus . . . that lies in me*: in the process of supplication (cf. notes at 145 and 274), any form of physical contact with the person supplicated put pressure on them to accede to the request being made. Such contact, as it were, activated Zeus, the god who watched over this sphere. Odysseus slides his right hand under his cloak and turns his face aside to make it problematic for Polyxena to touch him and so circumscribe his independence. Ironically enough, he has nothing to fear. She has no intention of supplicating him.

354   *Ida*: see n. at 325.

379   *stamp*: this metaphor, taken from stamping an impression on

a coin, is favoured by Euripides when he is concerned with establishing the relationship between internal truth and external show. Cf. Robert Burns, *For a' that and a' that*:

> The rank is but the guinea's stamp;
> The man's the gowd for a' that!

387–8   *It was I . . . destroyed him*: Paris had caused the Trojan War by abducting Helen, the queen of Sparta. Hecuba was culpable for keeping him alive, despite having been warned in a dream of the consequences of doing so. Paris, with the help of the archer god Apollo, had killed Achilles by shooting him in the heel, the only part of his body in which he was vulnerable.

396–401 *I must die . . . leave here without her*: stichomythia. See p. 116, n. at 242–50.

407   *lose your dignity*: Polyxena's insistence on dignity is fundamental to Euripides' characterization of her.

415–31   *Yours is a pitiable fate . . . Calamity has killed me*: stichomythia. See p. 116, n. at 242–50. J. Diggle has reordered the lines between 414 and 421, and I have followed his arrangement.

421   *I have lost my fifty children*: according to Homer, these fifty children were Priam's; 19 (or 38) of them were by Hecuba.

441   *the Dioscuri*: Castor and Polydeuces, the brothers of Helen and Clytemnestra.

443   *hellish ruin*: I have tried to reproduce a play on words here. The Greek verb meaning 'ruin' can contain the syllable 'hel-', and this can be exploited to emphasize the destruction wreaked by *Hel*en.

444   *Breeze*: 'the opening address provides a direct and poignant link with the preceding scene, as Polyxena dies because the [breeze, ocean breeze] is being held back by Achilles (cf. 37–9, 111–12—see n.); 445–6 thus have ironic overtones when applied to this situation, for these ships are becalmed' (Mossman, p. 78).

         The wind only starts blowing at 1289–90. (See notes there, at 539–40, and at 900.)

450–3   *in the Dorian land . . . enriches the plains*: the Dorian land is the Peloponnese, where Agamemnon and Menelaus come from Argos and Sparta respectively; Phthia in Thessaly is the home of Achilles' son Neoptolemus; the Apidanus is a tributary of the Enipeus, and both rivers water the fertile Thessalian plain.

458–61   *where the first . . . Zeus' children*: Leto gave birth to Zeus' children Apollo and Artemis while clasping a palm-tree on the island of Delos, which lies in the middle of the Aegean. Zeus is said to have created the palm and the bay-trees to help Leto to bear the divine siblings.

466   *the city of Pallas*: i.e. Athens.

468   *her saffron robe*: a magnificent new robe, always representing Athena doing battle with the Giants, was carried in a procession to be presented to the goddess on the acropolis at Athens every year (in the Panathenaea festival).

Collard (n. at 468–71) observes how words such as saffron 'exemplify Euripides' interest in light and colour'. Cf. n. at 150–2.

472-4   *the race of the Titans . . . his thunderbolt*: the Titans were the sons of Uranus and Gaia who rebelled unsuccessfully against Zeus after he had conquered them and their king Cronus. Zeus blasted them with his thunderbolt, on whose 'double blaze' Collard comments (n. at 472–4) that the bolt was often represented in vase-paintings as a shaft with fire at both ends.

497   *I am an old man, but even so*: Talthybius means that, since he is old, he has little life left to live. Therefore the short time remaining to him is very precious. Even so . . .

503   *adjutant*: I have borrowed Collard's translation here.

507   *old man*: Talthybius' age is stressed (cf. 497). F. W. King (Euripides, *Hecuba* (London, 1938), n. at 484–628) comments: 'The sympathetic and respectful attitude of the old herald, Talthybius, is a striking change after the callousness of Odysseus; he too, like the rank and file of the Greek army, has been captured and humbled by the noble beauty of Polyxena's end. Though he plays a small part, he is not without individuality—an amiably self-important man, resolved to give a full account of the fearful scene at which he has just been present, not least of the part which he himself played in the ceremony.'

510   *The two sons of Atreus*: Agamemnon and Menelaus.

518   *win a prize*: while this is likely to be ironical, Collard quotes an ancient critic (n. at 518): 'as a friend, Talthybius thinks it gain to mourn Polyxena a second time'.

526   *your poor girl*: the Greek word which I have translated 'poor girl' in fact means 'calf'. See notes at 142 and 205–6.

536   *this libation which summons up the dead*: the ghost will rise to drink the blood.

539–40   *we may untie the ropes which hold our ships' sterns fast*:
         Neoptolemus is in effect asking the ghost of his father Achilles
         to allow the wind to blow again. Cf. notes at 444, 900, and
         1289–90.

548   *I am happy to die*: with these words 'the sacrificial victim gains
         control over her own death' (Nicole Loraux, *Tragic Ways of
         Killing a Woman* (English trans., Cambridge, Mass., 1987), 46).
         The young girl makes a pattern of nobility out of her grim
         slaughter.

566   *he wavered between reluctance and eagerness*: cf. Shakespeare,
         Measure for Measure, II.ii.33: 'at war 'twixt will and will
         not'.

568–70   *But even though she was dying . . . from men's eyes*: a com-
         mentator from the second century CE praises a statue by
         Polygnotus which showed Polyxena performing this decorous
         action. Decorum is surely the keynote of Euripides' presenta-
         tion of his heroine, who succeeds in bringing due order to a
         scene of horrific brutality. See notes at 407 and 548.

573–4   *Some of them threw leaves on the dead girl*: an ancient com-
         mentator remarks, 'as upon a victor in the games'.
              King (n. at 573–80) comments: 'The enthusiastic admira-
         tion aroused in the common soldiers by Polyxena's courage is
         perhaps the most human and pathetic touch in this vividly
         beautiful and imaginative narrative. It has upon Hecuba the
         calming effect that it must have on all its readers. It is passages
         like this which led Aristotle to describe Euripides as the most
         tragic of the poets.'

607–8   *the sailor's indiscipline blazes fiercer than fire*: Aristotle writes of
         the 'naval mob' as the scum of the population (*Politics*
         1327[a]10 ff.).

609   *old*: like Talthybius (see n. at 507), the Serving Woman is old.
         They join Hecuba to create a trio of old people. The queen does
         not have a monopoly on old age in this play.

612   *the bride that never was a bride, the maiden who is a maiden no
         longer*: Polyxena has 'married' Achilles in a hideous perver-
         sion of a marriage. More truly, it is death that she has mar-
         ried—and to which she has lost her maidenhead.

632   *Alexandros*: the Trojans' name for Paris.

641   *Simois*: one of the rivers of the plain of Troy.

644–6   *and the rivalry was settled . . . on Ida*: while working as a herds-
         man on Mount Ida, the Trojan prince Paris judged a beauty

competition between the three goddesses, Hera, Athena, and
Aphrodite. He awarded the prize to Aphrodite, who bribed him
with the offer of the most beautiful woman in the world. This
proved to be Helen, queen of Sparta, and when Paris ran off
with her, he provoked the Trojan War which the Greeks
fought in order to win Helen back.

650–1 *by the fair-flowing Eurotas | a Spartan girl*: the river Eurotas
flows through Sparta. By causing his Chorus of Trojan women
to empathize with the widows and bereft mothers of the
Greeks, Euripides movingly conveys the tragedy of war for the
women on both sides. They transcend any narrow factional-
ism.

It is interesting to note that, at the time of the play's production, there may have been 292 Spartan captives in Athens
(taken from the island of Sphakteria off Pylos in 425 BCE).

657 *s.d.*: 'The corpse will remain on stage until the very end of the
play' (Mossman, p. 60).

671–2 *But why have you brought the body of Polyxena here to me*:
'There is little in all Greek tragedy more terribly ironical than
Hecuba's question [here]' (King, n. at 652–6).

684 *O my child, my child*: Hecuba here bursts into song, while the
Chorus and the Serving Woman keep to spoken verse.

703–4 *I understand the dream | which I saw in my sleep*: King (n. at
702) provides an explanation here which some will consider
over-interpretation, bringing too clear a logic to a conscious
lack of definition on the playwright's part: 'The mention of the
sea-shore reminds Hecuba of the vision of Polydorus which
appeared to her at the beginning of the play. What the audience hear as the prologue spoken by Polydorus' ghost, Hecuba
had heard as a dream within the tent, and she now knows that
the dream spoke true and that Polymestor is the murderer.'

736 *s.d.*: *turning away and speaking to herself*: Mossman pro-
nounces (p. 62) this 'the longest sustained series of asides in
extant tragedy'.

737–8 *Should I fall here at Agamemnon's knee*: for the conventions of
supplication, see notes at 274 and 342–5.

750 *for my children*: in fact she is referring simply to Polydorus.

759–85 *I am not begging . . . Lady Fortune herself*: stichomythia. See
p. 116, n. at 242–50. Mossman (p. 182) comments sensitively
on the use of this convention here: 'there are a number of
devices that Hecuba uses to engage Agamemnon's sympathy

... Line 762 emphasizes the intimate bond between mother and child, 766 the waste of his young life, 768 the useless care of his father; and 771 ff. tell the wretched story of his death and the finding of his corpse. The stichomythia drags the miserable tale out slowly, and Agamemnon's contributions express a sympathy which we are bound to share as we gaze on the pathetic corpse on the stage.'

795   *He received all that he should, was given all consideration*: the meaning is that Priam sent to Polymestor enough—and more than enough—money and gifts to cover the expenses of looking after Polydorus.

825   *Cypris*: i.e. Aphrodite, goddess of love, who was born from the foam of the sea and carried first to Cythera and then to Cyprus—hence the name Cypris.

837   *hair*: is Hecuba's hair cropped (Collard, n. at 836–40) or disarrayed (Mossman, p. 129) in mourning?

838   *Daedalus*: Daedalus was the 'type' of the inventive genius. There may be a reference here to the belief that Daedalus' statues could speak as well as move, but that could well be an idea that post-dates the fifth century BCE. To objections that this passage is 'bizarre' and 'ghastly', Mossman responds (p. 129) that she is 'praying not to be transformed into some strange beast, but that she might undergo a similar kind of liberation of energy to that which Daedalus and the god are envisaged as granting to the statue, affecting every part of her body, which she may then use to its utmost in persuading Agamemnon'.

875   *As for the rest—have no fear—I shall see that all turns out well*: cf. Lady Macbeth's supremely sinister 'Leave all the rest to me' (*Macbeth*, I.v.72).

880–5   *These tents conceal . . . women's strength*: stichomythia. See Introduction, p. 00.

886–7   *Was it not women . . . of its all males*: the fifty daughters of Danaus married the fifty sons of his brother Aegyptus. Danaus presented each of his daughters with a knife and made them swear to murder their husbands on their wedding night. However, one did not go through with the crime. This was Hypermestra, who spared Lynceus since he had not violated her virginity.

A parallel story tells how the malodorous women of Lemnos killed all the men on the island when their husbands imported

Thracian concubines, save that Hypsipyle spared her father Thoas.

888   *so be it*: i.e. as Hecuba wishes in 870-5.

900   *the god does not send us favourable winds*: see n. at 444. The wind does not blow to any effect until 1289-90. See notes there, at 111-12, 444, and 539-40.

923-4   *I was arranging . . . binds it up*: 'There is a great deal of pathos in the picture of [the chorus] arranging their hair: hair is unloosed and disfigured and cut in mourning, and their *coiffures* will soon be ravaged by grief' (Mossman, p. 89).

       the cap: 'an Oriental head-piece (e.g. Herodotus 1.195), with sides covering the temples'—Collard, n. at 923.

926   *my bed's coverlet*: i.e. in order to make love (Collard, n. at 926).

934   *like a Spartan girl*: Mossman (p. 90) notes that the comparison 'refers to the comparatively exiguous clothing of Spartan girls. Placed here, in the chorus's mouths, it conveys a bitter irony: the sheltered eastern matron is having to run like a tough Spartan girl. At the same time it recalls in a curiously off-key manner the sympathy for the mourning Greek women in the previous ode' (see n. at 650-1).

943   *the Dioscuri*: see n. at 441.

953   *O Priam, dearest of men*: with this address to the now-deceased Priam, the hypocritical Polymestor is laying it on with a trowel in his very first words. Mossman, writing interestingly (pp. 185-6) of how an Athenian audience might be expected to view Thracians, comments that they are 'consistently portrayed in Greek literature as greedy, savage, and cowardly'.

955   *your daughter who has just been killed*: in fact, it is the corpse of his own murder victim Polydorus, now presumably covered, that lies on the stage. See n. at 657. Mossman argues that 'it was necessary for Euripides to undercut Polymestor so utterly by the presence of so eloquent a corpse if he was to make convincing the violence of Hecuba's action and achieve the intensity of tragic pity and terror which the plot he had chosen required' (p. 178).

960   *run ahead*: the metaphor is from an army's pioneers.

983-5   *But you must let me know . . . disposal*: Collard (n. at 984) notes that the 'irony continues; an already false friend offers further help'.

989–1017 *Certainly he is . . . Are there no men*: stichomythia. See p. 116,
          n. at 242–50. This exchange finds Euripides mining his rich-
          est vein of irony. As Hecuba counters Polymestor with her bril-
          liant exploitation of his own weapon, hypocrisy, it is possible
          to feel that she becomes corroded by it. She may be suffering a
          degeneration of her character, a degeneration which will be
          furthered when she puts her terrible plan into effect. While one
          can agree with Mossman (p. 165) that it 'seems simplistic to
          identify one clear-cut point in the play at which her moral
          deterioration irreversibly sets in', there is surely a gleeful
          malevolence and chilling control evinced—indeed height-
          ened—by this irony-laden stichomythia which suggest that
          such a deterioration is by now at least under way.

1008   *treasure-caves*: the translation is that of Collard, who notes (n.
          at 1008) that 'Euripides apparently credits the Trojans with
          structures like the great Mycenean *tholos*-tombs for royal buri-
          als—the so-called "Treasury of Atreus" at Mycenae or of
          Minyas at Orchomenus—or even shaft-graves, which were
          sometimes made inside *tholoi*'. *Tholoi* are circular structures
          rising to a cone.

1019–20   *for the Argives are eager to set sail for Troy*: presumably Hecuba
          is implying either that the Greeks' minds are otherwise occu-
          pied and so they will not notice Polymestor entering the tent,
          or that he must make haste because their departure is immi-
          nent.

1035   *I am being blinded, cruelly robbed of my eyes' light*: Collard has
          an admirably detailed note (at 1035–295) on why Hecuba
          blinds Polymestor rather than killing him. I quote just one sen-
          tence: 'The purpose of blinding, as of any mutilation, is both
          to incapacitate and to stigmatize indelibly.'

1050   *blind steps*: as a comparison with the 'transferred epithet'
          here—in literal fact it is Polymestor who is blind, not his
          steps—the editors J. Bond and A. S. Walpole (Euripides, *Hecuba*
          (London, 1922), n. at 1050) quote Milton's *Samson Agonistes*,
          1–2:
                A little onward lend thy guiding hand
                To these *dark steps*, a little further on.

1055   *s.d.*: *ekkyklēma*: this stage machine was a platform on wheels
          that could be pushed through the central door of the stage
          building. It would usually display the corpses of those who had
          been killed off stage, as here.
              The corpse of Polydorus, slain by Polymestor, now shares

the stage with the bodies of Polymestor's sons whom Hecuba has killed. Cf. notes at 657 and 955.

1061   *man-slaying*: 'possibly an allusion to the *Iliad*, where the adjective commonly describes Trojan Hector' (Collard, n. at 1061).

1068   *O you Sun god*: Polymestor 'feels the warmth of the sun as he comes further out on to the stage, and appeals to the Sun as the supreme giver of light to restore the light of his eyes' (King, n. at 1067-8).

1069   *quiet*: Polymestor 'hears the rustling of drapery as Hecuba's women steal out on to the stage from the tent' (King, n. at 1070).

1076   *hellish Bacchants*: in Euripides' later play, *The Bacchae*, the frenzied followers of the god Bacchus tear animals and a human being to pieces.

      Polymestor's freedom of movement is circumscribed by his need to stay close to his children to prevent the mutilation of their corpses.

1077-8 *a cruel and bloody banquet for the dogs*: these flesh-eating canines of Polymestor's imagination are an ominous prelude to the prophecy, reported by him to Hecuba, that she will be transformed into a dog (1265).

1080-1 *furls its sails*: 'the imagery [in these lines] is both condensed and confused, expressing Polymestor's frenzy' (Collard, n. at 1080-4).

1089   *Aiai*: presumably a cry of pain here. (The word often seems a Greek equivalent for 'alas'.)

1101   *Orion or Sirius*: Orion, a giant huntsman, became a constellation after his death. Sirius—his name means 'scorching'—was the Dog-Star.

1109-11 *For Echo . . . the army*: 'With this stilted and highly artificial language, Agamemnon hides the fact that he is playing a part, pretending to be a disinterested and uninformed spectator and arbitrator in an alien quarrel' (King, n. at 1109-11).

1122   *Did you do this deed*: whatever sympathy the audience may feel with Hecuba's motivation in her treatment of Polymestor, the language of the play is insistent that a *deed* has been *done* (cf. 1038, 1048, 1085, 1169). Indeed, at 1187-8 Hecuba herself insists on the primacy of deeds over words. What she has *done* surely affects the way we now view her. As De Flores chillingly tells Beatrice Joanna (in Thomas Middleton's *The Changeling*,

III.iv.138) after she has led him to commit a murder: 'Y'are the deed's creature.'

1142–4   *Then they would plunder . . . a short while ago*: Thucydides (1.11) tells us that the Greeks at Troy farmed the Chersonese and conducted raids.

1153   *Edonian*: the Edonians were a tribe in western Thrace.

1162   *like octopuses*: I fear that I share Collard's scepticism (n. at 1162) over Verrall's brilliant conjecture. These octopuses, so exactly right for the hands groping on all sides, are a little too good to be true! The manuscripts read 'like enemies'.

1170   *clasps*: these fastened the garments of both men and women at the shoulder. As Collard observes (n. at 1170–1), Oedipus blinds himself with his mother's in one play (Sophocles, *Oedipus the King* 1268 ff.) and his own, as we are told, in another (Euripides, *Phoenissae* 62).

1173   *these murderous dogs*: the dog, the animal into which Hecuba is to be transformed (1265), is being far from sympathetically presented in this play. Cf. n. at 1077–8.

1178   *if any man has spoken ill of women in times gone by*: one example would be Hesiod with his myth of Pandora (*Theogony* 585–612, *Works and Days* 53–82).

1181–2   *neither the earth . . . knows this well*: for this kind of sentiment cf. e.g. Aeschylus, *Choephori* 585 ff. Aristophanes' *Thesmophoriazusae* is based on the assumption that Euripides presents an extremely damaging picture of women in his plays. This is good material for comedy, but does no justice to the tragedian's often highly sympathetic presentation of his female characters.

1185   ⟨*unjustly*⟩: this and the following line are almost certainly interpolated. I have inserted the word 'unjustly' in order to make reasonable sense of them.

1197   *a second ordeal*: i.e. a repetition of the Trojan War (cf. Polymestor's words at 1138 ff.).

1219   *his*: referring to Polydorus.

1230   *that man*: presumably referring to Agamemnon, though possibly to Polydorus (since Agamemnon has not yet adjudicated against Polymestor and shown publicly that he is no friend of his).

1249   *So how can I escape criticism if I judge that you are innocent*: King comments (n. at 1249), 'This is the old Agamemnon again; fear of the criticism of others is his strongest motive.' Cf. Mossman (p. 41); 'When in *Hecuba* Agamemnon acts as judge in the final debate between Hecuba and Polymestor he displays some genuine authority (for example at 1129 ff.), perhaps indeed cuts a more impressive figure here than at any time in the *Iliad*. But as with the Homeric Agamemnon, even when he is acting as admirably as he ever does, we remain aware of serious flaws in his character.'

1254–83   *Isn't this just . . . Stop his mouth*: stichomythia. See Introduction, p. 00. The last line is shared between two speakers.

you have done evil deeds: Hecuba insists that what Polymestor has *done* defines him. Will the audience insist on the same criterion in her case? See n. at 1122.

1261   *masthead*: this is a 'truck', 'an inverted triangular structure receiving the sail ropes' (Collard, n. at 1261).

1265   *You will become a dog with fire-red eyes*: the general consensus among critics is that Hecuba's transformation into a dog is in some way a reflection of the dehumanization she has suffered during the action of the play. (See the notes at 1077–8 and 1173 on dogs in this play.) This is the view of her metamorphosis that Cicero reports, when in a discussion of reactions to bereavements, he points the contrast between Niobe's silent sorrow and Hecuba's grief (*Tusculan Disputations* 3.63.13): 'but they think that Hecuba is imagined as having been changed into a dog on account of a sort of bitterness and frenzy of spirit'. But see n. at 1273 for A. P. Burnett's different view.

1267   *The Thracian prophet Dionysus*: the cult of Dionysus had spread through Thrace. His oracle was near Mount Pangaeon.

1270   *Shall I die . . . there*: this line does not make convincing sense and is probably corrupt.

1273   *Dog's Tomb*: this was the name of a headland on the southern side of the Thracian Chersonese. Anne Pippin Burnett (*Revenge in Attic and Later Tragedy*, California, 1998) writes more fully of this location (Kynossema in Greek) and what she sees as the significance it gives to Hecuba's transformation (pp. 175–6): 'Kynossema is a rough promontory jutting out from the Thracian shore of the Hellespont so as to create a narrow passage that takes a hidden turn. Whether entering or leaving, a ship risked disaster there, and the danger was increased by the powerful current running down from the Bosporus. In daylight the difficulty ahead was recognizable by the doglike shape of the headland, but after nightfall there could be no safety unless the place were marked. Nowadays at Kilid Bahr there are two beacons mounted so as to be read from either direction, and probably bonfires and torches were lit on the same spots by grain merchants even in archaic times. Certainly there was a fire post here in the fifth century, for just before the battle of 411 B.C. the Athenians at Sestos received signals telling them that the Peloponnesian fleet had entered the Propontis (Thuc. 8.102.1), and these could only have been relayed by a fire watch on Kynossema's heights . . . The metaphoric emblem that closes the play is thus not Hecuba as an enraged beast, but Hecuba as a flagrant landmark that saves ships and their crews.

'The geographical Dog's Tomb marked a point where a ship's course had to be changed, and so it was literally a *tekmar* [landmark] for sailors (1273). In a larger sense it was a natural threat transmuted into a warning, its baleful beneficence concentrated in its fire signs, and this was evidently the aspect of the place that attracted Euripides.'

1275–81   *And fate decrees . . . in Argos*: the story, most famously told in Aeschylus' *Agamemnon*, is that Agamemnon took Cassandra back to his home in Argos where his wife Clytemnestra (the daughter of Tyndareus) killed his mistress and hacked him to death in his bath.

1276   *I spit out your words*: the single Greek word translated here simply means 'I spit out'. It denotes a reaction of disgusted rejection. Collard's arresting translation is 'Spit in your face!'

1278   *I pray that the daughter of Tyndareus may never run so mad*: after this line, as J. T. Sheppard remarks, 'Hecuba remains transfixed, in tragic silence'. Why? Sheppard believes that she is appalled by the destiny that awaits her daughter. 'The doctrine of revenge,' he suggests, 'has recoiled on Hecuba herself. In Cassandra's fate, Polymestor will be avenged . . . Agamemnon may bluster, and order the Thracian to a desert island; the Trojan women are marshalled for the voyage to captivity. But we see Hecuba still, hardly human, on the brink of the final transformation, yet human enough to feel the sting of this last, worst grief' (quoted in King, n. at 1278–9).

1289–90   *For I see the winds are here now to escort us home*: the play is strangely silent about the absence of winds that has stalled the action on the Chersonese. See 444-8, 539-40, and 900 (and notes ad locc. and at 111-12). Is it fanciful to believe that the Greek theatre made use of some kind of wind-machine, which could be operated here? The *noise* of such a machine would add dramatic force to the sense of stalled motion starting up again as the characters move off towards their grim futures. It could also suggest—but surely only suggest—actual motion, e.g. of the characters' clothes blowing in the wind, and so justify the expression 'I *see* the winds'. King (n. at 1289-90) writes charmingly: ' "See", because the breeze was fluttering the tents and the plumes of the soldiers' helmets'. But it is hard to imagine how such an effect could be managed on cue in an open-air theatre. A sound effect, on the other hand, could surely be easily contrived and would give a powerful emphasis to the winds which have not loomed large in the play's verbal imagery.

1291-2   *may we discover . . . release from our troubles*: the devastating irony here is underscored by the proximity of these blithely optimistic lines of Agamemnon to Polymestor's horrific prophecy of the future that awaits him (1277-81).

THE TROJAN WOMEN

A note on Alexandros

The Trojan Women was the last play of a trilogy (three plays performed one after the other) by Euripides. The first play was *Alexandros* and the second—of which we know little—was *Palamedes*, which dealt with the conflict between the dastardly Odysseus and Palamedes, the inventor of the art of writing, at Troy. The fact that Euripides chose to revive the old tradition of the dramatic trilogy—the most famous example of which is Aeschylus' *Oresteia* (458 BCE)—must be of some significance, especially since the plays are set respectively before, during, and after the Trojan War, which gives a clear sense of patterning to the project. But before 1971, the extremely fragmentary nature of the surviving passages meant that any attempts at reconstruction were highly speculative. In that year, R. A. Coles made known his work on a papyrus containing a hypothesis (plot summary) of *Alexandros* which had been discovered by Grenfell and Hunt at Oxyrhynchus, in Egypt, in 1905/6 (subsequently published as R. A. Coles, 'A New Oxyrhynchus Papyrus: The Hypothesis of Euripides' *Alexandros*', *BICS* Supplement No. 32 (London, 1974)).

With the caveat that the order of events in the play may well be awry, I give Coles's translation of the papyrus. Hecabe is the Greek name for the Latinized Hecuba.

The *Alexandros*, which begins:

. . . and glorious Ilium.

The hypothesis:

. . . Hecabe [seeing?] visions in her sleep, [Priam?] gave the infant [to a herdsman?] to expose . . . he reared him as his son, calling Alexandros Paris. But Hecabe, in sorrow for that day and at the same time deeming it deserving of honour, bewailed her exposed son, and persuaded Priam to establish . . . games in his honour. After the passing of twenty years, the boy seemed to be [nobler?] in his nature [than?] the herdsman [who had brought him up?], but the other shepherds, on account of the arrogance of his relationship towards them, bound him and brought him before Priam. Questioned in the presence of the ruler, he . . . and caught out (?) each (?) of those who were slandering him, and he was allowed to take part in the games arranged in his honour. They were beaten (?) in the running and in the pentathlon and even in the boxing, and . . . enraged those around Deiphobus who, thinking themselves defeated by a slave, urged Hecabe that she should kill him. When Alexandros appeared, Cassandra in a raving state recognized him and prophesied about what would come to pass, but Hecabe who wished to kill him was prevented. The man who brought him up appearing on the scene because of the danger was compelled to tell the truth. So Hecabe discovered her son . . .

(Reproduced with the kind permission of Dr. R. A. Coles and the Egypt Exploration Society.)

1   s.d.: *Hecuba lies on the ground*: though on stage for the opening scene (the Prologue) between Poseidon and Athena, Hecuba appears to be unaware of their presence.

1–3   *I am Poseidon . . . so gracefully*: Poseidon is the god of the sea and the brother of Zeus (48). The Nereids were sea-deities, the daughters of Nereus and the granddaughters of Oceanus.

4–7   *For since the time . . . my heart*: Zeus had forced Apollo and Poseidon to serve Laomedon, king of Troy, for a year and they had built Troy. Cf. n. at 814. The 'straight rules' are the rules or ruddled lines used by masons. The city walls, punctuated by towers, play an important part in the tragedy. They will collapse before it has ended.

            Euripides makes Poseidon a friend of the Trojans. In Homer's *Iliad* he is their uncompromising enemy.

8   *Argive*: this simply means Greek, as does the word 'Achaean'

in 19. However, when Hera, the queen of the gods, is called Argive in 23, the reference is to her important cult centre in Argos in southern Greece.

9–10   *For through Pallas' . . . Parnassus*: Pallas is Pallas Athena, the pro-Greek (see 65 ff.) goddess of wisdom. Epeius comes from Mount Parnassus in western Phocis.

13–14   *As a result . . . spears of wood*: probably an interpolation, with a somewhat frigid play on words: the Greek for 'wood' and 'spear' is the same.

17   *Zeus the Protector of the Hearth*: the epithet 'Protector of the Hearth' sounds with a savage irony: Zeus, the protector of suppliants, afforded no protection to Priam, the king of Troy, at his altar in Priam's own home. The Roman poet Virgil gives a thrilling account of this episode at *Aeneid* 2.526 ff.

24–5   *Ilium . . . the Phrygians*: Ilium is Troy; the Phrygians, Trojans.

29   *Scamander*: one of the rivers of the plain of Troy, it is called Scamander by men and Xanthus by the gods.

41–2   *As for the virgin . . . mad*: Cassandra rejected Apollo's advances, and he condemned her to possess the gift of prophecy and the frenzy that attended it, but not to be believed (that is, until she prophesied her own death). Thus, though she prophesied truthfully, she was thought to be mad.

67–8   *Why do your feelings . . . dictates*: K. H. Lee (n. at 67–8) notes that 'Poseidon sounds very like a mildly reproachful uncle!'

69–76   *Do you not know . . . on the salt sea*: stichomythia. See p. 116, n. at 242–50. The gods have up till now been addressing each other in pairs of lines. K. H. Lee (n. at 70) writes, 'Is the change to single-line stichomythia significant? Perhaps it reflects an intensifying of the emotional climate.'

70   *It was when Ajax dragged off Cassandra by force*: Ajax, son of Oileus (not the great Ajax), had dragged Cassandra from Athena's altar, where she had sought sanctuary, clutching a wooden image of the goddess.

88–91   *I shall whip up . . . many dead men*: the islands and other places mentioned cover most of the crossing over the Aegean from Troy to Greece. The scale of the damage which Poseidon intends to inflict is emphasized.

The promontories of Caphareus are on the island of Euboea. Here Nauplius, the father of Palamedes, a Greek treacherously murdered at Troy, will light misleading beacons to lure Greek ships to destruction.

102   *Sail*: there is much nautical imagery in Hecuba's lament. S. A. Barlow (n. at 98–152) suggests that this indicates a 'subconscious preoccupation' with 'the fact that the Greek ships are lurking just offshore to take her and the other women away'.

108   *cast down*: the word I have translated 'cast down' in fact continues the nautical imagery. The literal meaning is that the sail of the ancestors' grandeur has been shortened.

126   *the flutes' hated paean*: a paean was often a war song. The Greek refers to pipes, not flutes, but I have used the word 'flutes' to avoid a repetition of the word 'pipes' in 127.

128–9   *hung your Egyptian ropes | from your sterns*: i.e. anchored. The Egyptian papyrus plant was used not only to produce writing material but also to make ropes.

132   *Castor*: one of Helen's brothers. The other was Pollux. The father of all three, as well as of their sister Clytemnestra, was Zeus.

133   *the Eurotas*: the river of Sparta, thus referring to Sparta itself.

169   *the frenzied Cassandra*: see n. at 41–2.

173   *Troy, unhappy Troy, you no longer exist*: Barlow (n. at 173) comments that 'the address to Troy here as a person, with its emphatic repetition, characterises the women's close identification with their city. It is as if Troy is also one of the suffering Trojan women . . . Hecuba mourns Troy's annihilation also at 99, 582, 1292.'

187   *Phthian*: from Phthia in Thessaly in northern Greece.

191   *where, where*: 'the repeated interrogative is intended to imitate the speech of a person who is excited or nervous'—K. H. Lee, n. at 190–3.

192   *like a drone*: as a slave, she will live supported by others. 'There is the further point that . . . she is too old and feeble to be of any use'—K. H. Lee, n. at 190–3.

205   *the sacred waters of Pirene*: the fountain of Pirene was a famous feature of Corinth. Its waters still flow in an elaborate courtyard dating from the second century CE.

       The content of this chorus is very similar to that of the first choral song of *Hecuba* (444–83). See pp. 13–14.

209   *the blessed land of Theseus*: Athens, of which the hero Theseus had been king. H. D. Westlake (*Mnemosyne*, 6 (1953), 181 ff.)

has been followed by others in arguing that by his choice of place names, Euripides is directing his audience towards contemporary events. S. A. Barlow, writing of his references to Athens here and to Sicily in 220-3 (n. on this ode on p.168), remarks judiciously, 'Perhaps Euripides was flattering his audience here, pandering to their pride in their city and to their current interest in Sicily which culminated in the great expedition about to be undertaken in 415 BC, but if so, he has sacrificed dramatic verisimilitude to topical allusions, which in this case are scarcely appropriately contained by their context.'

214   *the holy land of Peneus*: i.e. Thessaly, through which the river Peneus flows. The Thessalian plain lies below Mount Olympus.

220-3   *And I hear that . . . garlands of excellence*: in popular mythology, the craftsman god Hephaestus had his forge below Mount Etna in Sicily—hence this volcano's eruptions. The 'garlands of excellence' are the prizes for Sicilian athletes. Pindar, whose career as a poet ended as Euripides was setting out on his, had celebrated the triumphs of Hiero and other Sicilians in his Victory Odes. It could be that Euripides is paying Pindar a compliment here and that the 'garlands of excellence' refer not only to the actual wreaths awarded to the games-winners but also to the poet's odes in celebration of them.

224-9   *the land . . . a country of fine men*: the land referred to is probably Thurii in southern Italy. The river Crathis, which had dyeing properties, flows into the Tarentine gulf south of Thurii.

231   *a dispenser of fresh news*: the herald Talthybius is introduced with a marked impersonality. However, despite Cassandra's violent denunciation of him at 424-6, he will in fact emerge as a highly sympathetic character, balancing his loyalty to the Greeks and his commitment to self-preservation (304-5) with genuine compassion for the Trojan women.

239   *It was this . . . long ago*: Talthybius speaks in iambic trimeters, the standard metre of Greek tragedy. Hecuba's violent emotion is shown by the fact that she sings in lyric metres right up to her last utterance before Cassandra enters (306-7).

242-3   *Phthian Thessaly . . . Cadmus' land*: Phthia was a country in Thessaly in north-east Greece. 'Cadmus' land' refers to Boeotia as a whole rather than just to Thebes, one of its cities and founded by Cadmus.

249   *King Agamemnon took her. There was no ballot for her*: Agamemnon picked out Cassandra as his special prize.

264   *She has been assigned to Achilles' tomb as an attendant*:
        Poseidon's words at 39-40 alert us to Talthybius' ambiguities
        and evasions in this and his next two lines.

282-8   *The lot has assigned me . . . held dear*: Odysseus is usually
        viewed in a detestable light in Greek tragedy. (The sympathetic
        portrayal in Sophocles' *Ajax* is the exception that proves the
        rule.) The qualities of shrewd inventiveness and deceit that had
        made him so attractive a hero of Homer's *Odyssey* are now
        viewed in a very different way. The indictment of Odysseus will
        have rung out here with especial emphasis since in the lost
        play *Palamedes*, which was performed immediately before *The
        Trojan Women*, his treachery was extremely evident.

292-3   *But which of the Achaeans or Greeks is master of my fortunes*: it
        may be that the distinction is between the inhabitants of
        southern Greece (Achaeans) and those of the north. There is
        pathos in the fact that the rank and file of the Trojan women
        never receive an answer to this question.

310   *Hymenaeus*: the god of marriage. He is also known as Hymen
        (314, 331).

323   *Hecate*: Hecate's functions overlapped with those of Artemis, a
        virgin goddess. She also had sinister chthonic associations.

326   *Euan, euoi*: cries of the frenzied followers of Dionysus, god of
        wine and unfettered emotion. Hesychius tells us that 'euan'
        comes from an Indian word for ivy, a plant which is sacred to
        Bacchus. Cf. 451.

338   *O daughters of the Phrygians | with your lovely dresses*: there is
        pathos in the irony that the Trojan women on stage are
        clothed in rags.

348   *Give me a torch*: presumably Hecuba takes one of Cassandra's
        torches. (She is already holding a stick to support herself (275-6).)

356   *Loxias*: Loxias is a name for Apollo. Two possible etymologies
        for it are 'the Ambiguous' and 'the Speaker'. Both would refer
        to his oracular function.

359   *Yes, for I shall kill him*: Cassandra, of course, will not literally
        kill him, but the fact that Agamemnon brings her back to the
        house where his wife Clytemnestra lives will be one of the lat-
        ter's motives for murdering him.

361-4   *the axe . . . the house of Atreus*: Clytemnestra will hack both
        Agamemnon and Cassandra to death with an axe. His son
        Orestes will take revenge on his mother by killing her, and will
        thus bring fearful pollution on himself.

370-3   *In a hateful cause . . . went willingly*: Agamemnon sacrificed his
          daughter Iphigenia at Aulis to enable the Greek fleet to sail to
          Troy. The Trojan War was fought so that Agamemnon's
          brother Menelaus could get back his wife Helen who had run
          off to Troy with the Trojan prince Paris.

381   *they had brought up their children in vain*: Greek parents would
          hope to be outlived by their children since they felt that their
          death rites could be safely left to them. If the children died first,
          this crucial wish would of course be frustrated.

381-2   *And there is no one . . . earth at their graves*: the blood of the
          sacrificial victim was thought to seep through to the dead.

383   *the praise*: 'i.e. the praise due to men who foolishly left their
          homes and country for the sake of a wanton'—K. H. Lee, n. at
          383.

384   *the shameful deeds*: possibly the murder of Agamemnon and
          herself by Clytemnestra.

422-3   *of a good woman*: Odysseus' wife Penelope was a pattern of
          wifely devotion.

424-6   *What a fine fellow . . . cities*: Cassandra's bitterness here may
          seem disproportionate. S. A. Barlow (n. at 425) writes sensi-
          tively of Talthybius: 'Although unable to comprehend
          Cassandra, Talthybius shows himself to be compassionate
          towards Andromache and Hecuba, and even goes beyond his
          duties later to take upon himself the preparation of Astyanax'
          body for burial (1151-2). One of the interesting things in the
          play is the way this Greek's sympathy for the Trojans grows as
          their suffering accumulates, and this dramatic touch robs the
          play of any crude division of characters into simple black and
          white.' See n. at 231. And cf. *Hecuba*, n. at 507, for the role of
          Talthybius in that play.

430   *by telling the rest*: Hecuba is to meet a bizarre end. She will
          drown at sea, having climbed a mast, turned into a bitch with
          blazing eyes, and then fallen into the water (*Hecuba* 1261 ff.).

433-43   *He will live through . . . troubles there*: this is the earliest sur-
          viving recapitulation of the events of Homer's *Odyssey*. The ref-
          erences to that poem are as follows: Charybdis (12.101 ff., 235
          ff.), Cyclops (9, 12.106 ff.), Circe (set by Euripides in the west-
          ern Mediterranean) (10.233 ff.), shipwreck (5.313 ff.), lotus-
          eaters (9.83 ff.), cattle of the Sun (12.262 ff., 394 ff.), journey
          to the Underworld (of which Hades (442) was king) (11).

435   *has her dwelling, on the rocks of a narrow strait*: something has

gone wrong with the text here. The line before this one seems
to have fallen out. I have inserted two short passages in brackets (see also 438) to help the sense. Apart from the textual dif-
ficulties here, the Greek is extremely compressed and
telegraphic.

444   *But why do I . . . like darts*: the metre for the final 18 lines of
Cassandra's speech changes to trochaic, an effect that
enhances the excitement and intensity of a powerful passage.
We hear no more from her.

446   *you ignoble man*: i.e. Agamemnon.

447   *Danaans*: i.e. Greeks. Danaus is said to have founded the
citadel of Argos.

451   *the god who is dearest to me*: K. H. Lee (note at 451) comments,
'Euripides is describing a very human development in
Cassandra. With the passage of time her antipathy towards the
handsome young god has waned and now . . . she sees things
in a far different light. Her tasks as priestess seem pleasant, and
Apollo, far from being the unwelcome suitor of earlier, has
become ⟨the dearest of gods⟩.'

451-4 *O garlands . . . O lord of prophecy*: as Cassandra flings her head-
bands from her, she gives us an action replay of a memorable
moment in Aeschylus' *Agamemnon* (1254 ff.) when that
dramatist's Cassandra does this just before she goes off to be
killed by Clytemnestra. Cf. 326 and n. The Greek word for 'joyful' (451) is in fact based on the Bacchic cry of ecstasy 'Euoi'
which Cassandra uses in the earlier line.

457   *you will be taking one of three Furies from this land*: the Furies
were terrifying chthonic goddesses who took vengeance especially for crimes against the house. Here Cassandra is saying
that three Furies 'will take vengeance on Agamemnon when
he arrives home . . . And these will be herself, Clytemnestra,
and Aegisthus' (J. Diggle, *Studies on the Text of Euripides*
(Oxford, 1981), 62).

474   *I was of royal blood*: Hecuba was the daughter of either Dymas,
king of Phrygia, or Cisseus, king of Thrace.

480   *and had this hair of mine shorn at their corpses' graves*: a lock of
hair was a customary tribute to the dead. Since the head and
the hair signified strength and life, the cutting of the latter
symbolized submissive grief. It was a *safe* sacrifice by the living
survivor.

504   *though I had many children*: according to Euripides, she had
         fifty children, but this figure is used in mythology simply to
         convey a large number. Homer tells us that she was the
         mother of nineteen of Priam's fifty sons (*Iliad* 24.496).

507–8   *my straw pallet on the ground with its pillow of stone*: presum-
         ably where she had started the play.

510   *Consider no prosperous man to have good fortune—until he is dead*:
         this sentiment finds frequent expression in Greek literature,
         perhaps most famously at Herodotus 1.32.

516–21   *the four-wheeled Wooden Horse . . . crammed with arms*: the
         Wooden Horse, which the Trojans in their delusion rolled into
         Troy on its four wheels, was full of armed Greeks, whose
         weapons clashed inside it. The gods made the Trojans deaf to
         this noise and what it signified. Virgil brings this scene unfor-
         gettably to life at *Aeneid*, 2.234–45.

526   *the Trojan goddess, the daughter of Zeus*: this is Athena, as is
         'the maiden with immortal steeds' of 536.

547–50   *and in the houses . . . for those who slept*: a problematic passage.
         I have followed K. H. Lee (n. at 548–50) in taking it that 'the
         bright light of the fires lit for the celebration produced a half-
         light inside where some were going to sleep'.

551–4   *the maiden daughter of Zeus | who dwells on the mountains*: i.e.
         the virgin Artemis, goddess of hunting (hence 'the mountains',
         a location for the hunt). In the *Iliad*, she takes the side of Troy.

556   *Pergamum*: the citadel of Troy.

561   *it was the maiden Pallas' handiwork*: Pallas Athena had inspired
         Odysseus with the idea of the Trojan Horse, which Epeius then
         built.

565–6   *a garland of victory | in the children they bore it*: we see the child
         of such a union, Neoptolemus' son by Andromache, in her
         name-play (also in this volume).

567   *s.d.*: Astyanax: according to *Iliad* 6.402, this name, meaning
         'lord of the city', was given to Hector's son by the Trojans. (It
         proved grimly ironical, as the action of this play will show.) His
         father called him Scamandrios (see n. at 29).

575–6   *will crown his Phthian temples*: it was standard practice to hang
         up spoils of victory in the temples back at home. Neoptolemus
         came from Phthia, as had his father Achilles before him.

581   *we were your children once*: K. H. Lee comments (n. at 581),

'The structure of this dialogue is effective. With short utterances the speakers cap one another's thoughts and so build up to a climax the picture of their misery and despair.' However, it would certainly be possible to bring out tensions between mother-in-law and daughter-in-law in the playing of this scene. They could be viewed as going beyond the standard 'I am more miserable than you' attitude entirely characteristic of Greek lamentation. Are they constantly needling each other?

588   *Hades*: the king of the Underworld, and hence (by metonymy) the Underworld itself.

597   *when your son eluded death*: Euripides' play about Paris, called *Alexandros*, launched the trilogy of which *The Trojan Women* was the concluding tragedy. *Alexandros* (see pp. 129–30) tells the story of the youthful Paris—unsurprisingly, since the two names refer to the same person—and thus the audience of *The Trojan Women* would be fully alert to the tale that Hecuba, when pregnant with this son, had dreamt that she gave birth to a firebrand which burned down Troy. The firebrand stood for the child to be born. However, he was not killed but exposed on Mount Ida. Here he survived and was brought up by shepherds who gave him the name of Alexandros ('the Protector' or 'the Protected').

618–19 *a second Ajax . . . your daughter*: Cassandra, who had been haled by Ajax from her temple (see n. at 70), is now the victim of Agamemnon, who is thus 'a second Ajax'.

660   *I shall be a slave in the house of a murderer*: Andromache may be thinking of Neoptolemus' impious and brutal killing of her father-in-law Priam. Of more terrifyingly direct relevance to her, however, is the fact that Neoptolemus' father Achilles killed her husband Hector.

673–4 *O my dear Hector . . . courage*: these lines are reminiscent of Homer, *Iliad* 6.429–30:

> Hektor, thus you are father to me, and my honoured mother,
> You are my brother and you it is who are my young husband.   (trans. Lattimore)

But, as S. A. Barlow sensitively observes (n. at 673–4), the nouns Euripides uses 'are abstract and therefore colder and more distant than Homer's simple persons . . . The extreme verbal neatness of 674 ['great in understanding, birth, wealth and courage'] is somehow at the expense of a strong emotional effect achieved in the Homer and just missed here.'

686-7   *I have not yet . . . from hearsay*: there is something bizarre
           about this comment of Hecuba's. After all, the sea is visible
           from Troy. But S. A. Barlow writes illuminatingly of the way
           in which the lines expose Hecuba's subconscious thoughts
           (n. at 686): 'She has never been on a ship before, but
           Euripides depicts her imagination working powerfully as she
           describes her own plight in terms of the thing she fears most—
           ships. These await her and she must face them at the end of
           the play.'

700   *seduce your husband into loving you for the way you behave*:
           Barlow (n. at 700) remarks: 'Hecuba's view is a much more
           pragmatic and practical one throughout than that of her
           daughter or her daughter-in-law.'

702-5   *may bring up this son . . . can still exist*: K. H. Lee (n. at 703-5)
           remarks: 'Hecuba's hopes for the boy Astyanax and his prog-
           eny have been deliberately placed at the end of her speech and
           immediately before the entrance of the herald who announces
           the boy's imminent death. This juxtaposition emphasises the
           pathos of the messenger's words and the tragic situation of
           Troy whose last hope will soon be crushed.'

711   *the Danaans*: see n. at 447.

           the grandsons of Pelops: Agamemnon and Menelaus.

712-25   *What is it? . . . the towers of Troy*: stichomythia, a device spar-
           ingly used in this play. (See p. 116, n. at 242–50.)

721   *Odysseus*: the villain of *Palamedes* (the play performed immedi-
           ately before *The Trojan Women*) is an apt proponent of this bar-
           baric infanticide. But of course Odysseus is right. The Trojans
           hope that Astyanax will survive to rebuild Troy (702–5), an
           eventuality that the Greeks understandably wish to prevent.
           Thus the *Realpolitik* of which Odysseus is the sponsor necessi-
           tates the child's elimination.

740   *my child so extravagantly honoured*: does Andromache here
           look back with a poignantly self-aware wistfulness from the
           catastrophic present to a time when esteem was heaped on
           Astyanax with hyperbolic generosity as the son of Hector? Or
           does she refer, as Lee thinks (n. at 740), 'to the honour paid
           to Astyanax by the Greeks, who regarded him as a foe dan-
           gerous enough to be killed even while a boy'.

747   *Danaans*: see n. at 447.

758   *O the sweet fragrance of your skin*: cf. *Medea*, 1075. S. A.
           Barlow (n. at 758) observes that 'sharp awareness of the

power of the world of the senses underpins Euripides' style in
many centrally dramatic passages'.

764   *O you Greeks, you who have devised atrocities worthy of barbarians*: 'these lines might be said to contain the heart of the play.
It is supposedly civilised Greeks who are really the barbarians,
and the barbarians who are the civilised ones—a slur on the
values on which the Greeks had prided themselves for so
long'—S. A. Barlow, n. at 764.

766   *You daughter of Tyndareus, you were never born from Zeus*: Zeus
coupled with Leda, the wife of Tyndareus, in the form of a
swan. Helen was one of the children that resulted (see n. at
132). Since Andromache is saying that Zeus was not Helen's
father, it is appropriate that she should refer to her as the
daughter of Tyndareus.

772   *With your lovely eyes*: Helen's eyes were the stuff of legend. In
Aeschylus' *Agamemnon* (418-19), Menelaus is described as
gazing into the eye sockets of Helen's statue, regretting their
unreality.

799   *O Telamon, king of Salamis, nurse of bees*: Telamon was king of
Salamis, an island quite close to Athens where tradition has it
that Euripides was born.
      Telamon and Heracles had sacked Troy in the previous gen-
eration. Laomedon, the king of Troy, had cheated Heracles of
the promised reward, the mares given him by Zeus (809-10),
for saving his daughter Hesione from a sea-monster. Heracles
took this revenge.

801   *the holy hill*: the acropolis of Athens.

801-3 *where Athena . . . gleaming Athens*: Athena gave the olive (a
major source of the city's prosperity) to Athens. 'Gleaming' was
an adjective of somewhat vague commendation which was
notoriously applied to Athens. Aristophanes makes his chorus
say in *Acharnians* (639-40): 'And if someone wanted to fawn
on you Athenians and called Athens "gleaming", he could win
anything from you just through that word "gleaming"—when
he's actually lauding you with an honour fit for sardines.'

804-5 *Alcmena's son, | the bowman*: the Greek word here translated
'bowman' conjures up the heroic world.

809-10 *cheated of the mares*: see n. at 799.

810   *Simois*: one of the rivers of Troy. Unlike the other, Scamander
(see n. at 29), it provided anchorage (Aeschylus, *Agamemnon*
696-7).

814   *Phoebus' fine handiwork*: Phoebus Apollo, together with
Poseidon, had built the walls of Troy for Laomedon, who failed
to reward them. In revenge, Poseidon sent the sea-monster
from which Heracles saved Hesione (see notes at 4–7 and
799). Laomedon's breaches of faith augured ill for the future
of the people over whom he ruled.

822   *O son of Laomedon*: Zeus fell in love with the boy Ganymede,
son of Laomedon, and took him up to Olympus to be his cup-
bearer. The argument in this stanza is that Ganymede's services to Zeus have brought no help to Troy, his fatherland.
And—a chilling touch—the cataclysm which has destroyed
that city does not cloud the beautiful face of Zeus' catamite
(835–7).

849   *Day*: i.e. Dawn, who fell in love with Tithonus, another son of
Laomedon (see n. at 822). The god of love (Eros) brought them
together. Like Zeus' liaison with Ganymede, this match was of
no avail to Tithonus' fatherland.

852–3   *though she had . . . to give her children*: Dawn and Tithonus had
the sons Memnon and Emathion.

862–3   *Helen . . . army*: D. L. Page (*Actors' Interpolations in Greek
Tragedy* (Oxford, 1934), 74) considers these lines as 'a pompous
melodramatic interpolation by an actor . . . [who] wishes to
make his identity clear at once, when the audience was no
longer quick to make inferences from allusions'. They are in
any case incoherent as Greek and they contradict 869–70.

884–6   *O you who support . . . intelligence*: the supporter of earth is the
aether; and the dweller on it is Zeus as the inhabitant of temples, with whom the aether is identified elsewhere. The 'necessity imposed by nature' may refer to Heraclitus' belief in the
balance of opposites in nature. Anaxagoras believed that intelligence was ultimately responsible for the universe.

891   *traps*: a Greek word for 'trap' (or 'capture' or 'take'—see notes
at 1114 and 1214) begins with the sound 'hel' and thus plays
on Helen's name. (I have found it impossible to reproduce this
effect in English.) The same Greek word can mean 'destroy',
and that in fact is the usual play on words in Greek where
Helen is concerned. The Elizabethan dramatists seize with an
equal alacrity on the similarity between the words 'Helen' and
'Hell'. Dr Faustus, in Marlowe's play of that name, apostro-
phizes the phantom Helen thus:

     Here will I dwell, for heaven be in these lips,
     And all is dross that is not Helena. (12.86–7)

922   *Alexandros*: the name that the Trojans normally use for Paris,
           the son of King Priam of Troy. Cf. 941–2.

924   *the trio of three goddesses*: Paris, temporarily an oxherd on
           Mount Ida behind Troy, awarded a golden apple as a prize for
           beauty to Aphrodite, goddess of love, who had offered him the
           most beautiful woman in Greece if she won. (This of course
           proved to be Helen.) The two goddesses who lost were Hera
           and Pallas Athena.

929   *Cypris*: another name for Aphrodite, who was born from the
           foam of the sea and eventually came to land at *Cyprus*.

940   *no insignificant goddess*: i.e. Cypris (or Aphrodite), goddess of
           love. See previous note.

948   *the goddess*: i.e. Cypris.

952   *when Alexandros had died*: Alexandros (or Paris) was killed by
           Philoctetes with one of Heracles' poisoned arrows.

959–60   *And that new husband . . . against the Phrygians' will*:
           Deiphobus was Paris' brother and married Helen after his
           death. The Trojans were against this marriage because they
           wanted to give Helen back to the Greeks and put an end to
           the war. There are good reasons for thinking that these two
           lines are spurious.

971–81   *I do not believe . . . stay a virgin*: if Euripides intends us to be
           more sympathetic to Hecuba's arguments than to Helen's, it
           may at first sight seem surprising that he causes her to begin
           by pouring scorn on a myth that, for the purposes of the play,
           is clearly true. However, the rationalizing of myth for the sake
           of argument is thoroughly Euripidean.

986   *Amyclae*: a cult centre of Aphrodite in the Peloponnese on the
           eastern bank of the Eurotas just south of Sparta.

990   *and it is appropriate that the name of the goddess begins with folly*:
           the Greek word used here for folly is **aphrosyne** (cf. Aphrodite).

991–2   *When you looked upon him . . . oriental raiment*: 'Paris's fine
           clothes impressed Helen because the Spartans generally wore
           plain attire and regarded as effeminate dress such as that worn
           by Paris'—K. H. Lee (n. at 991–2)

1000–1   *And young Castor and his brother . . . amid the stars*: Castor and
           Pollux, Helen's semi-divine brothers (see n. at 132), abducted
           the daughters of Leucippus and were pursued by his nephews.
           Castor was killed, and Pollux agreed to share life in Hades with
           him provided they could both be immortal and spend half their

time on Olympus (in heaven). This was granted and they were identified with the constellation which the Romans called Gemini.

However—and this is the point here—at the time of Helen's abduction they were, according to Hecuba, present in Sparta and could have heard Helen if she had shouted out for help (999–1000).

1021   *and wanted the barbarians to prostrate themselves before you*: prostration was an oriental custom (Herodotus 1.119) which Helen would not have experienced before she went to Troy since the Greeks regarded it as degrading.

1023–4   *you have breathed the same air*: I have borrowed S. A. Barlow's translation here. The literal meaning of the Greek is: 'you have looked on the same light'. This is a Greek way of saying that she and Menelaus are both alive rather than dead, and the implication is surely that, unlike her Spartan husband, she has no right to be still in the world of the living.

1034–5   *Rebut the charge of cowardice that the Greeks level at you*: since there is nothing in the rest of the play to suggest that such a charge had been levelled at Menelaus, J. Diggle (*Studies in the Text of Euripides*, 68–70) proposes a small change in the text which would make this an 'appeal to Menelaus to remove from *women* the blame which, because of Helen's conduct, Greece has heaped upon them'. This would give the words of the Chorus much more point and would look forward to 1055–6.

1039   *Let them stone her*: stoning is a form of execution for which the whole community shares the responsibility. Thus Menelaus evades personal initiative.

1042–3   *I beg you . . . the madness of the gods*: Helen 'supplicates' Menelaus, i.e. she kneels before him and touches his knees to make her request. Contact with the body of the person you were supplicating was the important thing, though the knees and the chin were the favoured areas. It was difficult for the person supplicated to refuse the request.

The 'madness of the gods' presumably refers to the participation of Hera, Athena, and Aprodite in the beauty competition and their disastrous promises to Paris.

1050   *Why? Has she put on weight since I saw her last*: this is one of a very small number of jokes in Greek tragedy. It chimes with the crass and foolish superficiality of Menelaus in this play. (He is sympathetically characterized in the *Iliad*.) It is now

generally seen as an attempt by Euripides to convey Menelaus'
evasiveness. See Introduction, p. xii.

1051   *Once a lover, always a lover*: I have borrowed this translation
from S. A. Barlow.

1063   *its sacrificial offerings*: the Greek word here translated refers to
a thick, batter-like fluid made of honey, oil, and meal.

1069   *the end of the land which is struck first by the dawn*: the eastern
boundary between the land and the encircling Ocean. It was
believed that Mount Ida received the beams of light that rose
from the Ocean and gathered them into an orb. This formed
the sun.

1075–6   *holy moon-cakes*: these were flat circular cakes used for sacrificial offerings.

1081–5   *O my love . . . unwashed*: the collective voice of the Chorus speaks
as if each woman was addressing her own husband individually.
    It was believed that the spirits of those whose bodies were
unburied could not find rest in Hades and had simply to wander about. The husbands' dead bodies were 'unwashed'
because there had been no opportunity for their wives to purify
them with lustral water.

1087–8   *the heaven-high Cyclopean walls of stone*: the walls of Mycenae
(just a few miles from Argos and probably the city referred to
here) were built of such huge masses of rough-hewn stone that
it was thought that mere humans could not have constructed
them. The gigantic Cyclopes must therefore have performed the
task. The other city with famously Cyclopean walls was Tiryns,
another place very close to Argos, and another—though less
likely—possibility as the Trojan captives' destination.

1097–9   *or the Isthmian peak . . . has its gateway*: the peak is that of
Acrocorinth which towers over the Isthmus of Corinth with its
two harbours on two separate seas, Cenchreae on the Saronic
Gulf and Lechaeum on the Corinthian Gulf. The Isthmus is at
the north of southern Greece ('the home of Pelops'—hence the
Peloponnese) and can justly be viewed as the gateway to it.

1107–9   *the daughter of Zeus . . . delight*: the daughter of Zeus is Helen.
'The chorus compares its plight with Helen's show of luxury
[cf. 1022–3]. The captives are dressed in rags and are covered
in squalor, their faces are furrowed with tears and torn by
their nails; appearance is of little account to them. Helen, on
the other hand, remains unchanged and is still anxious to pre-
serve her beauty.' K. H. Lee (n. at 1107–9).

1112–13   *the district of Pitane . . . bronze gates*: Pitane was one of the dis-
           tricts of the city of Sparta. Athena had a famous temple on the
           acropolis of Sparta surrounded with bronze plates.

1114   *hellish*: the Greek word that means 'trap' or 'destroy' here
           means 'capture'. See n. at 891.

1127–8   *Apparently . . . from his country*: Euripides appears to have
           invented this story. However, in a passage of great pathos in
           the *Iliad* (24.488–9), Priam tells Achilles that Peleus his father
           is being harried by those who dwell round him, and that, since
           his son is away in Troy, he has no one to protect him.

1151–5   *As I crossed . . . journey home*: S. A. Barlow (n. at 1150 ff.)
           remarks that 'Talthybius has taken the task which would nor-
           mally belong to relatives entirely upon himself—a sign that his
           initial detachment has been changed by observing the suffer-
           ing of these women.' Cf. 709 ff., 736–9, 786–9, 1130–3, and
           notes at 231 and 424–6.

1160–1   *Was it in case he might some day restore our fallen city*: cf.
           703–5 and n. at 721.

1182   *O mother*: Astyanax should, of course, address Hecuba as his
           grandmother, not his mother. There is in fact no single Greek
           word for 'grandmother', and the use of the word 'mother' here
           need not cause us problems. However, J. H. Betts has suggested
           to me that, while she is addressing the body of the infant
           Astyanax, Hecuba is constantly thinking of Hector, and this
           adds a note of poignancy, as well as some confusion, to her
           speech.

1200   *Bring, bring*:   Hecuba is probably speaking to stage extras,
           not to members of the Chorus. The extras bring on the adorn-
           ments at 1207–8.

1209–13   *But you have won . . . pursue them to excess*: 'Euripides seems
           to be criticising the over-emphasis which, in his opinion, his
           countrymen gave to athletics'—K. H. Lee (n. at 1209–13). Lee
           may appear to be confusing playwright and character at this
           point, but perhaps Euripides is putting in Hecuba's mouth an
           obituary defined in Greek terms—the Greeks, as Lee observes,
           were fanatically keen on athletics—and then withdrawing by
           noting that the Phrygians were less enthusiastic about sport.

1214   *Helen has taken*: see n. at 891 for the play on the name Helen.

1216–18   *Ah, ah! . . . in my city*: the Chorus may be referring to Astya-
           nax rather than Hector. The child had not had the opportunity

to become 'a great lord', but he would have done so had he
lived. Alternatively there may be a kind of conflation of the
identities of Hector and Astyanax. K. H. Lee notes here (n. at
1216–17) that the 'members of the chorus can no longer contain their grief and cry out in sobbing dochmiacs', a metre
associated with heightened excitement and emotion.

1223 *this adornment*: i.e. the corpse of his son Astyanax.

1224–5 *the arms of that monster of cleverness, Odysseus*: we have
already heard how much Hecuba hates Odysseus (278–88)
and, of course, it was he who had successfully argued that
Astyanax should be killed (721–5).

 Odysseus was now the proud possessor of the immortal
armour of Achilles which he had won after that hero's
death.

1244–5 *we would vanish . . . in their song*: editors refer to *Iliad* 6.357–8
and *Odyssey* 8.579–80 for the idea that the gods send men sufferings so that they may become the subjects of song. A key
passage in the *Iliad* (22.304–5) is Hector's declaration when
he realizes that his death is imminent: 'Even so, let me not die
ingloriously, without a fight, without some great deed done
that future men will hear of.'

1258 *brandishing*: the word used in the Greek literally means 'row-
ing about'. S. A. Barlow (n. at 1258) asks, 'Might the nautical metaphor here (untranslatable in English) not indicate that
the women still have ships on their minds or at least that the
poet wishes to keep the idea of them constantly in play?'

1264 *start our journey home from Troy with gladness in our hearts*:
there is devastating irony here since we know what Athena
and Poseidon are planning for them on their journey home
(75–94).

1265 *let my single order have two effects*: i.e. (1) that Troy should be
burnt and razed to the ground, and (2) that the women should
go to the ships.

1282 *Come, let us run into the pyre*: in her frenzy Hecuba attempts
to run into the pyre that is burning Troy. Presumably she is
restrained by Talthybius or one of his men.

1285–6 *But take her off . . . into his hands*: it seems as if Talthybius
intends that Hecuba should be dragged off here by Odysseus'
men. In view of the fact that she does not exit till the end of
the play, I take it that the collapse of Troy, however it was con-
veyed in the original performance, makes such an impact on

the soldiers who should have taken her off, that they simply
stand in stunned amazement.

1287   *Otototototoi*: an extreme cry of pain. The Oxford editor has pared
it down from a possible Ottototototoi because 'scribes are prone
to expand exclamations' (J. Diggle, *Studies in the Text of
Euripides*, 106).

1288   *Son of Cronus, lord of Phrygia*: i.e. Zeus—or alternatively
Dardanus, another descendant of Cronus, and the founder of
Troy, now invited to witness its extinction.

1300-1 *Our halls . . . by the enemy's arms*: these lines are bracketed
because they are superfluous to the metrical pattern; in any
case, they seem to relate more to 1297 than to the lines that
immediately precede them.

1305-9 *Yes, and I . . . from the shades below*: Hecuba and the Trojan
women kneel and beat on the ground to attract the attention
of their dead husbands.

1313   *unburied*: Virgil (*Aeneid*, 2.557-8) describes Priam's corpse
with memorable grimness: 'His mighty trunk lay upon the
shore, the head hacked from the shoulders, a corpse without a
name.'

1316   *holy amid unholy slaughter*: the slaughter was holy for Priam
in that it occurred at an altar, but at the same time the savage impiety of the act rendered it unholy.

1326   *an earthquake . . . overwhelms the city*: the Greek word which I
have translated 'overwhelms' is a watery one (= 'swamps' or
'deluges') and to make an earthquake its subject is bold. It is a
classic mixed metaphor. But the use of such a word ties up
with the nautical imagery that is a strong feature of this play.

1326   *s.d.*: *The trumpet sounds*: this sound effect, perhaps the most
memorable in Greek tragedy, is missed by all the editors. It is
prepared for in 1266-8.

1332   *the ships of the Achaeans*: 'the Greek ships have the last word
after all . . . They have bounded the women's thoughts and feelings throughout, recurrent nautical imagery ensuring that they
have never been far out of mind'—S. A. Barlow, n. at 1332.

ANDROMACHE

1   *Thebe*: this town (the name has two syllables) in Mysia (in
modern Turkey) was the birthplace of Andromache. The

Greeks had sacked the city (Homer *Iliad* 1.366–7) and Achilles, the father of Neoptolemus, had killed all Andromache's brothers as well as her father (*Iliad* 6.413–24).

2   *with a lavish dowry of rich gold*: Andromache here reminds the audience of the vast wealth of the East.

4   *bear his child*: in contrast with the present barrenness of the royal family of Phthia: Peleus' son is dead and his wife has left him, while Neoptolemus is married to the infertile Hermione. Ironically, he has had an illegitimate son by Andromache (24, etc.).

14   *islander*: Neoptolemus was born on Scyros. The term 'islander' tended to be used with contempt by mainlanders, to whom islands generally appeared barren and unproductive.

17–19 *Here the sea-goddess Thetis. . .with Peleus*: Thetis was one of the Nereids. These sea-deities, who numbered fifty in most accounts, were the daughters of Nereus and the granddaughters of Oceanus. The goddess could only endure her marriage to a mortal if she was isolated from all other human beings. Even then, the marriage did not last.

23   *he refused to hold the sceptre while the old man was still alive*: some ageing kings in Greek literature have abdicated to make way for their sons and grandsons, e.g. Laertes (Homer, *Odyssey*) and Cadmus (Euripides, *Bacchae*), who have handed over the rule of Ithaca and Thebes to Odysseus and Pentheus respectively.

29   *the Spartan girl Hermione*: Hermione is the only daughter of Menelaus and Helen whose union is now sterile. According to A. R. F. Hyslop (Euripides, *Andromache* (London, 1900), n. at 29), Andromache's words here 'strike the keynote of the play, which is undisguised hatred of the Spartans and the Spartan character'.

32–3   *I am using secret drugs to make her childless and hateful to her husband*: the play offers no support to this conviction of Hermione's. Michael Lloyd (Euripides: *Andromache* (Warminster, 1995), n. at 29–38) observes that 'Hermione herself later envisages the possibility of children (938–42). Her sterility should not be seen as a merely biological problem, unrelated to her more general inadequacy as a wife.'

36   *In fact, I never wanted a relationship with Neoptolemus*: in a later play (*Trojan Women* 665–8) Euripides causes Andromache to express the fear that she might overcome her initial reluctance

to sleep with Neoptolemus, though she expresses contempt for the woman who lets such a thing happen.

46   *the Nereid*: i.e. Thetis (see n. at 17–19).

51   *Loxias*: Loxias is a name for Apollo. It means either 'the Ambiguous' or 'the Speaker'. Both would refer to his oracular function. His most famous cult centre on the Greek mainland was at Delphi, which was said to be situated at the centre of the world.

52   *Pytho*: an old name for Delphi. The first possessor of the oracle here had been Earth and next had come her daughter Themis. A monstrous serpent called the Python, another child of Earth, defended the shrine for his mother and sister (hence the name 'Pytho'). Apollo slew the Python and took possession of the oracle, banishing Themis.

       Euripides appears to have invented the version of the myth of Neoptolemus which makes him go to Delphi on a second visit to make amends for a previous one on which he had madly demanded satisfaction from Phoebus Apollo for killing his father. (See next note.)

53   *for the murder of his father*: Achilles, the father of Neoptolemus, had been killed by an arrow shot into his heel—the only part of his body that was vulnerable—by the Trojan prince Paris but directed to the victim's heel by Apollo, who was the god of archery (among other things).

76   *the man they call your father is still lingering in Delphi*: there is a sense in which most of this play could be justly entitled *Waiting for Neoptolemus*.

79–87 *Is there any news . . . in their need*: stichomythia. See p. 116, n. at 242–50.

85   *You will find no shortage of pretexts. After all, you are a woman*: Lloyd notes judiciously here (n. at 85), "Euripides' plays contain many critical comments about women. Attention should always be paid to speaker and context, but some of these comments, like the present one, still seem somewhat gratuitous." Hyslop's comment here (n. at 95) is a charming demonstration of the confusion that can result when views expressed by a dramatist's creations are attributed to him: 'The unhappiness of [Euripides'] own married life probably gave him some reason for this dislike. The intriguing woman is his *bête noire*.'

100–2 *No mortal . . . goes below*: this sentiment finds frequent expression in Greek literature, perhaps most famously at Herodotus 1.32.

103   *Sings*: Andromache now sings the only lament in elegiac metre in extant Greek tragedy. In this metre hexameter lines alternate with the slightly shorter pentameter lines.

106   *on a thousand ships*: the canonical number of Greek ships that sailed to Troy is a thousand—cf. Christopher Marlowe, *Dr Faustus* 12.81 (FAUSTUS of Helen: Was this the face that launched a thousand ships . . . ?). The *Iliad* gives the number as 1,186 while Thucydides rounds it up to 1,200.

107–8   *whom the son of the sea-goddess Thetis . . . around our walls*: in *Iliad* 22, after killing Hector, Achilles, the son of Thetis, cuts through his heels, puts ox-hide straps through the holes, and ties him to his chariot so that his head will be dragged in the dust. Homer does not specifically tell us that he drags him round the city, around which he had chased him three times before killing him, though he does inform us that he drags him round Patroclus' pyre-tomb (24.16). (Virgil follows Euripides' version at *Aeneid* 1.483.)

109–10   *I myself . . . over my head*: M. Lloyd (n. at 109–10) notes: 'Paris' bad marriage destroyed Andromache's good one. He brought Helen into the bedroom as a bride (104), with the result that Andromache departed from her own bedroom (112) leaving her husband as a corpse (107, 112). She put slavery around her head like a bridal veil. On Andromache's departure from Troy as a perverted bridal journey, see R. Seaford, *JHS* 107 (1987) 129 f.'

112   *my husband in the dust*: at the end of the *Iliad*, Hector's corpse is in fact granted due burial after Achilles has given the body back to his father Priam.

116   *like a trickle dripping from the rocks*: is there a reminiscence here of Niobe who was turned into a stone which always streamed with tears for her children?

121   *find*: the Greek word here is 'cut'. Perhaps, as P. T. Stevens suggests (Euripides, *Andromache* (Oxford, 1971), n. at 121), 'the reference is to the cutting of herbs or roots for medicinal purposes'.

145   *the child of Zeus' daughter*: i.e. Hermione, daughter of Helen, herself the daughter of Zeus by Leda.

146   *s.d.*: 'There is a striking visual contrast between Andromache, whose status as a slave would have been manifest in her costume, and the gorgeously attired Hermione' (M. Lloyd, n. at 147–273).

156–8   *it is your wish . . . in barrenness*: cf. 32–5.

166   *sweep my house*: the reduction of royalty to the base task of sweeping is a commonplace in Euripides. In this volume, see *Hecuba* 363.

167   *the water of Achelous*: the river Achelous in western Greece, the largest of the Greek rivers, is used, as often, by metonymy for water. Hyslop (n. at 167) quotes Lovelace, *To Althea, From Prison*:

> When flowing cups run swiftly round
> With no allaying *Thames*.

170–6   *You have fallen . . . of these things*: Lloyd (n. at 170–6) writes that Hermione's 'chauvinism is undercut both by the manifest nobility of Andromache and by the fact that the crimes which she condemns as typically barbarian are regularly committed by mythical Greeks (e.g. Orestes, Hermione's former suitor and future husband)'.

200   *encumbrance*: the metaphor is from a small boat which is towed after a larger one. It may be that the word 'encumbrance' overloads the metaphor. The reference could simply be to a mother with her haulage of children.

216–17   *one man shares his bed with many women in turn*: Herodotus (5.5) says of the Thracians that 'each has many wives'.

220–1   *Admittedly we women . . . than men*: the prophet Teiresias, who had had experience of life both as a man and a woman, said that women gain nine times as much pleasure as men from sexual intercourse.

222–3   *For my part . . . for your sake*: there is evidence later than Euripides for other children of Hector, but even so the picture Andromache here gives of her relationship with her husband seems very surprising indeed. Lloyd (n. at 222–8) thinks that it is 'probably an *ad hoc* invention'.

229   *your mother*: the adulterous Helen.

236–60   *The arguments on which . . . She will come after you*: stichomythia. See p. 116, n. at 242–50.

257   *I shall use fire against you*: this threat proves effective at *Heracles* 240–4. Contact with a holy place should have granted a suppliant protection, but ancient history contains examples of such sanctuary being violated by both Spartans and Athenians. Herodotus (6.80), for example, tells how the Spartan king Cleomenes I (reigned *c.*520–490 BCE) used fire to

burn several thousand Argive survivors to death in a sacred grove. (Though tried for impiety at Sparta, he was acquitted.)

If Andromache can be dislodged from Thetis' shrine, she becomes vulnerable. In Athens in the mid-sixth century BCE, Cylon and his fellow conspirators took sanctuary in Athena's temple, and when they left the temple to stand trial they attached a braided thread to the image of the goddess and carried it with them, thus demonstrating their reliance on literal contact with the divine. The thread broke, and the archons (the city officials), claiming that this showed that Athena was refusing Cylon and his followers the rights of suppliants, slaughtered almost all of them. As a result the archons were called polluted men (Plutarch, *Solon* 12.1–2).

Supplication is discussed in an important and illuminating article called 'Hiketeia' by John Gould (*JHS* (1973), 74–103).

266–7   *even if molten lead were to hold you fast*: melted lead was poured into a hollow in the plinth of a statue to fix it in position.

270   *some god*: i.e. Apollo, the god of healing.

274   *Ida*: the mountain range behind Troy.

275–6   *the son of Zeus and Maia*: Hermes, the god who communicates between gods and mortals.

277–8   *leading the lovely trio | of goddesses*: literally, 'leading the fair-yoked triple team of goddesses'. The goddesses Hera, Athena, and Aphrodite came to Paris on Mount Ida to be judged by him in a beauty competition.

287–92   *outdoing one another . . . the citadel of Troy*: Hera offered Paris kingship, Athena military power, and Aphrodite (= Cypris (289) because the newly-born goddess emerged from the sea on Cyprus) Helen. Their words were malignant and deceptive presumably because they took no thought for their consequences. Paris' choice of Aphrodite and his subsequent abduction of Helen brought ruin on Troy.

293–7   *If only his mother . . . to kill him*: when pregnant with Paris, Hecuba had dreamt that she gave birth to a firebrand which burned down Troy. The prophetess Cassandra, warning that the firebrand stood for the child about to be born, urged that he should be killed. Hecuba, however, could not bring herself to kill him but exposed him on Mount Ida. Here he survived and was brought up by shepherds.

rejected him, casting him over her head: a polluted object could be got rid of by throwing it behind one's back.

by the oracular bay-tree: the bay was Apollo's tree and doubt-less grew by his temple at Troy. Cassandra was his prophetess.

300   *the elders*: 'the elders of the people were sitting by the Skaian gates with Priam . . . Old age had put an end to their warfare, but they were excellent men of words' (Homer, *Iliad* 3.146–51; translated by Martin Hammond).

306   *wandered*: T. C. W. Stinton (*Euripides and the Judgement of Paris* (London, 1965), 22) comments on the use of this word here: 'the brilliant heroic exploits of the Trojan War shrink in the end, like Stendhal's Waterloo, to the aimless toing and froing of bewildered patrols'. The word thus 'deflates the pomp of martial manoeuvres'.

369   *more important to him than taking Troy*: this is probably a pro-verbial expression. As Lloyd points out (n. at 368–9), 'Menelaus himself actually did take Troy, and the result of [his language here] is to subordinate his own greatest achievement to success in a domestic dispute.'

374–5   *As for slaves . . . members of my family*: Menelaus is of course referring to Andromache when he talks of slaves and to Hermione when he speaks of members of his family.

399–400   *I saw the butchered Hector dragged behind the chariot*: see n. at 107–8. The Greek of 399–400 could be taken to mean that Hector died by being dragged behind Achilles' chariot. If this is the meaning, Euripides is probably treading in the footsteps of Sophocles (*Ajax* 1030–1). My translation follows the *Iliad*—though not 8–9 of this play—in assuming that Andromache did not witness the killing of her husband. According to Homer (*Iliad* 22. 440–72), she had been at home weaving and getting her maids to prepare a hot bath for Hector's return when the sound of lamentation reached her. 'She rushed out of the house like a woman in a frenzy, her heart jumping. . . . When she came to the tower and the crowd of men gathered there, she stood on the wall and stared out, and saw him being dragged in front of the city, and fast horses pulling him ruth-lessly away to the hollow ships of the Achaians. Black night covered her eyes, and she swooned backwards, and her spirit breathed out of her. And she flung away from her head her shining headdress, the frontlet and the cap, the woven hair-band, and the mantle that golden Aphrodite had given her on the day when Hektor of the glinting helmet led her as his wife from Eëtion's house, when he had given a countless bride-price for her' (translated by Martin Hammond).

419–20   *Those who have no children . . . an unhappy fortune*: these words
         contrast with those of the Chorus in *Medea* (1090–3): 'And I
         say that those of mortals who have not had children and have
         no knowledge of this, none at all, win greater happiness than
         those who are parents.'

427   *I have you in my grasp*: the metaphor is from wrestling.

431–2   *As for the fate of this child . . . to kill him*: G. Norwood (*The
         Andromache of Euripides* (London, 1906), ad loc.) writes, 'An
         excellent example of the way in which official cruelty veils itself
         under a pretence of legality . . . Menelaus . . . tries to trump
         up some theory that he has a right to one life and Hermione a
         right to the other.'
              Menelaus' refusal to guarantee the life of Andromache's son
         despite his earlier assurances (315–17, 381) is contemptible,
         especially in view of his deceitful exploitation of the rules of
         sanctuary (see n. at 257).

435–44   *O my sorrow . . . awaits him*: stichomythia. See p. 116, n. at
         242–50.

437   *Eurotas*: the river which flowed through Sparta.

441   *What, and this nestling too, snatching him from under my wings*:
         presumably when she left the altar Andromache rushed to
         embrace her son whom she has been clasping ever since.

445–9   *O you inhabitants of Sparta . . . involved and tortuous*:
         Andromache's anti-Spartan outburst is altogether justified by
         her treatment at the hands of Hermione and Menelaus (see n.
         at 431–2). There is the further point that the play was probably
         written in the first phase of the Peloponnesian War which
         Athens and her allies fought with Sparta and hers, and it is
         extremely likely that Euripides will have seized the easy oppor-
         tunity to play on his Athenian audience's hatred of their lead-
         ing enemies. Commentators refer to various war crimes
         committed by the Spartans (e.g. Stevens n. at 445–53: 'Here
         the objective narrative of Thucydides indicates some basis of fact
         for Athenian accusations, e.g. the treacherous slaughter of two
         thousand helots in 424 (Thuc. 4.80); the massacre of the
         Plataean prisoners in 427 (Thuc. 3.68.1); the betrayal of Scione
         (Thuc. 5.18.7)'). However, as far as the matter of sanctuary, the
         main point at issue here, is concerned, as Gould notes (art. cit.
         74), 'two cases of a breach of the rights of suppliants [one by
         Athenians, the other by Spartans] played a dominant role in the
         diplomatic propaganda of the Spartans and Athenians on the
         eve of the Peloponnesian War' (see n. at 257). Neither side was

guiltless of violating divine law and human decency.

453   *My curse upon you*: I have taken this as Andromache's curse
        on all Spartans, but she could be narrowing and intensifying
        her hatred here to aim it specifically at Menelaus and
        Hermione.

456-7   *my famous husband . . . on land*: Andromache here asserts that
        Hector's assaults on the Greek ships had proved so fierce that
        they had frequently driven the cowardly Menelaus to take to
        his ship in flight. While in the *Iliad* Hector did drive the Greeks
        in among their ships (15.653) and was undoubtedly a greater
        warrior than Menelaus (7.104–5), Andromache is speaking
        with extreme rhetorical exaggeration.

458   *a grim-faced warrior*: Spartans traditionally scowled (see e.g.
        Plutarch, *Phocion* 10).

471-4   *In cities too . . . than one*: it is hard not to see an allusion here
        to the dual kingship of Sparta.

476   *When two craftsmen create a song*: a running joke in
        Aristophanes' *Frogs* (944, 1408, 1452 f.) suggests that there
        is a possibility that Euripides himself collaborated with a cer-
        tain Cephisophon.

504   BOY: according to tradition (and the list of characters in the
        manuscripts), the name of this child was Molottos. But his
        name is not given in the text of the play, and it seems prudent
        to keep him anonymous.

504-5   *Mother, mother . . . your wing*: editors like to quote Macduff's
        description of his murdered children as 'all my pretty chickens'
        (Shakespeare, *Macbeth* IV.iii.218). Cf. the word 'nestling' at
        441.
            G. M. Grube (*The Drama of Euripides* (London, 1961), 136)
        remarks that 'the boy is far too much a miniature adult'. A.
        M. Dale is perhaps nearer the mark when she observes
        (Euripides, *Alcestis* (Oxford, 1954), 85) that 'the child sings the
        sentiments its elders feel for it'.
            'Children in tragedy are pathetic victims, whose role is to be
        threatened, killed, or orphaned. Andromache's son, onstage
        throughout the third and fourth acts, is not only important to
        the plot but also embodies a central theme of the play. He will
        survive to unite the royal houses of Troy and Phthia'—Lloyd,
        n. at 501–44.

518-19 *my child Hermione | does away with your child here*: Menelaus
        has left the choice of whether the boy should live or die to

Hermione (431–2, 442). Both her father and Andromache had felt it likely that she would make the brutal choice (443–4)—they know her well—and she has done so. She is no innocent.

530   *O my friend*: according to Stevens (n. at 530–1), these words are 'euphemistic and propitiatory'.

533–4   *dripping like a spring . . . from some smooth crag*: cf. 116, perhaps again with a reference to Niobe, 'all tears'. Compare Homer, *Iliad* 16.2–4: 'Patroklos came up to Achilleus, shepherd of the people, letting his warm tears fall like a spring of black water, which trickles its dark stream down a sheer rock's face' (translated by Martin Hammond).

537–8   *You may as well . . . with your prayers*: see n. at 533–4. Later in *Iliad* 16 (33–5) Patroclus says to Achilles that 'your father was not Peleus the horseman, or Thetis your mother—it was the grey sea that spawned you, or the stark cliffs, such is the hardness of your heart' (translated by Martin Hammond). Cf. Euripides, *Medea* 28.

546   *his old age*: the old age of Peleus is repeatedly insisted on.

568   *those away from home*: i.e. Neoptolemus, and possibly Peleus.

573–4   *it is not possible for me to touch your beloved chin with my hand*: Stevens (n. at 573) comments: 'a pathetic touch; Andromache holds up her fettered wrists to show that she cannot perform the usual act of supplication.' My own reading of this poignant parenthesis is that the fallen Andromache can touch Peleus' knees with her bound hands, but she certainly cannot reach his chin.

589   *You'll see!*: this splendid translation is taken from Lloyd.

593   *when you left . . . without locks*: at *Trojan Women* 943–4 it is said that Menelaus sailed off to Crete leaving Helen with Paris and his retinue.

595–6   *Spartan girls could not be chaste even if they wanted*: Spartan girls did participate in athletics and wore dresses that revealed their thighs.

611   *many souls*: this is a clear reference to line 3 of Homer's *Iliad*, which begins (1–4): 'Sing, goddess, of the anger of Achilleus, son of Peleus, the accursed anger which brought uncounted anguish on the Achaians and hurled down to Hades many mighty souls of heroes . . .' (translated by Martin Hammond). Euripides wryly inverts the traditional view that it was Helen and Paris—rather than Menelaus—that caused the destructive Trojan War.

616   *without a single wound*: in the *Iliad* (4.139–40) Menelaus is in fact wounded by Patroclus.

621   *daughter*: literally 'filly'. Does the animal metaphor denote contempt in this context? The daughter is, of course, Hermione, the child of Helen by Menelaus.

624–5   *how outrageously . . . cut his daughter's throat*: before the Trojan War, Menelaus' brother Agamemnon sacrificed his daughter Iphigenia to create the weather conditions that would allow his fleet to sail to Troy. In one of his last plays, *Iphigenia at Aulis*, Euripides shows Menelaus putting considerable pressure on Agamemnon to kill the girl, though he later relents.

628   *you did not kill your wife . . . grasp*: Euripides later staged this episode in his *Trojan Women* 860 ff.

629   *you dropped your sword*: two fine Attic vases illustrate this scene. One of them, which is in the Toledo Museum of Art in Ohio and dates from about 440 BCE, makes the details of the story very clear. Susan Woodford (*The Trojan War in Art* (Duckworth, 1993), 112) describes it thus: 'Helen, terrified of her angry husband, has rushed to the sanctuary of an altar. Her clothes have become disordered and her beautiful body is partially revealed. Menelaus is overcome and drops the sword . . . This is unmistakably the work of Aphrodite.' The other, by the Altamura Painter, dating from 475–450 BCE (in the British Museum), shows Helen holding up her skirt as she flees to the right. Menelaus is at the centre of the vase, his sword falling from his hand.

636   *three times a bastard*: 'three times' probably simply intensifes the idea of bastardy. Cf. *Hamlet* III.ii.326: 'We shall obey, were she ten times our mother.'

647   *a famous father*: i.e. Aeacus, son of Zeus and Aegina.

650–1   *beyond the waters of the Nile, beyond the Phasis*: Phasis was a river in Colchis to the east of the Black Sea into which it flowed. Menelaus is here referring to the southern and north-eastern limits of the world.

668–77 *And now consider . . . help my own*: these feeble and not altogether coherent lines were thought by D. L. Page (*Actors' Interpolations* (Oxford, 1934), 65) to be 'an expansive interpolation, probably histrionic, specially written for this passage'.

682   *though they knew nothing of arms and warfare*: Thucyides tells us (1.3. 1) that the Trojan War was the first common enterprise of Greece. Even so, the sentiment sounds absurd on Menelaus' lips.

687   *Phocus*: together with his brother Telamon, Peleus had killed
           their half-brother Phocus, the son of Aeacus by the nymph
           Psamathe.

706   *Paris of Mount Ida*: a reference to the judgement of Paris on
           Mount Ida, where the prince adjudicated the beauty competi-
           tion that led to the Trojan War. See notes at 277–8 and
           287–92.

711   *girl*: the Greek word which I have translated by 'girl' in fact
           means 'heifer'. Cf. n. at 621.

717   *Up with you! For despite my trembling*: Andromache has pre-
           sumably been on her knees since 572. Peleus trembles not in
           fear but because of his old age.

724–6   *Except for . . . than anyone else*: Thucydides (1.70) puts into the
           mouths of a Corinthian delegation a devastating comparison
           between the innovatory, quicksilver dynamism of the
           Athenians and the sluggish and dilatory ultra-conservativism
           of the Spartans.

733–5   *There is a city . . . agressively towards us*: Lloyd (n. at 733–6)
           observes that 'since this is a feeble *ad hoc* excuse . . . it is idle
           to speculate about the identity of this city. Menelaus makes a
           veiled threat: Peleus also is a former friend who is now hos-
           tile.' Even so, since it is probable that Athens was fighting a
           war with Sparta when the play was first performed, the lines
           may well have carried a piquant charge. The original audience
           may have wondered whether the city Menelaus was going off
           to sort out was Athens itself.
              'Collapse of Stout Party' would seem an apt comment on the
           Menelaus of this speech.

754–5   *when they realize . . . this boy is*: they clearly will be without
           an escort.

760   *our cavalry*: the Thessalians were famous for their cavalry.

761   *I'm not the dodderer you think I am*: Lloyd (n. at 761) observes
           that 'Peleus has temporarily cast off his old age, but he will soon
           be reduced to even greater decrepitude (cf. 1076–8, 1225 etc.)'.

773   *who are proclaimed as the sons of goodly houses*: a reference to
           the custom of the announcing by heralds of the name and lin-
           eage of the victors at the games.

774–5   *Time does not . . . leave behind them*: Hyslop quotes the opposite
           statement from Shakespeare's *Julius Caesar* (III.ii.80–1):
              The evil that men do lives after them:
              The good is oft interred with their bones.

790   *you ancient son of Aeacus*: i.e. Peleus.

791-801   *you joined with the Lapiths . . . came back to Europe*: the chorus
           describes three of the great events of Peleus' life: the Lapiths, a
           Thessalian tribe, fought the Centaurs (creatures half-man, half-
           horse) when the latter got drunk at the wedding of Pirithous,
           one of them even trying to rape the bride; Peleus sailed with
           Jason on the Argo through the Clashing Rocks which guard the
           Black Sea (when the Argo avoided being crushed by them, they
           ceased to move) in order to win the Golden Fleece from the land
           of Colchis on the eastern side of that sea; the son of Zeus referred
           to is Heracles, who sacked Troy in an attack antedating
           Agamemnon's which the hero undertook because Laomedon,
           king of Troy, had failed to reward him for rescuing his daugh-
           ter Hesione from a sea-monster.

817   *You go inside the palace*: there is something teasing about this
           invitation since it would violate the conventions of Greek
           tragedy if the Chorus actually did go into the stage building.
           Euripides may be aiming at an effect of dislocation.

825-65   *O my agony . . . the first ship ever built*: while Hermione sings
           in dochmiacs, the most agitated and unnerving of Greek
           metres, the Nurse sticks to less emotional iambics, the pre-
           dominant metre of Greek tragedy and an equivalent of English
           blank verse.

831   *my finely woven veil*: the Greek word which I have translated
           'veil' usually means 'cloak'. I have taken Stevens's suggestion
           (n. at 831) that it is 'a kind of veil covering head and shoul-
           ders'.

833   *Why must I cover my breasts with my robes?*: Lloyd (n. at 833)
           asks us to 'contrast Hermione's first entrance, when her gor-
           geous costume expressed her sense of her own status (148)'.
           We cannot be sure how the male actor playing Hermione
           would have conveyed the exposure of her breasts.

843   *my friend*: the Greek makes it clear that this is not the Nurse
           but a male attendant.

847   *the fire's welcome flame*: presumably Zeus' thunderbolt.

854-5   *You have abandoned me . . . to save me*: Hermione sees herself
           as someone stranded on the coast with no ship to take her
           away. Contrast the nautical image with which Peleus
           addresses Andromache at 748-9. This vein of imagery is very
           common in Greek tragedy. Cf. 891.

863-4   *where the ship . . . the dark blue cliffs*: this refers to the voyage of the Argo. The 'dark-blue cliffs' are the Symplegades. See n. at 791–801.

881–2   *You foreign women . . . the son of Achilles dwells*: Stevens (n. at 882) writes, 'The fullness of expression strikes a note of stateliness and formality.'

885–6   *the oracle of Zeus at Dodona*: this, the oldest oracle in Greece, is in Epirus. It was believed that the god gave his responses through the rustling of the leaves of oak trees.

887–9   *it seems a good idea . . . alive and well*: 'This pretence that he is paying a casual call on Hermione and his questions in 901, 907 are shown by Orestes himself in 959–63 to be mere subterfuge, presumably adopted to avoid committing himself too soon' (Stevens, n. at 887–9).

892   *by these your knees*: as Lloyd remarks (n. at 891–5), 'Hermione's supplication of Orestes is a mirror scene of Andromache's supplication of Peleus' (cf. 572–6).

894–5   *Suppliant branches . . . touch your knees*: Hermione does not have an olive branch wreathed in wool, a frequent emblem of supplication. She hopes that her arms will prove as effective.

898–9   *Yes, the only child . . . in his house*: while Helen bore Hermione to Menelaus, it is interesting that her marriage to Paris proved infertile.

906–19   *Yes, that is precisely . . . afraid of your husband*: stichomythia. See p. 116, n. at 242–50.

908   *Yes, the captive woman who shared Hector's bed*: 'Hermione uses the disparaging term ["captive"] of her rival (cf. 155 and 932), and deliberately stresses her relationship with Hector' (Stevens, n. at 908).

914   *the old man . . . the inferior side*: Hermione lays stress on the weakness of the slave Andromache and implies that old Peleus showed considerable folly in supporting her. (See Stevens' n. at 914.)

919   *I understand*: Lloyd (n. at 919) observes that a stichomythia of this type 'normally culminates in an expression of sympathetic understanding by the interrogator'.

921   *Zeus, protector of kindred*: Orestes and Hermione are first cousins.

930   *It was the visits of bad women that proved my undoing*: Stevens (n. at 930) quotes Norwood: 'Hermione speaks as an ordinary Athenian wife of the poet's own day, not as a princess of an earlier age'.

934 *By Hera the queen*: this was a woman's oath, and it is particularly suitable here since Hera was the goddess of marriage.

936 *these Siren words*: the reference is to the Sirens, the mythical bird-women who lured sailors to their death on a rocky coast by their overwhelmingly beautiful singing. The story of how Odysseus sailed by them unscathed is told at Homer, *Odyssey* 12.158–200.

938–41 *After all . . . have been legitimate*: Stevens points out (n. at 938 ff.) that this 'is inconsistent with 32–5 and 156–8, where the charge against Andromache was that she had by magic arts made Hermione barren with the object of alienating Neoptolemus and ousting Hermione from her position, presumably with some chance of success'.

947 *to destroy a marriage in hope of gain*: Lloyd (n. at 947) suggests that the motive for destroying the marriage will be to earn bribes from a lover.

950 *so keep a good guard*: in an admirable note (at 950–3), Lloyd remarks: 'Hermione addresses husbands in general. She has now abandoned her earlier independence, and accepts Andromache's belief that women are inferior to men (220 f., 353 f.) and should be controlled by them. Neoptolemus failed to exercise appropriate control over her, just as Menelaus left his wife (Hermione's mother) unguarded (593).' Compare 622–3 where Peleus addresses suitors in general.

957–8 *It was a wise fellow . . . from the opposing side*: Stevens suggests (n. at 958) that Orestes means that he has listened to tales coming from the household of his enemy Neoptolemus.

972 *I forgave your father*: since it had been prophesied that Troy could only be taken with Neoptolemus' participation, Orestes may have understood how important it was for Menelaus to win him over.

976–8 *because of the exile . . . with the bloodshot eyes*: Orestes had killed his mother in revenge for her murder of Agamemnon, her husband and his father. This act of matricide raised up the Furies, the appalling goddesses who embody conscience and who have the bloodshot eyes, as editors suggest, of the victim whose madness they cause.

982 *this reversal*: Aristotle identifies 'reversal' (*peripeteia*—*Poetics* 1452[a–b]) as a key element in Greek tragedy. The use of this word is particularly appropriate in a play that contains as many reversals as *Andromache*.

998   *the rock of Delphi*: Delphi is perched on the side of a gorge and
           above it tower the massive rocks called the Phaedriades.
           Orestes' words (Hyslop, n. at 998) 'indicate a plot to murder
           Neoptolemus at Delphi'. See the Messenger's information at
           1074 ff.

1002–4   *His demand . . . makes amends to the god*: it is clear from 50–5
           and 1106–8 that Neoptolemus went on a first visit to Delphi
           to demand satisfaction from Apollo (see n. at 53), but has
           thought better of it and is now paying a second visit to propi-
           tiate the god.

1005–6   *he will die a grim death thanks to that god and my slanders*: does
           the silent Hermione show any physical reaction to these men-
           acing words about her husband? This is a matter for the direc-
           tor, who, in Euripides' time, would have been the dramatist
           himself.
              For Orestes' slanders, see 1090–5.

1008   *s.d.*: does Orestes participate in the murder of Neoptolemus
           after taking Hermione to Sparta, or does he leave the killing to
           others? While he is certainly present at Delphi, the evidence
           offered by the play for his actual involvement is inconclusive.

1009–11   *O Phoebus . . . and Poseidon*: Phoebus (Apollo) and Poseidon
           conspired with Hera and Athena to bind Zeus in chains and
           hang him in the sky. The plot failed, and Zeus forced Phoebus
           and Poseidon to build the walls of Troy for its king Laomedon,
           who later refused to pay them for their work.

1011   *blue-grey*: this colour is associated with the sea.

1014–17   *why did you give . . . of the spear*: since Laomedon had refused
           to pay Apollo and Poseidon for building the walls, the surpris-
           ing thing is that Apollo favoured the Trojans at all (Homer,
           Iliad 21.450 ff.).

1018   *Simois*: Simois and Scamander were the two rivers of Troy's
           plain.

1021   *no garland was the prize*: Homer makes this contrast between
           the world of athletics and that of war when he speaks of
           Achilles chasing Hector round the walls of Troy: 'it was no
           sacrificial beast or ox-hide shield they were competing for . . .
           but they were running for the life of Hector the tamer of
           horses' (*Iliad* 22.158–61; translated by Martin Hammond).

1028–30   *killed by his wife's trickery . . . her children's hands*:
           Agamemnon's wife Clytemnestra had killed her husband on

his return from Troy. According to Euripides' *Electra* (1225), their children, Orestes and Electra, both held the sword that killed her in their revenge for this murder.

1034   *the sanctuary*: i.e. of Apollo at Delphi, where the god ordered Orestes to kill his mother.

1036   *O divine Phoebus, how am I to believe this*: for this kind of indignant exclamation against the role of Apollo, cf. *Electra* 1245-6 and *Orestes* 28-30.

1037-41 *Many a groan . . . with another man*: these lines are something of a cliché (cf. e.g. *Hecuba* 650-4) to convey the effect of war back home.

1041   *you*: presumably the Chorus is referring to Andromache. Lloyd (n. at 1041) is one of the editors who raises the possibility that it may refer to Hermione, who has left her home with a new 'husband' (989, 991, 1049) just as Andromache had been 'remarried' to Neoptolemus.

1046   *s.d.*: there is a possibility that Andromache and her son come onto the stage with Peleus. Cf. n. at 1043. 'If so,' Stevens remarks (n. at 1047-288), 'no doubt even her silent presence during the closing scenes would help to give unity to the play, though only of a rather formal kind.' Cf. n. at 1246.

1051   *those who are away*: Peleus must be referring to Neoptolemus.

1053-65 *What was she afraid of . . . in co-operation with Delphians*: stichomythia. See p. 116, n. at 242-50.

1065   *Loxias*: a name for Apollo. It means either 'the Ambiguous' or 'the Speaker'. Both would refer to his oracular function.

1079-80 *if you really want to help your friends*: presumably by avenging Neoptolemus and looking after Andromache.

1088   *this awoke suspicions*: in a helpful note (at 1088), Lloyd remarks, 'Sight-seeing was presumably common enough at Delphi, but in view of his previous record (51-3, 1106-7) Neoptolemus was perhaps inviting suspicion if he spent three days at Delphi without informing the authorities of his desire to propitiate Apollo.'

1098   *unofficially*: i.e. without waiting for the decision of the authorities.

1100-1   *our sheep reared on the foliage of Parnassus*: provision of animals for sacrifice was perhaps a profitable line for local inhabitants (Stevens, n. at 1100).

1102   *the altar*: Euripides may have had the Altar of Chios in mind.
        For a summary of the problems relating to the geography of
        the last moments of Neoptolemus, see Lloyd, n. at 1100–57.
        The basic question is whether all the action after 1111 takes
        place inside the temple, or does Orestes leave the temple at
        1123 and re-enter at 1140?

1103   *the consuls*: these officials acted on behalf of visitors, enabling
        them to approach the oracle.

1108   *my father's death*: for the circumstances which caused
        Neoptolemus to blame Apollo for his father's death, see n. at
        53. Cf. n. at 1002–4.

1115   *in the shadow of a bay-tree*: there is evidence for a bay-tree near
        the tripod in the sanctuary itself (Aristophanes, *Wealth* 213,
        with the scholiast's comment).

1115–16 *the son of Clytemnestra, the contriver of all these things, was one
        of the number*: an alternative translation gives the meaning:
        'and Orestes was the sole contriver of all these things'. If this
        is correct, Orestes may not have been present at the murder of
        Neoptolemus. See n. at 1008.

1135   *Pyrrhic dance*: this, according to Stevens (n. at 1135), 'as
        known in the fifth century' was 'a lively dance in armour
        derived from an ancient war dance, recalling the crouching,
        springing, bending aside, all the movements, evasive and
        offensive, of actual fighting'. There is surely a punning refer-
        ence to Neoptolemus' other name, Pyrrhus.

1139   *leapt the Trojan leap*: if the reference is to Achilles' leap from
        his ship to the Trojan shore, it is appropriate to his son. If it is
        to Neoptolemus' own leap from the Trojan horse, it is still more
        appropriate.

1140–1 *like doves when they spot a hawk*: the more famous of two sim-
        iles in Homer's *Iliad* involving these two birds is that describ-
        ing Achilles in pursuit of Hector (22.139–42; translated by
        Martin Hammond): 'As a hawk in the mountains, quickest of
        all flying things, swoops after a trembling dove with ease: she
        flies in terror before him, but he keeps close behind her,
        screaming loud, and lunging for her time after time as his
        heart urges him to kill.'

1145   *re-echoed from the rocks*: Orestes' prophecy at 998 is fulfilled.

1147   *someone*: no doubt Apollo.

1151   *of the Delphian who killed him*: the tradition gives his name as

Machaereus (? = sacrificial knifer).

1153 *there was no one who did not stab him with his sword*: this moment may gain power from a Homeric antecedent. After Hector is safely dead at the hands of Achilles, 'the other sons of the Achaeans came running round, and stared with admiration at the size and wonderful looks of Hector—and none who came up to the body left without stabbing it. And a man would glance at his neighbour and say: "Look, Hector is much milder to handle now than when he fired our ships with burning flame".' (*Iliad* 22. 369-74; translated by Martin Hammond).

1061-5 *Such is the treatment . . . he be wise*: in a sage note in which he makes clear the distinction between the playwright and the words he puts into his characters' mouths, Stevens observes (n. at 1165), 'The loyal servant of Neoptolemus is naturally full of bitterness against the god who has helped to destroy his master; he may also be the mouthpiece of the dramatist, but it is more significant for the outlook of Euripides that he has chosen to present, if not originate, the version of Neoptolemus' death that is most favourable to him and discreditable to Apollo and Delphi.'

1174 *receive into my house with a touch of my hand*: it was customary for mourners to touch the corpse, especially the head.

1182-3 *if only fate . . . Simois*: the wish that a hero had died a noble death at Troy rather than a degrading one later goes back to Homer (e.g. *Odyssey* 1.236-43).

1186 *O marriage, marriage*: Stevens feels (n. at 1186) that 'Peleus is proclaiming as causes of disaster the marriage with Hermione, which roused the enmity of Orestes, and the feud with Apollo (1194-6), which enabled Orestes to invoke the help of the Delphians and of the god himself'.

1194-6 *you, a mere mortal . . . the archer's skill*: see notes at 53 and 1108.

1195 *a Zeus-born hero*: Achilles was not the son of Zeus, of course; he was his great-grandson. 'Zeus-born' is an epithet which Homer uses to describe kings.

1212 *my two children*: Achilles and Neoptolemus.

1218 *It was for nothing that the gods blessed you in your marriage*: for the ecstatic wedding of Peleus and Thetis with its extensive guest-list of divinities, see *Iphigenia at Aulis* 1036-79.

1223   *Away with you, my sceptre*: 'Peleus' staff is a means of support,
       a symbol of his power, and the weapon with which he threat-
       ened Menelaus (588)' (Lloyd, n. at 1223).

1224   *you daughter of Nereus in your gloomy caves*: Thetis lived in her
       father's home under the sea.

1226   *What is it that moves*: Thetis travels through the air, like the
       Dioscuri in *Electra* (1233–7). She will either appear on the roof
       of the stage building or suspended from a *mēchanē* (=
       machine), a kind of crane which was used in flying scenes. The
       sky is the element of the gods. It is not uncommon in Greek
       tragedy for a god to appear at the end to foretell the future and
       to bring the action to a conclusion. A god in this role is referred
       to as a 'deus ex machina', the Latin for 'the god from the
       mēchanē or machine'.

1231   *in recognition of our former marriage*: Thetis had entered on the
       marriage with Peleus with considerable reluctance and it did
       not last long.

1236   *swift-footed Achilles*: the epithet for Achilles is Homeric.

1244   *the land of Molossia*: the Molossi were a group of tribes who
       formed a tribal state in Epirus in north-west Greece. The boy
       of this play became known in myth as Molossus, the epony-
       mous founder of this state. Lloyd observes (n. at 1243–52) that
       'Tharyps, the Molossian king, a boy in 429, was educated in
       Athens and given Athenian citizenship (Thucydides 2.80.6)'.
       (*Andromache* may date from 425.)

1245   *Helenus*: a son of Priam and Hecuba, this Trojan emigrant was
       now resident in Molossia.

1246   *this boy*: the Greek word for 'this' is a pointing (deictic) word,
       and its use certainly suggests that the boy is on the stage. Cf.
       n. at 1046.

       Aeacus: the son of Zeus, he was Peleus' father.

1252   *Pallas*: the goddess Pallas Athena had been bitterly opposed to
       the Trojans throughout the Trojan War.

1256   *a deathless god*: this transformation of Peleus appears to be
       Euripides' invention. In Pindar (*Ol.* 2.78–80) he is merely
       translated to the Islands of the Blessed.

1259   *with your feet dry*: this is the consequence of his divinity.

1261–2 *his island home on the shore of Leuce within the inhospitable sea*:
       the island of Leuce (modern Phidonisi), on which stood a tem-
       ple to Achilles, is opposite the mouth of the Danube in the

Black Sea ('the inhospitable sea'). The name means 'white',
and it was so called either because of the white birds which
abounded there or because of its white cliffs. The ghosts of
Achilles and other dead heroes were supposed to have run
races there.

1266   *Cuttle Reef*: 'so called either because it was like a cuttlefish, or
because it was haunted by cuttlefish, near Iolcus, and not far
from Mt Pelion, where (see 1278) Peleus and Thetis were married' (Hyslop, n. at 1266).

1277   *Pelion*: see the previous note.

1279–83 *And in view of that . . . from the gods*: these extraordinarily
banal lines begin incoherently and, as Norwood observes
(quoted by Lloyd in n. ad loc.), they are 'vulgar and trivial to
the last degree'. It would certainly be pleasant to believe that
they were not written by Euripides.

1284–8 *The divine will . . . happened here*: the 'stock' ending of four or,
with a variation in the first line, five of Euripides' plays.

The Oxford World's Classics Website

www.worldsclassics.co.uk

- Information about new titles
- Explore the full range of Oxford World's Classics
- Links to other literary sites and the main OUP webpage
- Imaginative competitions, with bookish prizes
- Peruse the Oxford World's Classics Magazine
- Articles by editors
- Extracts from Introductions
- A forum for discussion and feedback on the series
- Special information for teachers and lecturers

www.worldsclassics.co.uk